SHADOW LIFE:
Aerospace, Love, and Secrets

JENNA WARE

SHADOW LIFE:
Aerospace, Love, and Secrets

© 2016, 2017 by Jenna Ware.

All rights reserved. No part of this publication may be reproduced, distributed, or transmitted in any form or by any means, including photocopying, recording, or other electronic or mechanical methods, without the prior written permission of the author, except in the case of brief quotations embodied in critical reviews and certain other noncommercial uses permitted by copyright law. For permission requests, contact the author @JediJW on Twitter or jennaware.com.

This book is my memoir, based on my life story. Some events and characters are composites or have been fictionalized to protect the privacy of others. This book does not give personal, lifestyle, medical or legal advice; please consult qualified professionals. If anyone disagrees with any part of this book, it is simply my opinion.

First available in print 01/2017.

First available as e-book 12/2016, United States, with color photographs and hyperlinks.

Print ISBN: 978-1-946438-02-7

"I hope anyone interested in an honest reflection on the issues Jenna discusses will read *Shadow Life*. It is a must-read for people who know Joe or Jenna or who are interested in heroes in aviation history. It's a great love story."

Richard Goff, Ph.D.
Aerospace Engineering
Virginia Tech

"Jenna Ware is a voice for free discussion and tolerance, even of ideas that have provoked angry controversy in the trans world. I think this can only be for the good of everyone."

J. Michael Bailey, Ph.D.
Psychology
Northwestern University

"I finished *Shadow Life* last night and when I awoke this morning I was still thinking about it. Well done, very well done. What an amazing life story. I liked the ending, which is really a beginning. It begs for a follow-on book."

Richard Kelty, MD
Pathologist
Fellow pilot

"This is one of the most beautiful love stories. The humor, understanding, the caring for each other has more depth than most romantic novels—and it's true, sometimes word for word."

Dot Minnich
From Joe's Church
Friend of Joe and Jen for 20 years

Shadow Life

TABLE OF CONTENTS

Title
Endorsements
Author's Note
Preface

PART 1: BEING MY NEW SELF

1 Is that real, or is it Memorex?	1
2 Need to Know	11
3 Dancing at the O Club	27
4 Transition	39
5 He Knew the Whole Time	55

PART 2: CAN'T STAND UP FOR MYSELF

6 Know Yourself	67
7 Heaven	77
8 Marriage	95
9 Ware Lab, Virginia Tech	109
10 So What Went Wrong?	123

PART 3: SEEMING ECCENTRIC

11 Woodhaven	139
12 Paris	157
13 Shallow Moat, Paper Castle	167
14 A Drink from the Ohio	175

PART 4: LIVING WITH DEATH

15 Fear and Prayer	197
16 Loving Him	211
17 Hell	235
18 *Joe!*	239
19 WV-2	243

PART 5: UNLEARN I'M NOT OKAY

20 Ashamed	255
21 Admitting What We Are	267
22 What We Can Do to Live a Normal Life	293
23 The Gravity of Gossip	307
24 Being	321

Glossary
Acknowledgments

AUTHOR'S NOTE

THOUGH *Shadow Life* delves into several controversial topics, no persons are disrespected. The essence of coexistence is respect despite difference.

Most books that relate to trans issues target a liberal audience, leaving others to interpret what is meant. *Shadow Life* exposes transgender issues usually downplayed and clarifies trans phenomena in a way that is more palatable for conservative people. Not buying everything you hear does not mean you don't accept human diversity or that you would not be kind to people who are different; it means you have questions that aren't being answered by the transgender political movement, which I think is because some stealth aspects obfuscate the true nature of what is sought.

Joe was a conservative man of the highest character, of national note, and he married me. He is an example of how love can happen between people who are different. He taught me how to be myself and come out with it.

There are dozens of photographs embedded in the text.

I am a former social worker, and as of 2016 I am 35 years in transition.

PREFACE

OUR LIFE together was the picture of difference. He was a man of national note, a conservative Republican Christian 40 years older, and I was private, a liberal Democrat Jewish transsexual, though conservative in this area. Joe was former Lockheed Skunk Works, who helped make the first two Air Force Ones for President Eisenhower and who was Department Manager of Engineering Flight Test over the U-2, and the SR-71; I was a social worker and, before that, in the National Security Agency, NSGA, NSOC, SIGINT, Ft. Meade, Maryland.

I'm here to share what a wonderful man my husband was, to correct popular misconceptions about transgender and transsexual living, and to make a suggestion. I've been in this since the 1970s, I've lived the life, and I've helped others. Inspired by Kenji Yoshino (*Covering: The Hidden Assault on Our Civil Rights*, 2006), I'm concerned about the current direction of the transgender paradigm: It's still hiding key stigmata.

I've done it myself. I tried to keep my sexuality away from other people's concern, but there is no such thing as actual stealth living. People knew. I wouldn't discuss it, and my husband and I caught hell for years. Now I see most transgender people doing the same thing in another way, unwittingly enabling prejudice and opposition they don't handle any better than I did. It's not the fact they're transgender they're hiding but what that really means, what they actually need or desire.

The transgender social movement is winning access to places most don't even want to go, where disrobing is required. If they can't *say* it, they can't *show* it. So they don't go, marginalizing *themselves* into a less than equal integration, furthering lack of awareness, preventing equal employment, and where it's discovered during sex, possibly even incurring surprise violence or murder.

Transgenders can never fully integrate into society if they're embarrassed to admit what they have and want. Leaders of the social movement cannot advocate for something they downplay. They need to bring these issues to the fore, not leave them to serve as doubt and denial, not relegate them to the periphery or treat questions as offensive. Rhetoric must be as clear in media as it would be in locker rooms so that those who are interested may more fully integrate. I've waited 20 years for leaders to do so. Most of them don't, so I did, herein. *Shadow Life* is explicit.

Joe and I put up with a lot in our life together, but I don't detail who did what against us. Rather, the focus is on what *I did*—that same mistake of stealth living—that made our life together much more difficult. I caused a lot of our problems because I didn't know how to handle my issues in society.

"Stealth" doesn't mean never being known. But it does mean excessive privacy, trying to fly under the radar, hiding something important—to pass without stigma—and if discovered to try and regain privacy. I transitioned in 1981, was stealth from 1985-2016, 31 years. I've been a magnet for other stealth for decades. Who is safer to talk with than someone else in the same boat? As a clinical social worker, MSW, LCSW, I've tried to help or support all varieties of trans persons in areas such as transition, medical interface, social integration, hate crimes, suicidality and rape.

There are two main reasons why trans people enter or remain stealth, about being trans overall or some key aspect: (a) to be the needed goal, and (b) to avoid repercussion. In earlier years of stealth living, the former may seem like the main reason, but the balance between the two will likely change through decades. Initially, stealth living can be healing, a salve over the old wound of being so painfully wrong before. I've been there; to my soul, I get it. But after decades in role, other issues may arise. Through healing, the need to *be*, without trans, can decrease, and *avoidance* of repercussion can become the impossible problem of managing unintended consequences.

Being an unwanted minority, shit will happen, and when it does—

(1) *Stealth cannot stand up for themselves* when needed, nor can they allow anyone else to stand up for them, as doing so may highlight the issue they need to hide. So when something happens—anything from gossip to hate crimes—the stealth trans person may feel unable to set the record straight, go to the police, or even so much as tell a doctor or therapist, with sharing electronic medical records. People talk, so don't tell. A revelation

to others could change the balance of other things in the stealth's life, or make it so someone could no longer pretend they don't know, which could be disastrous to living stealth. Much of the time, a stealth person can't even share that she is hurting inside. For if one is upset, what is the reason?

(2) *A stealth person may seem eccentric* when responding to things unknown to others. People may sometimes know or suspect that someone is trans, but they likely do not know about a large number of situations the stealth has been hiding. According to the U.S. Dept. of Justice, the majority of trans people have suffered sexual assault and other hate crimes. If we, ourselves, have not been attacked, we know we could be—and we know of others who have, or who have committed suicide. Even if someone stealth appears happy and well adjusted, he or she is likely carrying a lot, will make decisions in daily life that seem to be without basis—changing jobs, avoiding a person, leaving a group in emotional outburst. The stealth may deflect or misdirect to avoid revealing a snubbing, the painful issue of an attack, or take elaborate measures to avoid Internet databases. Some people refer to stealth as "secret agent stuff." Stealth may not even know how others perceive them, because they can't ask. Social skills easily degrade.

(3) *Stealth cannot unlearn they are not okay.* They can learn, in the head, they *are* okay. But they cannot *unlearn*, in the heart, the ingrained message they are *not* okay. Most trans persons get the message from childhood they are not okay as trans, and that message does not suddenly disappear with transition. Stealth carry that burden privately. They can't talk about it or blow cover. That needed face-to-face message that "you're okay"—a person saying so to your face—is not generally there in life *because the topic is not available for discussion.* A doctor or lover may say it from time to time, but the stealth person is mixing mostly with other people, and when someone disses trans people in some way, that message rams home to the stealth as well, confirming her nature is unwanted. Self-esteem can drop dramatically if stealth is held too long.

After a few decades, a long-term stealth person may care less about privacy and may want to stand up for themselves, set the record straight, or be recognized for extreme things survived.

When this happens, I refer to it as "busting out." Which brings me to this book, why I'm standing up, finally.

People have always pressured me to be small or not exist. After Joe passed away in 2012, it was my initial intention to remain quiet, be a non-person, through the rest of my life, to let myself disappear to protect his memory and his laboratory—the Joseph F. Ware Jr. Advanced Engineering Laboratory, the "Ware Lab," at Virginia Tech, Blacksburg, VA—*until I began to see that my stealth living was playing into the hands of those who wished me to not exist.*

Other people had sought, painfully, to make me small, and there I was—making myself small to please them.

Of all the crazy things to do!

I re-evaluated what was working in my life. I had carried stealth too long: 10 years would have been adequate; I went 31.

I realized that hiding myself was indirectly supporting ignorance and prejudice—that thing that had hurt me all my life—and that my unwillingness to stand up for myself seems to have made me an easy target for those inclined, who may have felt justified when I wouldn't defend.

I realized that disclosing myself was, instead, the *best* thing I could do for Joe's memory, as he was a man of far greater moral courage and wisdom than people knew. What do you care about? What kind of person are you? Those are the things that mattered to him. And when the going got tough, he stayed, as was his vow in church, before his pastor, at our marriage.

I also realized, to the delight of my rock-bottom self-esteem, that *I was the one he chose*. Joe Ware, that great man, held me higher than anyone else ever had—that amazing, magnificent man.

My mind was rocked.

I was ashamed of myself for letting the message creep in so deep that I am not okay as transsexual, and I was ashamed of myself for allowing myself to think that I had to play it small to protect him—for it's not true there is something the matter with me, or any of my trans brothers and sisters.

Then I remembered I had learned shame from transphobic oppressors, so I dropped that, too.

Freedom!

This nation should be proud to have people like my husband caring both for its dignity and its defense, and the nation should also be proud he had a good wife whom he loved and who loved him. Joe is a shining example of what it means to be both an American and a Christian.

To all trans people, let me share: Though it can be hard for each of us to see, there are sometimes things we do, ourselves, which make life more painful or difficult. In my case, it was stealth living. Being yourself, standing for who you really are, can be difficult, but without it there is no life, no *yourself* you live. There is only someone else's life you reflect.

And to all those who love us, who don't have the courage to say so or who find oppression painful, let me also refer you to *Covering* for the acceptance movements in societies for women, race, religion, and sex orientation. How may acceptance evolve? For an image, think of interracial marriage, how it used to be, and how it is regarded today. There's more to go, but it's better. These examples are all part of our social T evolution in respect for us as equal and valued human beings. Real love is such a rare thing in life. Can anyone who needs love throw it away because of a third party's preference, to choose to live, in loneliness, some prejudiced person's views? To emulate someone who is hurting you?

Also, several people have asserted to me that "transsexual" is a slur, a dirty word, a denigration used to imply sex workers or autogynephilia. I think sometimes when they say that, it's to pressure me to use "transgender" instead, but where it truly is used in a derogatory manner, I need to say that my phenomenon is not a slur. I am not a slur. I am a dignified human being, trying to live with and stand up for something little understood, that has been painful in the extreme, for which people have hurt me greatly over my entire life. I ask, please do not use my phenomenon to insult people.

I've been told sharing the truth of my life and various trans phenomena will cast me in a negative light, but I believe for research, the tone of the book must be in open sharing of inner thoughts—a level of disclosure found at the core of issue revelation—even if some of it is unpopular or leaves me exposed as flawed. I've made mistakes I'm not proud of. Others have experienced some of the same things I have, and I hope that my sharing will help them avoid some of the mistakes I've made.

Shadow Life is empowering, full of life and love. It is strength out of weakness. It's the bond between husband and wife that no one could break. It decries age bigotry. It shares aspects of trans living most prefer to hide, and it offers what might be a better way forward.

Jenna Ware
Oxnard, CA
2016

For Joseph F. Ware, Jr.,
my husband.

He was aerospace,
I was secret,
and we had love between us.

PART 1

MY NEW SELF

"To be yourself in a world that is constantly trying to make you something else is the greatest accomplishment."

Ralph Waldo Emerson

1

"Is that real, or is it Memorex?"

1990

THE 1951 T-28 FENNEC loped over the desert north of Los Angeles at an easy 160 knots, 184 mph, 1,500 feet above ground level. The French Air Force attack airplane was a "War Bird," which had seen military service in its day. Powerful and light, it was highly maneuverable and responsive. The monster's engine, a Wright Cyclone R-1820 with 1,350 horsepower, vibrated through the frame into the form-fitted, plastic joystick in my right hand.

Figure 1.1. Cockpit of T-28 Fennec NX28FE.

I banked the plane hard to the right to get directly over Rosamond Blvd. We were flying to Edwards Air Force Base for the air show that weekend, participating as Static Display Aircraft.

Joe, at 73, was pilot in command in the front seat, letting me fly from the back seat. At the age of 33, I was not yet checked out in the T-28, but he was letting me gain proficiency.

I gave him a position report over the intercom, so he would know that I knew where we were. "Rosamond." My voice sounded mechanical, through my own headset, like an astronaut, with a slight click before and after.

He could hear me in the front seat through his helmet's integrated headphones. It would have been impossible to hear each other over the roar of the Cyclone, otherwise.

"Follow their instructions to the letter, Jenna."

"Roger that," I said, and repeated for him: "Stay over the road at one thousand five hundred." The thought brought a smile to my face, because I knew the road made a sharp turn ahead.

Figure 1.2. Joe with helmet in cockpit of his T-28.

In the T-28, all I usually saw of Joe was the back of his helmet. Sometimes, when he scanned left or right for other airplane traffic, I would catch a glimpse of his favorite, old, gold, Lockheed Ray Bans. But the rest of the time in the cockpit, he was an off-white orb with shoulders—bright under the sun, with long, curved, transparent streaks from front to back, reflecting off the underside of the clear canopy overhead. His helmet, the seats, even his instrument panel up front, blended with the hard image of the southern California high desert rushing by beneath us.

Other aircraft talked on the radio. My mind sifted through it for our own calls.

I scanned left and right for traffic converging on Edwards.

"You can see the road under us from back there?" Joe asked.

The largest area of the fuselage was in front of us, which blocked my view forward and down.

I rolled the plane briefly and looked down through ghostly reflections to the road beneath the fuselage streaming into the right wing root, then leveled the wings.

"I've got you worried?" I asked.

I keyed the mike. "Edwards Tower, North American Two Eight Foxtrot Echo, east of Rosamond, Landing with November, PPR." Prior Permission Required was a code military bases gave civilian aircraft to confirm we have permission to arrive. It helped prevent little things like missiles or Marines with M-16s.

"North American Two Eight Foxtrot Echo, Edwards Tower. Say PPR."

It was taped to the panel, top center, but I had it memorized. I pressed the radio's transmission button on the stick. "Eight Fox Echo is PPR: seven, eight, two, four, seven."

Edwards Tower paused a moment. "Affirmative, Eight Fox Echo. Stay over the road: report the bend. Make right traffic Runway Two Two."

"Over the road," I repeated the clearance to Edwards Tower. "Report the bend. Right traffic Runway Two Two. Eight Fox Echo." The road we were to follow made a sharp half-left in a few miles.

"I'm doing okay, Joe?"

From the back seat I saw his helmet nod. "Yup."

Great. A Private Pilot with only 200 hours, I was fairly new to flying the T-28, especially into major military air bases—where Joe was Commercial grade with over 6,000 hours, experienced since the 1930s in everything from a Fleet Biplane to all the Lockheed Constellation variants, and had flown into military bases for decades. We'd previously talked about how I should make the approach. He was a natural teacher.

"Joe, Pancho Barnes and the Happy Bottom Riding Club were around here somewhere, weren't they? Where, exactly? The 'Right Stuff' guys? Yeager and all?" I asked him, straining to see ahead and to the right. We were running out of time to look.

"See over there?" Joe said, pointing to the right, ahead of the wing.

"Yes."

He nodded again.

"It's just open desert, now," I said. "It's gone."

He nodded again. "Yeah."

The bend was on us, but I didn't begin the turn. My smile grew larger.

Joe said calmly from the front, "You're gonna miss the turn."

"Edwards Tower," I said on the radio. "Eight Fox Echo at the bend." On the intercom, I added, "Here's to you, guys."

Figure 1.3. Joe on L. wing root of 28FE.

I yanked the stick hard left and throttled the engine for extra power, to make as much noise as possible. The right wing snapped high in a hard left turn. I could see the bend in the road beneath us and feel the cheeks on my face pull 2 Gs. I immediately yanked the wings level again, throttled back to cruise.

Joe chuckled in my headphones.

Edwards Air Force Base was visible ahead and to the right, Two O'clock Low. Runway Two Two was massive—twice as large in every dimension as Camarillo Airport—and it was famous. My heroes from Joe to Tony LeVier and the guys from Happy Bottom had all landed there.

Neil Armstrong couldn't get me more excited.

"Eight Fox Echo, Edwards Tower. Make right traffic Runway Two Two, number two, follow Mig 17, two-mile final. Report in sight."

"Right Traffic Two Two, No joy, Eight Fox Echo," I said, using the military reference I'd learned for not yet seeing the traffic.

The Mig checked his clearance to land with the tower, confirmed.

"Are you 'Right Stuff' also, Joe?" I asked over the intercom. I'd only known him a year. He didn't talk about it much, but I'd been suspecting more and more.

"Oh, no," Joe said, always humble.

I found the Mig approaching the runway and keyed the radio mike. "Edwards Tower, Eight Fox Echo has the Mig on final."

Our radio squawked. "Eight Fox Echo, follow that traffic. Cleared to land, Runway Two Two. Check gear down."

I pressed the little button on my joystick. "Cleared to land, Two Two, gear, Eight Fox Echo."

Flying northeast, we were downwind abeam the runway.

"I have the field," I told Joe up front, completely prepared to land the plane if needed. Runway Two Two was directly abeam us, to the right.

"Set it up," he said.

"Okay."

With my left hand, I brought the throttle and propeller back to slow us a little. At the lower speed, there was slightly less lift on the wings. I had to move the stick back a little, pitch the plane up slightly to maintain altitude.

"Gear down," I said to Joe, moving the lever to lower the gear. Then immediately, "Flaps down." I hit the lever to lower the flaps all the way down.

The plane began to immediately slow further and pitch down a little more, as if we'd applied the brakes. I adjusted the elevator trim to compensate.

We began our descent.

Runway Two Two drifted behind us, to our five o'clock.

I sequenced the power and RPM back to our landing settings and made a descending right turn to base leg. Runway Two Two was again ahead and to the right, getting closer.

"Good job," Joe said. "I'll take it from here. I have the plane."

"You have the plane," I repeated. We had to be clear who was flying. There were certainly no visual cues. I let go of the stick and spread my knees wide. It was not ladylike, but it was necessary to stay clear of the stick for whatever Joe may need.

"You stay on the radio," Joe said.

"Okay."

Joe turned the plane right from Base leg to Final, lining it up with the runway, dead ahead. He eased the power back, slowly, then back a little more, never adding.

The broad runway threshold passed under our wheels, and the T-28 touched down softly, well past the numbers, halfway to the first taxiway intersection.

Joe let it coast, very little braking, exited the runway at centerfield and stopped the plane.

I flipped the radio to ground frequency. "Edwards Ground," I said, "North American Eight Fox Echo off Two Two, taxi Static Display, Hangar 1600." I had no idea where Hangar 1600 was, but I felt sure Joe did.

Edwards Air Force Base! I felt more than thought.

My rapid heartbeat was not just excitement at arriving. I'd had a problem with the military, before. I scanned the ramp for trouble.

"Eight Fox Echo, Edwards Ground. Welcome. Toward the tower. Follow the follow-me truck."

That sounded okay.

"Tower, Eight Fox Echo looking," I said.

Joe headed the plane northwest toward the ramp, then northeast along the parallel taxiway up the length of the flight line. The air show had already been largely staged, with aircraft, vendor booths and displays all over it for a mile in either direction.

On the ramp, my anxiety levels rose notably. Air shows were fun, but military bases were still a concern. Military personnel moved about to our left, on the ramp, engaged in their own work. No one stared at us. A truck drove southwest along the ramp carrying a load of something.

Joe opened the canopy half way, per norm in taxi, to give us a little ventilation. The noise of the Cyclone engine's throaty beat flooded the cockpit—with a slight, higher-pitched *"pang,"* distinctive on a T-28. Its nine cylinders were fed through only six pipes, situated 3 on each side of the engine compartment, ahead of the cockpit, so we got the full brunt of the noise, and the smell of the exhaust.

The monster's prop blast tossed my hair in all directions like a Medusan mad scientist. I tried to hold part of it down with my hands, but it was a losing battle.

I shouted to Joe in the intercom. "What truck?"

"Eleven o'clock," Joe said.

I looked to find a ramp tug working its way toward us.

I keyed the mike and said loudly to Ground: "Eight Fox Echo has the truck."

The tug turned in front of us—sported a large sign on its back that said, "Follow Me"—and began to move northeast up the taxiway.

"I think they don't want us to get lost," I told Joe.

The truck took us along the flight line toward the tower and turned left toward a mammoth hangar that could house a building. The follow-me truck broke away. An airman pointed us toward a marshaller, at the northeast side of the hangar, with large wands to catch our attention.

Joe waved to him.

In easy taxi, we inched forward, closer to the Air Force sergeant, near the large open door of the hangar.

Our engine noise reflected off nearby hangars and rang even louder, with a steel twang, in steady rhythm. Joe had been a Wright Cyclone test engineer in Paterson, New Jersey, back in the late 1930s, and he knew how to tweak them. If our idle fuel/air mixture had been too rich, it would have loped: blump, blump, blump. Ours was a steady chug, the way Joe liked it.

I scanned Air Force personnel nearby: mostly enlisted, the occasional officer.

The marshaller waved us closer, closer, until he crossed his wands over his head and we came to an abrupt stop.

Air Force personnel kept their distance for the time being, as our propeller was still turning.

Joe talked to me over the intercom, checked aircraft systems, then shut the engine down and let the propeller stop.

For the first time since Camarillo, it was quiet. Airmen put wooden 4x4 contoured chocks around both main tires.

"Welcome to Edwards," a major said, approaching the plane.

"Hi," Joe called back to him.

The major greeted me also. "Hi. I'm Major Weeks."

An officer is talking to me?

I hesitated for a second. I knew I was a civilian, but old experiences had taught me to be careful. I tried to give him a smile and what I hoped was a friendly wave.

Joe and the major exchanged some information with Joe still in the cockpit.

"You two get settled and come inside," the major said. "I'll show you where to go."

I exhaled, unbuckled my military 4-point restraints, put my hands on the canopy section in front of me, stood up, and stepped out onto the left wing root. I felt its thick aluminum under my feet.

In the forward seat, Joe put his helmet on the floor in front of him, still wearing his favorite, old Ray Bans, and put a T-28 ball cap on his head.

"You need any fuel?" another airman asked from the ramp.

"Never turn down fuel," Joe said, standing up in the cockpit.

The airman nodded, left.

Joe stepped out on the wing, looked at me with a smile in his confident way. "You did fine."

That evening, sporting A-2 leather flight jackets, Joe and I went to the Officer's Club for a little enjoyment. People were relaxing, sitting at different tables, talking, laughing. A few stood at the bar or danced a little.

Joe and I sipped our Diet Cokes at a table with one of his sons. They were chatting about life, how it's going, how the plane's doing.

"Will you two excuse me? I need a refill." I showed them my empty glass. "You want anything?" I asked.

"No," they indicated.

"Fine."

I got up and made my way to the bar, amazed I was at the Edwards O Club—when a man stepped in front of me to block my path. It was General Chuck Yeager! I hadn't known he was there. He had a bottle of beer in his hand, and his grin was Yeager-classic, from ear to ear. When he smiled, his whole face smiled. The laugh wrinkles at the sides of his eyes were the most endearing.

Of course I knew who he was! He was one of my idols. I should have said, "Good evening, General," with just the right amount of deference, but, instead, I blurted the inelegant "Chuck!" I'm the one who has been afraid of officers since I was in the Navy at Ft. Meade—think third class petty officer, with one red chevron, on the arm of a scared teenager—but Chuck was such an aviator that his rank didn't occur to me. To me, he was a *pilot*, and I could handle that.

Chuck's smile grew larger, if that was possible. *Charisma!* He looked at my jacket and said without hesitation, "Is that real, or is it Memorex?" quoting a line from a popular television commercial.

My jacket was not military issue. It was a copy, so I said, "It's Memorex."

"Well," he said, as casual and friendly as a man could be, "you get drunk and puke on it a few times, it'll be just as good."

I smiled, but I didn't say anything in response. I just raised my right arm near his bottle of beer, tipped his bottle over with my left hand—his hand still holding it—and poured some of his beer on my sleeve.

He laughed at me and massaged it into the leather, "There." He smiled at me again then turned to jaw with friends at the bar.

I went back to our table, without my new drink, a grin as wide as Chuck's, completely star struck. "Joe! *Did you see that?*"

He laughed at me. Yes, he did.

"I will never ever clean this jacket! It has *Yeager Beer* on it!"

2

Need to Know

1975

THE NATIONAL SECURITY AGENCY stood frozen in the snow before me, a long, multi-story building, off-whitish in general, with 20-foot golf balls on the roof and the little credit union on the south end. It was by far the largest building I'd ever seen.

I was a teenager, barely in the U.S. Navy. I didn't even know what the NSA was.

Why did the building need to be so long?

I walked for a week across the sprawling parking lot to get inside as soon as possible. Windblown snow stacked between cars, settled into cracks, filled door jams with just enough frozen fractals to keep a shivering driver outside ten seconds longer than needed. A gust threatened to blow my Navy "cover" off, ball cap, so I angled the bill down, huddled into my pea coat and trudged forward, Zen-walking, one step after another. The building would get there in time.

Landing the previous day at Baltimore-Washington International, I walked out of the airline terminal to stare at a winter landscape completely foreign to my previous few months in the Navy. Snow blew over frozen, irregular ice that looked like it had half melted the day before under traffic. The air was so cold I thought it would freeze my face.

I was hopelessly lost.

"Where you going?" a taxi driver asked me outside the terminal at BWI.

"Uh." I was new to my Top Secret SI clearance. They'd drilled protocols into my brain with more than a few cautions—institutional paranoia. Should I tell him? *Could* I tell him? Yes. The fact that I will work there is not classified. "I'm going to

Fort Meade, Maryland," I said, in as general terms as possible. "An Army post."

"But you're Navy?" he asked me?

I nodded.

"Yes, sir. Get in. I know where you go."

He seemed like a good man.

A little wind buffeted the taxi while I entered. I was glad the heater was on.

The driver headed out. "What you going to do here?" the driver asked.

I literally can't say. I don't even know.

"Eat Shit on a Shingle, I think," referring to chipped beef in gravy on toast, "If they do that in the Army."

"Yeah, yeah," he said, waving his hand at me.

At the time, there were no gates at Ft. Meade. Anybody could drive on-post, and the taxi did, wandering around a bit to find his way.

Eventually, he found the barracks. My view was from the parking lot in the back. I could see no sign on it, but it looked warm, a good enough starting point.

I paid him then got out, took my duffle bag into what turned out to be the correct place: a Zumwalt Award-winning, three-story, twin-tuning-fork-shaped barracks of brick (an east and west wing) that would have resembled a hotel in civilian life.

Checking in was easy, and I was shown to my room. There was a large lobby area with pool table, ping-pong, a mail center, tables, and chairs. The suites, when I got to mine, were situated so a room with 2-3 men linked with a central bathroom/shower, then to another room with 2-3 men.

Most people there worked in "the building," as we called the NSA. It was nondescript with no emphasis. We could say "the NSA," but that would draw attention, and we felt we shouldn't as a rule, so we usually just said "the building." Security was a practiced habit. No one talked about what they did.

I'm not sure what I can share about my work inside the NSA, even as far back as the 1970s.

There are a few things I can share, however.

First, I have to say that modern concerns about the NSA tapping phones had nothing to do with our work. We were

Naval Intelligence, Naval Security Group Activity or NavSecGruAct, "NSGA." Our work was wholesome, admirable.

Secondly, I can say that I worked in the NSA as a member of a signal intelligence "SIGINT" operations center called "NSOC," the National Security Operations Center, pronounced "EN-soc" —because they told us at the time we could say so.

I was a blank canvas before I got there. The Navy, and more specifically the NSA, opened my mind the first of two times in my life and had a major influence on my thinking. It was as if a million things existed I'd never known about before. My life had been so narrow before that. I'd never even thought before of anyone going to college. I had no idea of other cultures in the world or what they were about. There, I learned about classifications, security procedures, compartmentalization, computers, minorities, religions, politics, colleges, the sciences, weather—other people and the world in general.

I found the NSA to be fascinating—by far the most interesting place I've ever worked, and it was so much more inclusive than my experience south of Dodge City, Kansas—not that they were all that tolerant. But by comparison, the NSA felt more accepting of human diversity, if only in the simple fact they openly embraced minorities of race and religion.

I'm sure I would have enjoyed spending my entire enlistment, there, but my time had to be cut short. My need inside was blossoming. I couldn't keep it in.

1990

Edwards Air Force Base personnel used to put air show people up in their own homes. That year, Joe and I were housed with a colonel and his wife in a modest and comfortable house on base. Previously, as enlisted in the Navy at Ft. Meade, I had never been allowed in "officer country," but as part of the air show, we got one of their bedrooms like visiting relatives.

I exited the bathroom in my nightgown to stand face-to-face with the colonel—

God—!

His wife turned off the light in the living room and made her way past us to their bedroom.

"Good night," she said with a smile.

"Uh—" I stuttered.

She disappeared into their room.

"Uh, Colonel—" The look on my face must have been obvious.

"Frank," he said. He was in his robe. He'd obviously been waiting for me to get out of his bathroom.

"Right. Frank." I tried to sound casual. "Thanks for putting us up, Frank."

That was appropriate!

"No problem. Glad you two came. It ought to be a good air show."

"Yes, Sir."

Shit! He told me not to do that.

I was sure my smile was fake. I scooched around him in the hallway and half ran the two steps back to Joe's and my room, quickly closing the door behind me.

Joe was in his pajamas, sitting on the edge of his bed, taking off his socks, tossing them onto a nearby chair where his clothes rested.

I stood by the door and pulled at my gown.

"What are you scared of him for?" he said.

"Joe, *Jesus*!"

"He's just a person, and she's just his wife."

I knew that was true, but—

"Check under the pillow for microphones?" he asked.

"You think he knows about me? *You know?*"

"He might," Joe said. "They have security on base. Probably checked us out before we got here."

"Christ!"

"You praying?" he asked, teasing me a little.

"I might!" I migrated toward my bed, across from him, the other of two twins, and sat on the edge.

Joe sat on his bed and looked at me.

"That's all I fucking need." I knew Joe hadn't been serious, but I lifted the pillow anyway to check—nothing—plopped it back down. "It's like, one wrong word from him, and I'm gone. He could do anything—"

"What's the problem with officers?"

"The Navy might have something to do with it." I sat on my bunk, in the center, cross-legged, and looked toward his silhouette.

"Boot camp?"

"Partly."

Joe was my confidant.

"I was scared before I even got there, Joe. San Diego recruit training center. You know I was abused as a child for being me. I just knew someone was going to lay into me in boot camp."

"Did they?"

Some actually tried once. I was 17, not butch, easy target—but this big strong guy, who looked like Clancy Brown in today's world, stopped them. Thank you, Clancy, whomever you are.

"Boot camp grated against my soul," I told Joe. "My older brother had taught recruits there as a CC Aid, and helped me learn some before hand, or I think I'd have never made it. I wound up as guidon bearer the whole time—carried the company flag out in front. Easy duty, but by the time Mom came out to see me graduate, I was so stiff, I couldn't move. I'd been so scared. She took me to some movie—'Blazing Saddles' or 'Young Frankenstein,' I don't know. I didn't smile the whole time."

Joe put his elbows on his knees and held his hands. "Hurt you."

"My biggest problem was at Ft. Meade."

I could see his silhouette nod.

"When I was in boot camp, they tested us, and I showed some talent for pattern recognition—not in spades like a genius, but they could drop me into a sea of something, and I'd sort it out. The NIS—Naval Investigative Service, like the Navy's FBI—got me out of class, one day, and asked if I'd like to join 'intelligence.' Anything to get me out of the main stream, I joined him.

"I flew through self-paced training in Cory Station, Pensacola to find myself facing a Lieutenant who promoted me up to E-4, Petty Officer Third Class, if I'd extend my 4-year enlistment to 5. Which I did. I was at Ft. Meade before I knew it. I learned my job at NSOC—"

"NSOC?" Joe asked. He pronounced it with familiarity, like me: "EN-soc."

I clarified before I caught up with myself, "National Security Operations—"

"I know," he said.

He told me that on purpose!

The tone changed between us, became even more serious.

"*How* do you know that?" I asked.

He shook his head in the dark.

I pressed. "People know about the NSA, but they don't know about NSOC."

He shrugged.

Need to know?

"By the way," Joe said, "the FBI has a lengthy file on you. If the Air Force checked, they'd get everything."

Nobody thinks about that stuff. Who is this guy?

"I know," I said. "That's one of the things I worry about going to military bases with you. I'm afraid they'll out me, or ridicule me— So you think they told the colonel about me?"

"That still depends on who was working in security."

"The colonel doesn't act mean," I said.

"Doesn't seem mean."

"So *is* he mean? I've faced more than my share of shit—"

"I don't think he is."

"Well—"

"Keep going," Joe said with a movie-reel turn of his hand.

With a wary look to Joe, I continued. "Okay. Soooo, while I was there—at Ft. Meade—I explored D.C. You know it's okay to drive backwards up one-way streets in D.C.?"

"How'd you make out with the White House?"

"I didn't make out with the White House, Joe. It's a *building*."

He made another movie-reel motion with his right hand.

1975

In the relative liberality of the NSA, my heart began to press that I needed to be female, that I should have been female all along—in the Navy, in life, before God, everywhere. I'd needed it since my earliest thoughts in life, but I'd been pressed into denial long years before, in the Midwest. Away from my culture, I couldn't block it out. My need seemed both crazy and natural to me at the same time.

At first, I shamed myself for such thoughts, dutifully trained in childhood. In the barracks, showering in my suite, walking down the hallway, trying to watch TV during off hours, I knew my needs were "wrong," but I couldn't stop them, so with no choice, I gave myself permission to feel them.

Walking in the corridors of the NSA, going to the head, interacting with my team in NSOC, asking what were those airplane pictures on the wall—the SR-71 and the WV-2—I tried to act like I was supposed to and suffered, privately, with my dilemma.

Who I was conflicted with *what* I was. That woman over there in uniform? That was me. That woman at the front desk? That was me.

I knew I'd be kicked out of the Navy, if they knew, and I couldn't take the shame for that, either, so I struggled to do my job and prayed my heart would follow.

Maybe it'll go away!

God, help me get rid of this!

Speaking of whom, God—the old man on a throne who spoke to enlightened people and threw sinners in hell—was a problem for me. I'd been raised as a fundamentalist Christian in the midwest. God knew my thoughts, I'd been taught. I'd go to hell for even thinking about my needs, but in the expanded culture I found at Ft. Meade, I began to understand that the picture of God I'd been shown in church was false.

For one thing, the whole concept of hell seemed more to me like a religious threat than a depiction of reality. I mean, if God was benevolent, omniscient and omnipotent, then he wouldn't want his children to go to hell, he'd know how to fashion the universe so we wouldn't go to hell, and he'd have the ability to put that into effect. Hell, as it was given to me, made no sense, so—to my great surprise—I concluded that people were wrong and Hell didn't exist.

One of my little social group was extremely well educated, said he had been to college. He agreed with me on the logic, which made me feel better—and in time, I actually raised my personal topic with him, obliquely, without disclosure.

"Can a person change sex?"

There was precedent, he shared with me. *Some people had!* "Look at Christine Jorgensen."

How could I not have known?

It was the 1970s, and the Internet had not yet developed, but I was immediately involved. I went to libraries. I got books, I read. I studied, grew, learned. And it happened, right about that time, alone late at night, I saw Canary Conn on Tom Snyder in the TV room at the barracks.

No one else was there. If anyone walked in, I'd quickly change the channel. I felt I was safe. There, with the two of them—a beautiful woman with long, straight, blonde hair, and Tom, before a black background—Canary told her story. I absorbed every word, everything about her manner. She'd been an award-winning, male teen pop singer who'd become female, and I was enchanted.

Canary was from Los Angeles.

I could go to Los Angeles—

B*ut I can't do that!* I fought with myself.

It wasn't as easy as coffee.

Boys could not be girls, and by extension, males could not be female. That was sick. To need to actually be female? Everywhere? Inside and out? In person and in society?

Sick!

It's not sick to be female!

It's sick to become *one!*

I had 3 years left to go on a five-year enlistment—forever. Every day was an eternity with my horribly wrong body.

I couldn't go to Los Angeles, anyway, and become this shameful thing, face the world and my family—and tell them? The truth? I had to go to work in the building, through numerous security checks each time just to get in there, be who they wanted me to be, or else.

My suite in the barracks at the time was on the 2nd floor, south end. I'd lay there at night, my mind whirling across the nation all the way to Los Angeles. It was impossible to contemplate, yet ever-present, and over time, pressure built. I began to consider that the only way for me to relieve the pain was to commit suicide. I could see no other way.

I cried in my bunk at night, racked my brain for a way out of it. My entire life, I had fought to suppress my need, put up with people slamming me for it, but I couldn't suppress it any more—and I couldn't do anything about it.

Clearly something had to change, so one night I confided in my smart friend about my actual need. I trusted him, for some reason.

He, actually, was receptive to the idea. Later, however, that same man attempted suicide, so there was more going on with him than I knew. They took him to a mental ward in Bethesda for a while, due to his attempt, and on visiting him, he pointed out two others who were in there as well.

"What about them?" I asked.

"They are transsexual. They want to be female." He did not elaborate for my sake, I'm sure.

"The Navy put them in a mental ward because of *that*?"

"Yes," he confirmed.

One day, while I was in the building, my friend disappeared. I don't know what happened to him. That was the Navy. He was there. He was gone. I was on my own.

Need and suppression are a formula for implosion, and I was close to it when my creative mind suggested the possibility of an alternative to physical suicide. I thought, what about the idea of dropping out of society instead of life, disappearing, as gone as if I had died? I called the idea "social suicide," where family could not find me, where I could try to be myself. I'd have shame from my own heart, but, at least, not with their condemnation on top of it. Other people around me would know. People, who saw me change, or doctors, or neighbors, would know. But not people I'd known from back home.

I'd never been myself, and I had to give myself a chance, no matter the risk. The vector sum of all variables pointed that way—or, more so, in a fog of pixels, that way appeared less dark, maybe a path to light.

One day, not long thereafter, working in NSOC, with my co-worker, Juice, the pressure built until I could take it no more. I got up suddenly to leave my desk. I didn't ask permission; I couldn't. I had to get out of there. I think Juice knew something was building in me, saw me leave, said nothing. He was compassionate, and wouldn't have wanted to stand in my way.

As I walked south in the impossibly long hallway of the building toward the credit union, Barbra Streisand sang "The Way We Were" through overhead speakers. Sentimentality was built into the song. She was reaching inward for a memory, and I needed to reach inward for myself.

I thought of the possibility there could be an alternate future for me. Could it really be possible? Would I ever stop the charade?

Tears began to form in my eyes, but I could not break down in the hallway, in front of everyone.

With Barbara's song in the hall, I turned on my heels, and walked the other direction, toward the building clinic, and demanded with tears in my eyes to see a shrink "right now." I didn't know how long I could last or what my future would bring, but there could be no further delay.

The psychologist was kind.

I was shaking.

He was patient.

I was scared.

Until, finally, by force of will, I told him what part of my story I could—that I was learning I was into men. He did not ask if I had any experiences. He did not ask if I needed to be female to love a man—which was true, though that talk would have taken us in the wrong direction. My problem was not about a desire to get laid. My need was to be the female sex, as a person.

His response to me was simple, calm acceptance of what I said.

1990

Joe leaned toward me from the edge of his bed, silently, his elbows still on his knees.

"Of the six or so guys I'd run around with from the building, two turned out to be gay and one was—me." I tapped my chest for emphasis. "They were obviously selecting for us, while shunning us at the same time. Just like Mom. For all I know, there were others—probably were. We didn't talk about such things. So maybe the psychologist had seen us before? The shrink listened to me as if I were okay. I sat there with my badge on my neck chain, with him acting comfortable.

"I can't tell you how shocked I was that a man of the establishment—in the building—acted like I was okay as someone different. It was the first time I ever told anyone official even that much. I think that's when it could have gone well for me."

Joe was sitting on the edge of his bed, looking at me intently. "So the trouble was ahead."

1977

"And what do you want?" the psychologist asked me, as if he didn't know.

"I think I need to be released from the Navy," I told him. "I would stay in the NSA if they would have me as I really am, but I know they won't. I had a friend who was kicked out for being gay." True.

"Okay," he said. Then he just sat there and looked at me.

"What do I do?" I asked.

"Nothing," he said. "I'll handle it."

I left his office in a daze and went back to my work in NSOC, an avowed gay, as far as they were concerned. It felt strange, as if I'd never seen the operations center before. I carefully looked at everything because of its importance to me, aware I was taking mental pictures, because I'd never be allowed to see it again: the lights, panels, computer screens, wall photos of aircraft, people, my desk—everything.

I went to the mess hall that evening. Ate.

Nothing happened.

I went to sleep. Got up.

Nothing.

I went back to work in the building the next day, as expected.

Still nothing happened.

I talked to Juice and said my good-byes. It was mysterious, I'm sure, because nothing had happened. He was pleasant, as if knowing without asking. Juice was easy to like. He wasn't a guy who needed to know everything about everything. He could be comfortable with me if I was being me, I think.

Then a lieutenant commander came to my desk and asked me to follow him.

I waved goodbye to Juice and followed.

On exit from the building, the commander told me not to leave the country for 10 years without notifying the FBI first, and that all this was classified for 10 years. I said, Okay. It's been 40 years, and I've still not told anyone what I did there, or what our mission was. If the NSA would ever let me know it's not classified any more, and I think it's not, because of the NSOC wall at the NSA's Cryptologic Museum, open to the public, then I'd be glad to discuss it. But I think I should get confirmation first.

Out of the building, I went back to the barracks, checked in for local duty there, and our three-month standoff began.

The problem was the NIS—like today's NCIS—didn't believe my claim. They didn't discuss it with me; they just seemed to think I was lying, a fake gay claim to get out of the Navy.

1990

I looked at Joe on his bunk. "I thought about saying, 'Shit, I work in the NSA. *Half* of us are gay!' But I bet they didn't have a sense of humor."

Joe's silhouette nodded in the dark. "Good, good."

"So what?" I asked. "The NIS thought I was making it up? Because I had an FBI Background Check, maybe? All of us had one of those."

"You weren't lying."

"Right. I just wasn't answering questions they didn't ask. I was holding out, and I needed a lawyer—but let's not be reasonable."

1977

A stumbling block was the NIS wanted me to take a polygraph—which is an *interview technique*, rather than a truth machine. Cooperate with someone trying to nail me? We entered a stalemate: the NIS demanded a polygraph, I wouldn't take one without a lawyer, and the Navy wouldn't give me a lawyer until after I took the polygraph.

The NIS didn't like the stalemate and threatened to have me put in prison for obstruction or something—I wasn't clear on the charge, but the guy was pissed.

I felt my choice was between a mental hospital if I owned up, and prison if I didn't. I envisioned heavy, government metal-frame doors with little, head-high wire-glass windows, or sliding doors of iron bars, slamming shut. I hadn't planned on either.

Time passed; no progress was made. I walked through the barracks, ate in the chow hall—people stared at me. I was the one who had gotten kicked out of the building, and since I was skinny, I had to be gay. I went for walks, and people stared at me. I avoided the recreation areas, because it was scary for me. I feared every day the NIS was going to do something. Stress mounted.

I stopped eating—down to only 1 meal a day, for those months. I lost some 30 pounds—skin and bones.

One afternoon, a big guy caught me in our foyer.

"Get out of here, faggot!"

"I have to be somewhere." I tried to leave. "I—"

His fist hit me in the chest. When I bent forward, his other hand, open palm on my forehead, slammed my head against the wall.

I really don't remember the details beyond that, more the emotional impact.

It only took a few seconds, but there were several blows. In the end, he grabbed my shirt and threw me against the wall again, then held me there by the front of my shirt, in front of my chest. I remember he leaned in close to my face. Little balls of spit came out of his mouth as he told me, "You hear me, faggot? You're out of here today, or I kill you!"

When he finished, he left me on the floor, a wreck, bruised, my uniform torn. I fought to catch my breath. I got myself to my feet and left the suite, hunched over, crying down the hall, through the lobby to the barracks commander's office and locked myself inside, alone. I was hysterical, not in control of myself.

I grabbed the desktop phone and called personnel, in the building behind us. I found our Executive Officer and in a crying fit, in a series of broken and run-on sentences, I shared my situation and a lot of the trouble that had been given me. I am certain some of it was unintelligible and that my language was inappropriate, but I couldn't take it any more.

"…You goddamn fucking Navy shit make this happen!? Goddamnit! *Fuck all of you!* I swear to *God*— I'm still a non-com in this goddamn Navy, and *I'll write every fucking one of you up so help me God! You don't give me a fucking lawyer! You make this shit happen…*"

When I was done, the XO said nothing I can remember. I refused to go back to that suite, and I was assigned two guys who went in to get my things.

After that, to my surprise, nothing happened. I know the Navy did nothing to me for cussing the brass, but they also did nothing to anyone else that I could see.

Seeing no change and fearing both the NIS and the sailors around me, I took my first pro-active steps since our stalemate began. I drove down to D.C. and walked in to my Senator's office, dumped everything all over a kindly aid who was there to listen.

1990

I wiped tears on the shoulder of my gown. It had been traumatic for me. I was sure Joe couldn't see me well in the dark, but I felt shame for my display.

"I was scared," I told Joe.

He sat quietly on his bed, apparently thinking.

Why is he so nice to me?

I checked my watch. "God, it's nearly midnight." I pulled the spread back on the colonel's bed and crawled in, laying my head on the pillow. "The thing I needed that was so horrible, Joe? You know what it was they couldn't stand?"

He shook his head.

"Do you?"

"No. What?"

"Imagine someone with her husband and kids, holdings hands, walking that National Mall down in D.C., under a blue sky, appreciating the blossoms in the trees that line the park, talking about where they'd like to go for lunch."

Joe hung his head. "So how did you get out?"

"Very briefly after my trip to the senate, I got a lawyer. Shortly after that, I was in the barracks cleaning a pool table, when someone walked up to me. 'You want out of the Navy?' I was tired, and my voice was dry, cracking, so I just said, 'Yes.' He said, 'Then go to personnel.' I was out by noon."

Second-guessing myself, many years later, I have wondered if I made things harder for myself in the Navy, or not. I feel the NIS' concern for me was disdain, with the suspicion I was not telling them everything, and I've wondered, sometimes, if I should have been more forthcoming, to win trust by disclosure. What if the two trans people at Bethesda were placed in that ward for suicidal ideation, not because they were trans, per se. What if they were not really TS? What if my friend just said they were? I hadn't considered those things.

My read at the time, being there, seeing the reactions of people involved, was as I shared. I felt they were looking to nail me. Whether true or not, I should have been given a lawyer when I asked for one, at the beginning. Yet I still wonder. Oppression of trans people had been horrendous, so it may have been good to withhold. I truly do not know.

When I was in the Navy, Christine Jorgensen, who transitioned to female in 1952, was still regarded as a joke by most people, at best a novelty. Harry Benjamin's *The Transsexual Phenomenon* (1966) was well received by some, but society, like a fleet of ocean liners, does not turn on a dime. In the 1970s, cases of people transitioning were less frequent than today, and partly because of social pressure, people who transitioned tended to "woodwork," blend in, or were relegated to less normalized lives, so I had very little guidance. Most early transitioners suffered the problem.

How many trans people were in the military then, who needed to leave to be themselves? No one knows.

How many trans people are in the military in modern times? The Palm Center's Report of the Transgender Military Service Commission shares there may be over 15,000 trans people serving in the U.S. military today and over 134,000 trans veterans who are alive today. But I think there are far more. My feeling is that only half of people who would like to transition, actually have.

Why should we be treated with equality instead of prejudice? Our concept is offensive? Why shouldn't our presence be taken as corrupting the moral fiber of this righteous, God-fearing nation we depend on for our freedoms?

Because we aren't *Homo habilis* any more. Because with our Ray Bans we can see past the Serengeti Plain. We've outgrown the Olduvai Gorge, and we need to outgrow suspicions we learned there.

3

Dancing at the O Club

2015

ELLEN, a visiting, five-foot-six brunette, long-term, deep stealth friend from Seattle, was foolish enough to walk with me into Six Flags Magic Mountain, roller coaster park in Valencia, California. The area inside the gate was typical tourist: shops to buy cute things, customer service, fast food... The park had just opened; a thousand people flooded in around us on their way to thrills.

"So which ride is the best?" she asked like a school kid.

"Well," I told her, "Scream is like flying a fighter plane in combat: smooth rolls and loops. Superman is all about acceleration, like shot off a carrier. Tatsu, you think you're gonna die, but X2 actually tries to kill you—"

"Lets try X2."

"I'll let you do that one by yourself."

"It scared you."

"Someone needs to notify your next of kin."

"Baby," she said.

My smile was almost sincere. "Like the first time you read from the Torah at your Bat Mitzvah and nearly fell over?"

She smiled. "Which way is it?"

I pointed and started walking that way at a good clip—inside the gate, up and to the left.

She and I had been talking about stealth issues before, while we waited to enter—talking in such a way that others didn't know what we were talking about, because we left out key words or relied on a little shared experience. Someone walking by might hear one sentence, but not the next, therefore not getting what we were discussing.

"Why is it you think you might want to come out," she said as we walked. "I don't think I could do that. Yet. Sometimes I wish I could, but—no, I can't." She transitioned in her teens and had been stealth for nearly 30 years, ever since. It was what she knew.

Her hair was long and straight. As was her habit, she moved her hand to tuck strands behind her left ear.

I tried to think. "I—am not sure there is that much of a closet, in reality. People usually know when we've transitioned. And I've been in that same county for most of the last 25 years."

Most people were walking faster than we were, cutting around us to get somewhere fast, before lines developed.

We walked a little faster through the beautiful amusement park.

"So you think people know about you?" she asked.

"I don't really know who does and who doesn't. Stealth can't ask. Sometimes I think someone knows, and I learn later they didn't—or they act like they didn't, or lie outright and say they didn't—"

"True. So why do you think you might point it out?" she pressed.

"You mean stand up? You remember I talked with you about pressures on me to disappear?" I was starting to breathe a little hard, but I think it was the uphill walk. Mostly.

"Yes."

We turned into the X2 line. It was early, mostly empty, with people walking quickly around us through the empty barricades toward the roller coaster.

"Well, should I disappear?" I asked.

"You can just live your life, without regard to the issue. That's what I do."

"No, you don't. You run scared half the time."

She deflected. "You could."

"Maybe as Jenna. But can I as Mrs. Ware? There are people who have dissed me because of that, and I'm letting them paint me as they wish. I can't say a blessed word about it, if I'm stealth."

People were climbing over one barricade to get to the next aisle, so we followed suit and began walking up the ramp toward the roller coaster proper.

"You can be Mrs. Ware. You've always been Mrs. Ware. Everybody around you knows that."

Someone walked in-between us.

"I haven't *confirmed* it."

"You're reaching," she told me.

"Maybe." I wasn't discussing all of my concerns.

Up the ramp, X2 stood large, and the line we'd been chasing formed out the side of its building and back a ways.

Someone else walked between us to get to his friend ahead. "Is this ride scary?" The young man asked his friend, excited.

"Sissy, dude!" his friend complained. "Come on!"

I butted in to their conversation and pointed down the hill, beneath the roller coaster. "See those dead bodies scattered on the ground? Probably crashed through support struts all the way down."

Dude looked as if the bodies were really there. "Awesome!" He ran ahead with his friend to join the forming line.

Ellen smiled. "This is gonna be fun."

We stopped walking to join the forming line down the ramp on the side of the X2 building.

One of the 20-year-old ladies in front of us commented to us. "You done this ride before?"

"Never," Ellen said.

"Once." I held up one finger for emphasis. "And that's enough for me."

"For sure!" Blonde said.

"They're old," Brunette said to Blonde.

"Like nearly 60," I said. "And she," I said thumbing Ellen, "is gonna die because she won't listen to me."

"You don't look dead to me," Blonde said to me.

"Trust me," Ellen said. "She's dead *up here*." She tapped her forehead. "She always thinks she's so *right*!"

Oh, we're "doing" these two with our "sister" gag?

"I *am* always right," I said back to her.

"You just think you're better because Mom always liked you best," she said.

The girls giggled at us. They usually did.

"No, Mom liked *you* best," I said. "She kept giving you all my clothes! *I always had to go out and get new ones—*"

With mock indignation, Ellen charged, "Those were your *hand-me-downs...*"

The two ladies teased us a bit, and then returned to their own conversation.

"That's fun to do," Ellen said.

The line moved forward a few feet and stopped again. We could hear mechanical clanging sounds within the ride's building.

Scanning the line, it seemed clear for us to continue talking.

"There's more to it," I said. "You remember I shared with you that Joe and I had trouble from others?"

She nodded, stepping to the side to lean on a rail, scanning people near us. "No details."

"Well, you know one of the reasons I think they happened? I think it was because I was stealth. I think when there are bullies, keeping quiet kinda empowers them."

"Joe's gone, now—I'm sorry. But why would anyone cause you any more trouble?"

"Maybe they won't. But there's more than that. What about the idea that I'm not good enough to be included with people's friends? That still happens. And people act friendly to me when they're not, wishing I was somewhere else. And every time someone disses us—"

The line crept forward again. We moved with it. "You know that other group I was in. The 'conservative group' as I call them? I couldn't avoid being kicked out of that one."

"Why?"

"I stood up for Caitlyn Jenner, when she came out. They didn't like her—but they loved Tom Selleck, so I pointed out that Tom wasn't against gays. Played a gay guy in 'In and Out.'" I smiled at the movie. "Smooched Kevin Kline on the lips for ten seconds! I thought they'd accept that, but they kicked me out."

"That's a stealth issue?" she asked.

"I think so. I think they could presume I was a social justice warrior for a liberal agenda. They didn't have to admit they were dumping on *me* for being trans, because I wouldn't discuss it. If I had been open, they may not have taken action against me, because it might show their prejudice. Stealth mistake: My assumption that they didn't know—which they probably did—allowing them to take action against me for another reason and pretend it's real."

"Or," she said, "they'd have derided you behind your back, made you look like a freak."

"Probably happens among those inclined, anyway. Most of the time, I don't know what's best to do."

Ellen rubbed her hands together, scanned people near us.

Our confidentiality was still okay.

X2 opened for us. Ride personnel showed Ellen how to get in.

"You, too?" a staff person asked.

"I know better," I said with a knowing smile.

"Chicken," Ellen said, all buckled in.

"Cross yourself," I said, showing her how.

"I'm Jewish!" Ellen acted astonished. "*You're* Jewish!"

"If we put the matter through committees, the ride's over before we're done. *You* have to cross yourself: North, South, East, West—"

She did in fun.

When the coaster got back, zombies got off and stumbled on their way.

I still haven't heard the last of it from her.

1985

Entering graduate school to get my master's in social work, I needed a cheaper place to live.

BURBANK: The lady at the door was curt. "I'm sorry. It's not for rent, now."

"But why? The sign—"

She closed the door.

NORTH HOLLYWOOD: The man looked at me with scorn. "You can fill out an application, but it won't do you any good…"

And I needed to adjust my part-time jobs to fit my school schedule.

WILSHIRE DISTRICT: "You can't work here."

GLENDALE: "No."

VAN NUYS: The door closed without comment.

1990

The twin-engine F-14D Tomcat raged across the Edwards Air Force Base flight line in full afterburner, its deep roar shaking windows and shattering ear drums for a mile. The crowd whooped its delight.

Hangar 1600 was full of what may have been forty airplanes, all on static display for the air show. People milled about, stopping to look at planes or talk with owners. It was hot outside. The Hangar doors were wide open. Barely a breeze floated through.

Against the southwest, inner wall of the hangar, I climbed onto the monster's wing and reached inside the T-28 cockpit to turn on the master and sump switches. I could hear the faint whir of the pump, as oil was recovered from the bottom of the engine.

I was feeling good that day because Joe had listened to me and cared.

"What are you doing up there?" a young man asked me.

I looked at him from the top of the wing root. "Pumping oil."

"How long's it gonna take you?"

"Half way," I said.

"Why you doing it?" the young man asked.

I held up one finger. "Stand by one."

I climbed off the wing—aft over the airplane's lowered flaps, the large, embedded, aluminum steps clacking as I went—and joined the young man on the hangar floor in front of the airplane. I glanced at Joe wiping oil off the belly of the plane.

He nodded to me.

I seemed to have his blessing to talk to the guy about the plane.

"The engine holds, I think, about seven gallons of oil—"

"Seven gallons! My Cessna only has four *quart*s."

"It'll grow."

The young man looked at me funny.

"This plane has nine cylinders," I told him. "A lot of oil is needed to splash around—and after we shut down, some of it drains down here." I showed him the bottom of the front of the engine. "And collects in these cylinders. So we pump it out now and then, give it to Jed Clampett, hopefully so it won't leak out, maybe prevent hydraulic lock when we fire up, but we turn the engine over 9 blades before we engage the magnetos—"

"Why is the engine shaped like that?" the fellow asked.

"Uh— Big and round? Flat to the wind?"

I looked. Normally Joe handled the questions. I just fended people off the wings.

Joe nodded.

"It's a 'radial' engine design, I said to the young man. "Back in the early days—about a hundred years ago—it was popular."

I heard Joe chuckle.

"All these cylinders get fresh air, for cooling," I said, "and to save weight, there's a master rod in there. All the pistons have a rod that connects to that rod, and it all rotates around the master rod bearing in the middle." I was showing the guy with my hand, animated at the front of the engine, like Tom Hanks, later, in "Dragnet."

"Nine cylinders?" he asked.

"Yes. They have to be odd, to keep the firing even."

"What's wrong with odd," the young man asked.

"The NIS can't stand it. They're probably still looking for Dorothy." I was referring to the NIS's embarrassing faux pas at misunderstanding the gay slang "Friend of Dorothy" that led to their manhunt in the early 1980s for the elusive, conspiratorial woman.

Joe laughed somewhere behind me.

He got my joke!

"Dorothy?" the young man asked.

"Yes," I said. "'The Wizard of Oz.' Well, she's not the wizard."

The young man seemed confused. "That's fiction."

I exclaimed sardonically. "She apparently has friends—"

Joe walked forward under the wing to call me down. "Jenna!"

I hurried before Joe got up there, "The rods are hooked to a cogwheel—"

"*Cogwheel?*" Joe asked. He loved quoting his old professor from Virginia Polytechnic. He started to push me gently away from the increasingly mixed-up young man.

"Bosco Rasche used to say," Joe said playfully, mocking righteousness, "'There is no such thing as a *cogwheel*!'"

I had to hurry to get my gag in. I spoke to the kid over Joe's shoulder. "I think that's called a 'planetary gear train' in the middle, which means it came from *outer space*."

"Cool!" the kid said, smiling, and moved on.

Joe stood by me, holding a roll of paper towels, oil on his hands and shirt.

"How'd I do?" I asked him.

He shook his head and went back to wiping oil off the plane.

I followed him. "I did just like you taught me!"

Joe and I sat at a table in the O club at Edwards. Pilots, officers, and air show people sat at other tables, danced a little on the floor, or traveled to the bar for another drink.

Joe was wearing his standard jeans, an office shirt, tucked in, and his North American T-28 ball cap. I was wearing my standard jeans and some shirt from J.C. Penny, no cap. My long, dark hair flopped around my shoulders like Bette Midler's after a storm. Air show people, or even just pilots or plane owners, from my experience, did not usually bother dressing up because they were as likely to crawl under an airplane as they were to go to dinner. It was no fashion show.

"Joe," I asked, leaning in to him so he could hear me over the music. "These are test pilots around here, mostly, right?"

"Some." He was always glad to converse, but he didn't usually speak much.

"Hottest jets in the military?"

"Some."

"Then why are they so subdued? The excitement isn't here, like there was at Miramar. They were raising hell there, partying and gung-ho." That was before the Tailhook Scandal.

Joe sipped his Diet Coke, appeared to think about the answer. "This is a test base," was all he said.

"Okay? So?" I prodded.

"Miramar is the Navy's Top Gun school," he said.

I sipped my Diet Coke and scooted my chair a little closer to his, so I didn't have to lean over. The music was not loud, per se, but we were close enough to some speaker that he had trouble hearing me.

"Okay. Like the movie 'Top Gun.'" I smiled. "I like that."

I think Joe sensed I still didn't see the difference.

"These pilots need to follow strict test flight profiles, each flight to test something. Precision is what's needed here, and the ability to calculate. These guys are gutsy, but not hot dogs."

I looked around at them, and it seemed true.

"So," I asked Joe, playing our favorite game of what if, "if I were a kid in college, and I wanted to be a test pilot out of Edwards, I'd have to—" I let that linger for him to finish.

He nodded. Continue.

I finished, guessing. "I'd have to be calm and steady, mature, good at math?"

He smiled.

"Oh! I'm blown out of the water! The only math course I ever took was bowling! I had a calculator, once, but it broke in the dishwasher. These guys wouldn't let me cook their breakfast."

He smiled. "You could do it."

"I don't think they'd want me," I said. "You know why."

"You can understand anything," he said. "And if you can understand it, you can fix it."

"I can't fix everything." I was sure.

"If something's not right, pull up a chair and study it. It'll come to you, if you try."

"How do you know so much?" I asked. "A year I know you, and I still don't know you. Where you from, Georgia or some place? Do they have schools in Georgia?" I teased him to egg him on.

"Va-GIN-ya," he said, mocking sarcasm. "Blacksburg."

"And you mentioned you've got family going back to the Civil War."

He nodded. "Revolutionary War."

"But you don't condone slavery."

The look on his face made it clear he didn't. "No." He looked down, furled his brow slightly.

A pilot walked to a nearby table with two drinks in his hands and a smile on his face. I noticed the wings on his chest.

"What did you do at Lockheed, again?" I asked Joe.

"I was, uh," he said, "a flight test engineer."

"You helped shape airplanes. Engineer them."

He nodded.

"Which was what?" I pressed.

"I'd design a flight test program, and people like these," he indicated the room, "would fly the profile. We'd modify designs to meet specs, improve safety or to perform a certain function."

"You worked with test pilots?" I asked, letting it soak in. Why hadn't I realized that before?

He shrugged.

It was because he hadn't said.

"You— Test pilots worked for you?"

He nodded.

"Like Tony," He said, indicating Tony LeVier. His face brightened a little at the mention.

"Oh, my God, yes!" I remembered him. Tony had come over to Joe's house when I'd been there. It was dawning on me where I was, what these guys were, and what Joe was.

Joe smiled at me for connecting the dots.

"Here at Edwards?" I asked him. "You work with prototypes? You were here?"

He nodded. "Here also."

"I'm so thick," I finally said.

Joe shook his head. "No."

"What planes did you work on?" I asked him.

"Oh, uh, a few." Joe wasn't holding back or playing hard-to-get. He just wouldn't brag to save his life.

"Cough it up. What?"

"Oh, I started out on the Hudson Bomber and the P-38 Lighting, 1941."

I didn't know what a Hudson Bomber was, but I did know the P-38. "No kidding?"

"Yeah. Tony used to fly those, too. And the Connie variants, the YP-3V1—"

"A what?"

"The P-3. Sub chaser. And the YC-130—"

"C-130 *Hercules*?" I said, thinking about it.

"Yeah, partly."

"And you were flight test engineer on jets, too?"

He nodded. "A few."

"Which ones?"

"Oh, uh, the U-2—"

"Holy shit!" I sat back in my chair and looked at him. "Holy shit," I said again, astonished. If this were music, I was sitting with Elvis Presley.

"So you've known Chuck Yeager here, too?"

He shrugged.

"Joe! Jesus!" I was thinking long hot mornings at Edwards on the flight line with the latest planes, hotshot pilots in the cockpit, Joe standing there with a clipboard—

"Tony?" I asked him.

"Yeah, he flew the U-2."

With Tony LeVier in the cockpit!

"And the SR-71—"

"JOE!" I had to catch my breath. "Are you kidding me?"

He smiled. "The SR was something."

"Who were you?" I asked him.

He shrugged it off. "Mostly I worked at Burbank or Palmdale."

"Lockheed," I said.

He nodded. "Skunk Works. I worked for Kelly Johnson."

"Why didn't you ever tell me?" I asked.

He shrugged.

Glenn Miller's "Chattanooga Choo Choo" began to play.

"You know what that is?" he asked me.

"Yes, Glenn Miller, the first gold record. I saw 'Sun Valley Serenade' with Tex Beneke and the Modernaires. I'm hip."

"Then come on," he said. "Lets dance."

He stood up and held out his hand to me.

Glenn Miller's band sounded like a train starting to move.

"I'm not good at dancing. I'm terrible."

He continued holding his hand out and smiled until I accepted.

A few more people walked out onto the small dance floor.

He took me into the square, put his left hand in my right, his right arm around my waist. I put my left hand on his right shoulder, and—

He reached up to turn his ball cap slightly to the side, put his right hand back on my waist.

"Now it's crooked," I said.

"It's jaunty," he said with a smile.

"Tex used to do that with his hat."

It was the first time I'd danced with Joe, and it was revealing. His manner was clipped. It had rhythm. It was dancing, but it wasn't showy or over-done. It was reigned-in with short movements that bounced in beat with the music. Someone watching might have thought we were simply swaying to the music, but really, Joe was quite animated—maybe even a little jazzy.

And then he broke into song with Tex:

"You—leave—the—Pennsylvania station 'bout a quarter to four,

Read a magazine and then you're in Baltimore..."

"You even sound like Tex!"

He laughed in my ear.

4

Transition

1991

I INTENDED to set a National and World Speed Record in a very slow Cessna 152.

Joe and I were at Van Nuys Airport loading my little rented plane. A gray-tan layer of haze and smog covered the San Fernando Valley, the northern half of Los Angeles, topping out at a couple of thousand feet. I could see it against distant hills on all sides. The weather report said it was clear above.

I raised my head and sniffed a little to smell.

"Good air today," I told Joe. "Chevrolet, I think?"

My humor was not his focus, just then.

"So, load your CG as far aft as possible," Joe said, for center of gravity. "Your horizontal stabilizer will produce less down lift, less drag, so you go a little faster. Your power level is fixed, but you can do a lot with drag."

"Okay."

"Stay within the envelope," he said with a smile.

Of course.

"This is so silly," I said, wondering why I was doing it. "A 152 is one of the slowest planes in the air, and from Oshkosh, Wisconsin to Van Nuys, California? You can outrun this plane with a bicycle."

"It's okay," Joe said. Everything was a teaching vehicle to him. "'Paired Cities' is historic. It's the way people back in Lindberg's day would have done it. At first, in aviation, it was as simple as wondering how long it took to go from A to B by plane."

"I'm going to fly to OSH anyway," I said. "So I might as well?"

Joe could see I missed the point. "It's worthy in its own right, if you try."

Joe explained it didn't matter that it was a slow kind of airplane. What mattered was working with it, using my head to apply the principles I'd learned about how to fly as true as possible—navigation, flight technique, weather management—over a long period of time. At 1,756 statute miles, it was more of an endurance run than speed, but technique would make a large difference in outcome.

For both of us, I knew it was something we were sharing.

He leaned over and gave me a hug.

I had been to Oshkosh before, but it was the first time I'd flown there by myself, and I learned a few things.

First, I learned that if you're flying into Wickenburg, Arizona airport after 5 p.m. expecting to gas and go, the fuel pump was closed.

Second, I learned that if you're sleeping under the wing of a 152, it's good to deploy about 10 degrees of flaps, because at 2:00 in the morning, rain will drain off the wing better, instead of onto your sleeping bag soaking your feet.

And Third, I learned the trip was worth it, regardless.

The American southwest, from the air, and apart from forests now and then, appears mostly as brown dirt. After Albuquerque it greens a little, and after Tucumcari, it greens even more. You make a left 45 at Tucumcari, and make a beeline straight through to OSH. Flying for hours over the Midwest, there is plenty of time for introspection. It was the land of my past, and ghostly as hell.

For a number of reasons, including my mother's marriages, we lived in several places in Tornado Alley. South of Dodge City, Kansas, I looked beneath the left wing of the Cessna to see Minneola floating by, our family seat, as it were, where Mom was born and raised, where her parents lived, the place to which we returned, repeatedly. I could see the Christian church on the corner—south of that central white building, and Grandma and Grandpa's house across the street to the south of that.

Figure 4.1. Minneola, Kansas

I saw my younger, tortured, eight-year-old self, stand on the sidewalk, staring at the church on Sunday morning, at girls who got to be themselves, who knew a parent's embrace as who they were, who may have guessed a future they could grasp. Her heart was already broken. She was a shadow of herself, barely alive, able to walk to church but unable to believe God loved her, unable to love herself.

It's me, I thought, sending love and courage through spacetime to my earlier self, who had no idea I was here, just above.

You can make it.
Hold on.
I'm here with you.

1981

By the time I was 23, I was beside myself with desperation. The mind-body incongruence felt like a congenital birth defect tearing me apart. It came with severe psychic pain, something from which I could no longer run.

When people have asked me in life how it hurt, what did the pain feel like, where was it localized, I've been known to answer, "Imagine someone stuck something in your brain and twisted it to make you scream." The brain wouldn't actually feel it, as such, in reality, but it's the best way I can describe what I've always felt, nonetheless. It felt like a deep pain nothing could touch, deep in the middle of my soul, as if in the vicinity of the hypothalamus, screaming for relief—as if something deep inside was biologically one way, incapable of tolerating things the other way. The physical sex I was in body did not match the sex I knew I was inside, which I'm sure exasperated more than a few people in my life.

I don't know if it was caused by diethylstilbestrol—DES, a synthetic estrogen, which was sometimes given to women in the years around my birth, in the belief it would reduce the risk of pregnancy complications—or if it was due to other chemicals, intrauterine fluctuations, a combination of genes, epigenetics, nutrition, or even a natural variation of the species. In my opinion, if the brain is part of the body, the brain/body discordance is an intersex condition, possibly a significant, prenatal nondifferentiation of the brain, which may be confirmed at a later date through research. But I do know the strong need has been with me since my first thoughts in this life, and remains with me to this day.

My mother gave birth to me in that small, wheat farming community, in 1957. I became the 2nd of 2 males, then the middle of 3, and several years later, the 2nd of 5. The three older children had the same father and mother, the 4th had a different father, and the fifth, a different father, still—but no matter how hard life became at times, we never thought of any of us as "half brothers." We had the same mom. We were raised together.

She and my father divorced in my early childhood. A succession of other husbands came and went through the course of her life. She married a total of 7 times to 6 men, if my count is right. Her marriages tended to be brief, only a few years or months. Most of the time, she wasn't married. I never met two of them. Women should care for the home, the culture complained, and if they worked, it should only be to help a little. Women should keep a husband, we understood, but Mom didn't.

And she fought hard to raise us. She usually had trouble earning enough money for us to live on. Sometimes the gas would be shut off at the house, because we couldn't pay the bills, or we would have to move because we couldn't pay the rent. Pennies were always counted at the grocery store.

Our mother was a good person, kind and loving, even outgoing, yet with a sensitive and fearful heart who struggled to find love in a culture that seemed quick to criticize. Life had to be a certain way or it was wrong, perhaps a character deficit—something she noticed, because she didn't fit expectations, and that I noticed as well, because I didn't fit, either.

My brothers may reasonably have a different view, but my childhood understanding of Mom was that, even though she cared for us deeply, her giving nature would sometimes erupt under pressure. Someone would say something, and she would sometimes react as if it touched a sore spot that we couldn't see. She never shared, but I think she had the feeling she needed to be a much better person than she felt she was, and that she could not measure up—never mind that her effort to raise us in that situation was heroic.

As a toddler, my problem had no words. It was just me, in pain with discordance, needing to exist, a silent scream inside. As I grew, I began to express some of my traits, feminine, which led to punishment from my mother with condemnation and battery. I grew to learn that I was shameful, unwanted, unloved, that I should be nothing, and indeed, that I actually was nothing. I remember one such event distinctly at about age 6 when she beat me, holding my arms with one hand while she hit me repeatedly with a belt until I had, perhaps, 50 welts and bruises over the entire back side of my arms, back, butt, and legs. *"Stop acting like a girl!"*

I didn't even know what "acting like a girl" meant, but I later learned she believed my nature had been perceived by others as yet another thing she had done wrong in her life, as if not only could she not keep a husband, she couldn't raise her children right, either. I think she beat me out of fear—then, at other times, she'd hold me and tell me I was so special.

At age 7, I realized I was alive, awareness dawning one day as I walked through the front yard of our house on Redbarn in Wichita, Kansas, before her husband #3, I think. After that, I was able to voice my pain in specific to God, naming the problem, pleading through tears for help. But as far as I knew, God agreed with Mom. I had to suppress myself everywhere. If

I shared myself, if I so much as said how cute something was, I would get that glance, be ridiculed or beaten.

Growing up I was also a person who needed to survive, somehow, hopefully to feel good about herself, in some way, so a duality developed of an inner me that could not be denied, on the one hand, and a series of conditioned expressions on the other that were meant to get me by, if I kept quiet. I had to pretend as though I was a boy and, to my humiliation, that I liked it.

I felt constantly alone, different and separate from others. Simple human connection was not possible because of the extreme disconnect in my own self. I could not relate to myself, so I could not relate to others.

By 1981, at about my age of 23, I was coming apart. I thought I was strong, but I wasn't nearly as strong as my need. Even if my family would know I was a freak, even if people in society would regard me with hate crimes, the only solution I could see was to bring my body in line with my soul, to be myself to the extent possible. It wasn't about dressing in women's clothes, and it wasn't about a social role as a woman or sexual orientation (being into men). It was just *me*, my state of being. It wasn't explainable as anything else, as if my brain knew what I had to be—again, it felt neural, something in brain formation, most definitely not a choice. My sex identity was distinctly female, and every move I made, every moment of existence, I knew I needed a completely female body, the ability to bear children, all of it—yet none of which could I have. I had a nightmare, instead.

I am not exaggerating. Many people who feel more strongly die by their own hand.

Yet, as strong as was my need to be female, so, also, was the conditioned need to make maleness work, a relic of the hostile culture in which I was raised. So, as inexplicable as it may seem—yet as I've seen in other transitioners—I waffled when I made a chance for myself.

In the Navy, my plan was to get out, go to L.A., switch. After I got out of the Navy, however, I made the mistake of going back home to the area of my former culture, and there was the same guy there, whom I had known in high school, who had captured my heart in a way I did not yet understand.

I didn't think to frame a romantic thought about him. The awareness wasn't there. In retrospect, I know it's because what I needed was not possible; I did not love him as a male. But at the time, all I could see was *him*. He captivated my mind. He was everything. It's amazing I couldn't see that at the time—denial born of discordance and social condemnation.

I was under his spell, without even knowing it.

What he did, I did.

He dated women. I dated women.

He got married. And I got married—to a female.

I would never be embarrassed to be lesbian; I was embarrassed because I was *not* lesbian. I admired her, tried to be into her, my body was able, but emotionally I wanted to flee. In time, I think she grew to understand.

I got her to read my copy of Canary Conn's book, and after a short while, I broke down and told her my problem. To my surprise, she was a friendly angel who tried to help—I think, partly, because she was not really in love with me, either.

We moved to Hollywood in 1980 and got an apartment on Normandy, just above Hollywood Blvd. With her knowledge, I found a doctor and began my transition. Academically, I knew all the details, but inside I didn't have a clue what to do. I recognized females two out of three times, but my whole life had been spent trying *not* to be one. I found the process of transition both elating and embarrassing, my old conditioning still with me.

What worked for me best was learning how *not to try*. Because I'd been trained to pretend as *other* most of my life, the most valuable thing I could do *was to let go*—*unlearn* behaviors I'd ingrained, let them dissolve, and begin to discover for the first time in my life what lay inside.

As I look back, now from 35 years in transition, I can see that the influence on my life from that earlier other-me training in my formative years continues to fade. Transition is not something that happens and is done. It's an ongoing process that lasts through life—like being raised traumatically in one country, moving to another as an adult to survive. You can forget an earlier life for long stretches of time, but it's still there, following you around for decades.

The angel helped me choose my name, helped me relearn myself, and helped me tell my family—me, the one who invented social suicide to avoid ever telling them. The guy I mentioned took it seemingly with good-natured humor, largely in stride. He wasn't prejudiced. A friend of his, however, openly laughed. Several family withheld opinion from me—which always felt like a negative, expressed with silence—but my mother was clear. She threatened to have me kidnapped and institutionalized so I wouldn't mutilate myself.

I moved.

In the Los Angeles area, in the early '80s, with her in the Midwest, it would be hard for her to find me.

Shortly after I began, my angel got a boyfriend, moved out, and we got an amicable divorce, going our separate ways. I was on my own from then on, with Canary's story of a difficult transition lingering in my mind.

Transition, for me, became a frenzied whirlwind of pressured change. I was beyond my ability to tolerate my old self a moment longer. I was a shot out of a gun. Everything I did was with one thing in mind, one thing only.

I found a job at Max Factor headquarters, in Hollywood, on the third floor, Corporate Planning Department, as a word processing secretary on a CPT 8000, right across the street from (then) Mann's Chinese Theatre on Hollywood Blvd. I'd begun female hormones, and I was developing, but I did not transition on the job, yet, until I changed enough to at least partially fit my new role, and also until I had permission from Personnel. Everything grew together at the same time. My hair was growing. I collected a meager wardrobe, not wanting to spend any extra money on it, because surgery was going to cost me just over $7,000, a huge sum to me.

The first day going to work in my new role, people didn't recognize me. The change was so profound. I had to re-introduce myself, and word got around, though no one expressed a negative word to me. It was all positive, as far as I knew. Max Factor even assigned someone to take me to the Max Factor make-up studio on Highland, a block away. I think the intent was to show support. I was thankful to learn the makeup artist was genuinely pleased to help.

However I seemed to people on the outside, inside I was barely able to hold on from my initial steps in transition until my Sex Reassignment Surgery (SRS) several months later. It was during that time that I experienced the worst pain of my life. Some people seem to feel I should have been happier with a transition of gender—"You're a woman, now"—but I found it excruciating, like being closer to survival, almost able to breathe, yet still denied.

I need to clarify because "gender" pervades discourse and transgenderism is being used as an umbrella term over disparate phenomena. I embrace my transgender brothers and sisters, each with his or her goals. They make a gender transition and feel happy, somewhere on a continuum where they feel more comfortable, "The [man or woman] I've always wanted to be." But for me, the need to be the other physical sex is different from the need to be the other gender/not wanting to be the other sex. Virginia Prince, Ph.D., then promoting transgenderism and herself as a "transgenderist," made it clear to me differences between sex and gender. For me, being in that state—cross gender yet same sex—was intolerable. At the time, I likened it to a person, emaciated, genuinely starving, who had been admitted to a banquet, yet not allowed sustenance—"You can be here, but *no food*," which was the point for being there, to me.

Living in a banquet hall, the starving was more poignant than before; it hurt between my ears and in my heart, my stomach and groin. The ugly, putrid growth that God had for some reason stuck on me, was so vile, so disgusting—I could no longer block it out. The dual game scenario I'd learned in childhood no longer worked. I had revealed myself.

One psychologist I met—not mine—at a university, once asked me as if perplexed, "How can you like men, if you hate male genitalia so much?" I was aghast at his question. I really didn't need ignorance like that from people who were supposed to understand. I told him as simply as I could, "How could any female? Don't you get the *basics*?" Thankfully, I never saw him again.

For a time, I was unsure how I'd ever get the money for SRS. It seemed like saving would go on forever. I moved into a one-room, cheap apartment in Van Nuys on Sepulveda. My old car broke down—I left it where it was. I had no money to fix it.

I took the bus. Like in the Navy, I dropped to eating only one meal a day, losing perhaps 35 pounds I could not afford to lose. I took a second job. The money wouldn't come in fast enough. Every day was earn a dollar, save a dime.

Starve and scream in silence.

The days dragged on—

I would lie in my one-room apartment at night crying, tears running down the sides of my face, through my hair onto the pillow, screaming in my mind for God to help.

When could I call the surgeon and make an appointment?

I schemed, getting letters of approval for surgery. Working at Max Factor, I was also in college with a full load, evenings, getting monthly money for the G.I. Bill.

Even though it had only been a few months. I remember going to a doctor in Encino and crying in the exam room about the delays, *"Why! Why does the system hold out its hand and say, 'I won't help you unless you cross my palm with enough green'? Can't they see we're dying?"*

My doctor was a good man, but, without knowing the extent of my pain, he answered the question, I had asked, with business realities.

I walked out of his office on Balboa, south toward the bus station on Ventura Blvd., while I pretended on the outside to be calm, as well as I could, for people around me. I moved my feet down the sidewalk, one step at a time, zen walking, praying the future would come. I tensed certain muscles to appear to smile at someone. I waited at the bus stop. When the bus got there, I held the handrail on the bus to enter and made myself sit down on the putrid growth as if it didn't hurt.

I began to fear that if I couldn't get surgery soon, my transition could take a lot longer than expected. I feared that as slowly as I saved, surgeon's fees could increase further out of my range. I was so desperate that suicide was again entering my mind, against my will, and I began to fear that some night, in pain, I could do it on impulse. I didn't want to. I knew I couldn't mention it to anyone, or I could be locked up for observation, which would both delay and hinder my request for surgery.

I just needed health care for an ailment few recognized as worthy.

Finally, thin as a rail, Max Factor health insurance agreed to pay part of it. I was then only $700 shy of my goal. I made phone calls, begging for money. One evening, to my surprise, my biological father agreed to give me the $700, and I got Stanley Biber in Trinidad, Colorado, then called "The Sex Change Capital of the World," to do it for me.

My time was coming!
I prayed nothing would go wrong.
Biber don't get sick.
Don't have an accident.
Myself, don't get sick.
Don't get mugged in my bad neighborhood.
Look before crossing streets.

When the day came to go, another of Biber's patients took me to Los Angeles' Union Station where I took a train straight to Trinidad. A nun met me at the train and was nice to me. A *nun*. Someone official with the Christian religion had been accepting with me. As chance would have it, I stayed in the Columbian Hotel in "Tom Mix' old room," I was told, on the 2nd floor, in the front corner.

I saw Biber the next day in his office and checked into Mt. San Rafael Hospital, spent my time counting minutes.

Nothing go wrong.
Biber don't get sick.
Don't slip on the floor...

Entering the operating room the next morning, I was under a pre-sedation, but even then I knew what I was doing. I thanked God for His help, over and over.

After a lifetime of screaming for help, the surgery, for me, only took ten seconds. A mask went over my face. I zen counted...

When I was awake enough to think, I tried to assess. They had me on my back in a bed, in my room, my knees slightly spread with a pillow beneath them. I was weak, but I had to check. I lifted the sheets to see if in fact— *It was done!* My heart leaped! I looked further. I had to lift my head, because there was not much to look at from my angle.

Swollen, with gauze— It was clear. It had been done.

To this day, I am thankful to that former Chief Surgeon of a MASH unit in Korea for his courage in saving my life. He was my Hawkeye Pierce, a gifted genius—who I wish could have explained things to my mother.

Accepting that I was past the horror, of my life to then, did not seat in my heart on that first day. I don't think well on pain killers. But I think it's also true that fear so deep, and held so long, won't disappear overnight. The traumatic hell of being so wrong in earlier life continued to spring to mind. I had to reassure myself, again and again, that it was over, at least that part of it, letting the effects of surgery, so profound, wash over the echoes of fear.

Figure 4.2. Jen, early '80s, hiking in Griffith Park.

I felt an internal battle that my relief might be a dream, part of a nightmare designed to hurt me even more when I would realize SRS hadn't happened, but reality slowly won over time.

In a matter of moments, a ton of weight left my chest. In hours my anxiety began to dissipate. In days, most of the panicked fear I had lived with before surgery fell to the side. Every time I woke from a nap and found the dream *true,* my embrace of this life grew stronger.

I was an important step closer to my unobtainable goal, to be biologically female.

I began to settle down, inside, became more relaxed. I began to let myself catch up to what I am—finally on the right side of correct—and the world began to turn *funny*, a new one for me. Events in the hospital, the curt way Biber talked, the way I waddled when I walked, at first, would break me up, and I'd laugh until I feared I'd tear something. It was a new thing, to feel so good about myself. The discovery was so rich and natural.

As the months went by, I began to find peace, for the first time—ever—to take more of an interest in other people. I was able to give genuine smiles to people I met and talk with them about things that mattered to them, instead of myself.

1991

In the North 40, the large camping area on the north end of the field at Oshkosh, I got the little spam can ready for the return flight back to Van Nuys—to a man who I was learning appreciated me for who I was, who cared about my life, and who called me "Jenna."

An official from the Federation Aeronautique Internationale saw me off, recorded the time. I flew with the maximum continuous engine RRM that was reasonable, while being kind to the engine. The altitudes I chose reflected my understanding of the winds aloft. Even my day and time of departure were planned per my anticipated fatigue through the night and into the next day.

Flying southwest across the Midwest, typical afternoon/evening convection built. By midnight, I was aware I could no longer see any stars ahead, and that was a bad sign. It meant something was in the way. A squall line had developed. I slept for 2-1/2 hours in Colby, Kansas, on the couch of an open FBO, while thunderstorms passed overhead.

Rain doesn't drip on your feet, inside an FBO.

Flying into Van Nuys the next evening, I pulled a Joe trick. From 10,500 feet, over the Mojave Desert, I put the plane into a 200-feet-per-minute descent, to gain true air speed over a longer period of time and screamed over Van Nuys as fast as my 152 could. I coordinated with Van Nuys tower over the radio to clock me as I passed over the VOR, the navigational aid on the field, which served as my finish. My time overall was 28 hours, 36 minutes, 9 seconds, if I recall, at 60.45 mph on average. The plane would go double that, but that time included such things as re-routing for weather, refueling, climbs, and the time I spent sleeping on the couch in Kansas. The numbers don't seem to reflect the work that went into it. The record was more of a testament to the ability to fly while tired—and it was fun.

Joe was there, waiting for me on the ramp at Van Nuys, a beautiful sight, his broad smile welcoming me. Exhausted and worn, I climbed out of the plane and ran to him for a hug that has never ended. I still feel his embrace.

Figure 4.3. Jenna, Bob Hoover, Joe Ware.

Like Joe said, I came to understand the "speed run" as an exercise in doing my best. Bob Hoover, air show pilot, former USAF pilot and friend to Chuck Yeager, seemed to look at me like Joe did and took it seriously when he later gave me my award plaques in Santa Monica. Joe was beaming the whole time, caring about my growth. He seemed proud of me—

Proud of me?

Years later, talking with Mom in a restaurant in Dallas, she asked me why transition was so important.

"Why did you have to put everyone through that hell?" She indicated me with a sweep of her hand. "You ran shod over everyone. Don't you care about anyone else but yourself?"

"Would you say that if it was a heart condition?" I asked her.

"That would have been *real.*"

"*This* is real."

She leaned on the table. "How could you have *known* it was *real*?"

"I couldn't *not* know it, Mom. And please understand: without it, I know I would have died."

She seemed disgusted. "It wouldn't have killed you—"

"Yes it would—as surely as if God cut out my heart with a knife. People do die from this."

"But how could you have *known*?" she asked me. "It was *crazy*. You were so young!" She leaned in to me and whispered. "People are so weird any more."

I leaned into her and whispered back. "*Everybody's* weird, Mom. You know that. We're people, like any other." I sat back up. "I knew because it was me, who I am."

"I gave birth to you!"

"You didn't know what I was born *with*."

"I sure as hell did!"

"Only on the *outside!* How do you think a three-year-old would dream this up? Think I saw it on Captain Kangaroo? There was no guessing, Mom. I couldn't avoid it!"

"People feel things all the time that aren't true. What about denial? Or delusions? *How did you know it was true?*" she demanded.

"Mom, it's not—" I had no way to say, but I tried. "If you were denied air, and you were gasping, how would you know you needed air?"

"That's biological."

"*This is biological!*"

"It's flaky!"

"My *physical sex* is not flaky!"

She sat back in the booth and crossed her arms over her chest.

Even through the worst of it, I never attempted suicide. I was struggling to live. But I'm sure I came as close to it as one could, and still live to write these pages.

Suicide is a major problem for all trans persons. Per the findings of the National Transgender Discrimination Survey, suicide attempts for trans people are alarming, summarized:

- 41% in general
- 51% for those bullied or harassed in school
- 55% for those with job loss due to bias
- 61% for those who had low household income or physical assault
- 64% for those who suffered sexual assault

The majority of us have suffered much of this, I pray for everyone to know. The next time someone mentions something negative about our "lifestyle," I ask someone to consider the hell we try to live through, struggling to be ourselves. My mind is stunned when I learn *some people would rather let us die than accept us*—and when healthcare is denied, when disgust substitutes for respect, when people criticize and denigrate us, that is what that is. When people hit us, rape us, and kill us, that is exactly what that is.

5

He Knew the Whole Time

1991

ROKUDAN SHIHAN TAKE SHIGEMICHI—actor Steven Seagal—looked at me sitting *seiza* along the edge of the mat with the other students. I wore a medium-weight dogi and a black, floor-length hakama, with "Je ni fa" embroidered in Japanese on my right hip. I had a brown belt at my middle, my long, dark brown hair was gathered behind my neck.

I also wore a brace on my right wrist, a joint strap on my left shoulder, and two knee braces, literally trying to keep myself together.

Aikido was the way of harmony with the energy around us. I'd begun it before he came out with "Above the Law." The harmony, when I could get it right, was beautiful, but in the end, I'd stayed with it because I was getting hurt. I needed to learn how not to get hurt, the whole business of *ukemi*.

Which meant better harmony.

Take Sensei (TAH-keh SEN-say) was the real thing. He was a master, and his skill was impressive. In *rondori*, where he was the *nage* (NAH-gay), the one who throws, alone against three black belt *ukes* (OO-kays), ones who receive, my health concern was for them, not for him. Thankfully by the time they went black, they knew how to get thrown, because he was a tornado. He could stand roughly in the center of the mat and move—not all that much, but so correctly they went flying, piling onto the mat, against a wall, anything.

My talent, however, at Aikido was limited, which is why I never went black, *shodan*. I could not get myself to move fast enough, as the effort would sublux my shoulders or knees. It would be years before I learned of my genetic syndrome that allowed that, which was also why my arms were longer than usual.

My rank was *ikkyu*, first level brown belt, just under black. I was the ranking female on the mat that day at Take Sensei's ranch near Santa Ynez.

He nodded to me.

I promptly placed both hands on the mat, bowed, and ran up to him, taking a stance, looking up to him, waiting. He was tall, maybe 6 foot 4 or 5 inches.

He looked at me like he meant business. He always meant business.

"*Katate dori*," he told me in Japanese. I knew I had to use my right hand to grab his left wrist—and whatever he did, I better move fast to keep up. I was a senior student. He was supposed to challenge my abilities, to help me improve.

I gathered whatever strength I thought I had for the technique—my right wrist was about to be torqued. I looked at him severely, mentally checked my joints, and stepped forward with my best intentions.

No chance!

I never reached his wrist.

Lightning fast, he cut my right hand very slightly to the side, grabbed it in his left, turned around by my side—*tenkan*—then stepped behind me and bent my wrist back over my elbow.

Kote gaeshi!

I knew it. I'd trained in it for years.

We were not dancing; he didn't play around. If I let him crank my wrist, it would break. And it's the uke's responsibility—me—to protect myself from harm. Throwing someone was only part of Aikido.

Move it or lose it!

I dove over my right elbow, flipped through the air, and landed on my left side, slapping the mat with my left hand.

My right wrist stung.

I didn't move with *him!*

He's so bloody fast—

Move faster!

I got up as fast as I could. I was on him in half a second, reaching for his wrist—.

He moved again—*tenkan*—and *wham*! I was back on the mat.

I had no idea, at the time, how or how often I would use Aikido, years later, to help prolong Joe's life. I offer my most profound thank you to Take Sensei and Reynosa Sensei.

1992

The nurses' station was busy as usual. One of them looked at me as I walked past.

I smiled and pointed ahead. "Joe's room." I carried a small envelope in my hand.

She nodded and went back to her work.

He was sitting up in bed, on his new, metal right hip.

"Good Morning, Joe! How is the Six Million Dollar Man?" I referred to a popular, former television show about a man with mechanical enhancements.

"Fine, fine." That was a big summation from him.

"You can run a hundred miles an hour, now?"

"Oh, sure."

"I got this in the mail for you." I handed him the card envelope.

He looked it over. "It's from Counselor Troi? From the Enterprise? This real?" He was still on some pain killers.

We watched "Star Trek. The Next Generation" on TV.

"No, no. It's real." I played along with my gag. "See?" I tapped the envelope with my finger to show him it was not imaginary. "It says it's from the 24th century, right there in the 'from' part." He looked better than the previous day. "Doc says I can take you home, today."

It had been a month with no flying, while he recuperated and could finally bend his hip enough to get into my little Cessna 120 taildragger.

I placed a footstool on the ground in front of the cockpit door.

"A month is too long," he said, opening the right side door, placing it in its groove against the right wing strut.

"There," I said. "Sit on the seat, scoot in backwards as far as you can—"

He did.

"That's right. Any problem so far? Your hip hurt?"

"No, fine."

Joe scooched butt-first onto the bench seat of the little, 1947 taildragger.

"A little more?"

He scooched in some more.

"Now maybe turn and put your left foot in the cockpit, against the bulkhead."

"No problem." He did it.

"Now, push with your left foot a little—scooch in some more. Now—" I placed my hands under his right foot so he wouldn't have to do it with his muscles, babying them. "Let's see if this will rotate in."

Figure 5.1. 1947 Cessna 120 "Jenna's Dream"

It was so refreshing, flying over the Oxnard plain, side by side, seeing the area he'd loved for decades: Channel Islands Harbor, Ventura Harbor, fields of crops, nearby mountains.

We could speak to each other through our headphones and the intercom.

Joe sat comfortably in the right seat.

"You want to fly?" I asked him.

He took the yoke and I let go. His turns were smooth. He had never been a fighter-pilot-type. He was precise and calculated.

Back in the traffic pattern for landing, on the down wind leg, Camarillo Airport under my left wing, I took back the plane.

"Camarillo Tower, One Three November, left down wind abeam, full stop."

The tower gave me my clearance. "One Three November, clear to land."

"We the only ones in the pattern?" I asked the tower.

"Yeah," he said.

I repeated the clearance to the tower. "One Three November, Cleared to Land."

"What kind of landing you want, Joe?"

"Safe one."

"Oh, different this time?"

"How about at the 1000 foot marker," he said, *"trailing edge this time—and you've lost all your power right now."* He reached over and pulled the throttle back all the way. "Pretend the engine's dead."

The plane slowed behind the windmilling prop and began to lose altitude. I looked at the runway, calculated a reasonable base leg, and adjusted the yoke to keep us at our best glide speed.

"Wheel or three point landing?"

"Wheel." He smiled at me. It was easy to make a simulated-forced landing to the runway, but to make his mark, dead-stick, and "wheel" it was a little different. He was giving me something to work toward.

"Okay! Watch this. I got this." I was so modest. I keyed the mike. "Short approach, One Three November."

"Approved, short approach," Tower said over the radio.

I made sure the fuel/air mixture was rich, pulled the carb heat on, to keep ice out of the O-200 engine up front, turned on my turn signals—

"Oh, no. Wrong plane." I teased Joe.

I focused on the image of the runway, more specifically the thousand foot markers, as the plane sank—then I applied nearly full right rudder and left aileron, putting the airplane into a hard slip. It's the kind of maneuver that makes people on the ground scream, *"It's gonna crash!"* But in reality, it's a common maneuver on landing for antique airplanes with no flaps. It pushes the fuselage into the wind, slowing it down, so I can bring the plane down faster without gaining speed. I was using it to shorten my glide.

Talking to myself helped me focus. "Lets see, 8 knot wind from two four zero. The windsock is medium. Runway heading is two six zero, 20 degree left crosswind, feel the drift..."

I glanced at Joe and checked my breakers, just in case he'd pulled one.

He hadn't, but nodded to me.

"I'm past downwind. Plan to overshoot the mark then shorten my glide—"

I turned base, focused on the runway.

"Make sure your gear is down," Joe said. He was distracting me, an old trick.

"Gear's welded down," I said with no delay, though in truth it was bolted. The Cessna 120 has "fixed gear," meaning it's always down, not possible to raise it.

"Drift, glide ... keep the air speed the same for now."

I held the slip all the way through a quick descent on base.

On final, it was clear I was going to safely overshoot my mark, so I increased the slip, full rudder, and nosed the plane down some to increase air speed a little, which was not a hotshot maneuver. I was within limits. The plane was designed for it. And drag increased as the square of the speed—shortening our glide further.

The runway threshold slipped by beneath us.

At 20 feet above the runway, I leveled the wings and kept the plane in a forward slip as our airspeed bled off.

The leading edge of the 1000-foot marker came—then the trailing edge went by.

I missed it.

The plane slowed enough I could straighten out the fuselage— "I need to be about 5 or so knots above stall for a wheel landing, with no power, so inertia will keep the tail up for a few seconds while I put her down—"

The two main tires greased onto the runway, and I promptly applied the smallest touch of forward pressure on the yoke. The elevator on the horizontal stabilizer angled down slightly, which raised the tail. The nose dipped. The angle of attack on the wing decreased, and suddenly we had no lift. The plane was stuck to the runway like fly paper.

Speed bled off, and the tail dropped onto the runway of its own accord.

"I think you over-estimated the wind," Joe said.
"I know."
"But nobody's bleedin'." His smile told the story.

I lay on the examination table for my annual physical examination, my feet in the stirrups.
"Doctor, you're sure I need a Pap smear?"
"Yup."
"But what does a Pap smear really do? Why—"
"It won't take a minute."
I felt the pressure inside as he opened his speculum.

We sat in the third pew from the front on the right side, in front of the choir, opposite the preacher.

The look on my face was brooding. I didn't like Christianity. I'd been condemned to hell more times than I could count—probably part of the reason I'd converted to Judaism in the mid-'80s.

In that day's sermon, the preacher had mentioned gay people only slightly, and in such a way that people could take it as a condemnation or not, however they wished—noncommittal, which didn't make me feel any better. I wasn't gay, but I used sentiment toward gays as a social barometer, a way of guessing how people might feel about me. If he was playing games with it, it wasn't good.

I looked around.

Who in here knows about me?

I couldn't ask. Except for such people as Joe, doctors or lawyers, other trans people, I hadn't raised that issue since the mid-'80s, because I'd had too much difficulty in the years before.

Joe was happy to be there and held my hand.

"All rise," the pastor said.

Everyone stood, except me.

Hell no!

Why does Joe bring me here?

Joe's eyes were not doing as well, due to macular degeneration, so he didn't bother trying to read the small print in the hymnal. But he knew the lines to this one.

"Holy, holy, holy! Lord God Almighty!
Early in the *mooorning* our song shall rise to thee…"

My right knee was in a bandage and brace: medial meniscal tear. The nurse handed me crutches.

My surgeon had a look of disgust on his face. "Don't torque it." He turned and walked away without a goodbye.

He hadn't been disgusted with me before the surgery.

My heart sank.

Doctors are as bigoted as anyone else, and getting it from someone I've come to for help—

It stung, and it was getting old.

By 11 years in transition, I'd had enough experience to notice the look. I think people who face oppressions notice, become more sensitive to them than other people—who seem to write them off as benign.

We reached my apartment building.

"Come on," Joe said, helping me out of his car.

My head hung, because of the doctor's stinging look, and Joe knew it.

"It'll be okay," he said.

That will never go away.

In spite of my sturdy appearance, we both knew I was fragile and I could be hurt with the slightest torque. My left ankle could sometimes fold without warning. Lifting anything could cause a wrist to sublux, particularly my right. Sometimes, my shoulders would sublux and drive a searing pain through me. It was the weight of the arm, itself, when standing relaxed, that did it. Sitting down—riding a motorcycle, driving a car, flying, boating—it never happened because shoulder muscles were either in use or the weight of the arm was resting on my leg. I was designed to sit and drive things.

I had tried to make up for my joints for years through exercise—which was none too helpful for feminization—and by learning physical coordination, hence the Aikido: how to move with my body and keep my joints in.

Joe helped me up the stairs to my apartment. I took them one at a time, kept my right foot on a stair braced with crutches, stepped up to the next stair with my left, repeat.

"You don't need to stay here alone," he said.

"It's where my things are."

"Come live with me."

I braced myself and climbed another step with my left foot.

I shook my head. "I'll be alright. The bed is two steps from the bathroom. It wasn't that big a surgery."

"You need to quit Aikido," Joe said.

I reached the top of the stairs.

"I know. The doc also said to—but, for what it's worth, I didn't hurt this knee in Aikido."

"How then?"

"All I did was turn around in the kitchen."

During those years, we'd increasingly spent our time flying and boating. Friends of his, such as Tony LeVier, test pilot, and Gil Cefaratt, technical writer from Lockheed, would come over to the harbor house and talk to me about Joe, go boating with us. Joe would take me to church with him, against my will, or on little trips to L.A. or Palmdale to see his family. We went to movies, sat at the beach, and walked around the ramp at the airport, with me asking questions about his life or aviation design, and him talking at my urging.

In time, he convinced me to come live with him in the harbor, which bothered me. I feared it would be another embarrassment in life and that I'd find myself, in a couple of months, having to find another apartment, but he assured me I would not. He always seemed to understand our process better than I.

So with some trepidation, I gave up my apartment and moved into the front bedroom of his house in the Channel Islands Harbor, Mandalay Bay. His house was the smallest design in the harbor, but it was magnificent to me because, steadily and over the course of time, it was clear that he cared about me.

Someone cared about me, who actually understood me?

One morning, not long afterward, we found ourselves hanging a bunch of his old Lockheed photos in the living room. I was pulling them one at a time out of a box and sorting them. He had the P-38, P-80, F-104 Starfighter, the YC-130, the P-3...

"And this one?" I asked.

"Oh, that's a bunch of the guys and me, out front of Nineteen Sixty-one. That was its serial number, not the year. The Skunk Works bought it off Howard Hughes to use as a prototype test bed. First thing I did was stretch it. Then we produced—" He showed me photos. "See this one? Notice 1961 here has three different kinds of engines on it? R-3350 Turbo Compound, a turboprop, and a turbojet. That was fun."

"R-3350?" I asked.

"Duplex Cyclone, from Wright."

I pulled photo after photo out of a box and laid them in groups.

"And this one? It's a Connie, too."

"That's the R7V-2. It had all turboprops on it."

I saw a couple I recognized. "And these?" I held them out carefully for him to see.

"That's the WV-2. And that's the WV-2E with the rotodome."

"You were flight test engineer on these?"

I saw the WV-2 pictured at NSOC.

I looked at Joe knowingly. I knew he knew, and I knew he knew I knew, but we also both knew there could be no discussion about it, so we didn't. Consideration for classified material was important to both of us.

Joe smiled.

All I said was, "You little shit."

He chuckled at me. "Well—"

"You knew your planes had done that—this whole time! That's how you knew!"

"Well, you told me at Edwards—"

"You couldn't reciprocate? I showed you mine—"

He shrugged and smiled, caught red handed.

"Okay." I said. "Little shit."

I found other photos in the box, the U-2 and the SR-71—

PART 2

CAN'T STAND UP FOR MYSELF

"You are never given a wish, without also being given the power to make it true."

Richard Bach
The Bridge Across Forever: A True Love Story

6

Know Yourself

THE BIGGEST PROBLEM I've seen in transitioners is learning how we present to others, how we come across. How do others perceive us? How do we look or act? In most of us, the need to be is so strong that we tend to think we come across as how we feel.

1992

Standing at the kitchen bar, in the harbor house, I held the phone's handset to my ear, to listen. The handset cord was so long, it touched the floor.

I spoke to Joe in the living room, 20 feet away. "Do you remember Jane from the party last month at Tina's?"

"The little one?" Joe asked. "Black hair?"

"Tina said she got beat up last week, and she won't talk about it."

"Another one." Joe hung his head.

"Jane wants to meet us for lunch after we're done at the doctor's."

"Okay," Joe said. "Fine."

I drove us south on the 405 freeway, over the Sepulveda Pass in lane number 2. The traffic was a little heavy, and cars were only doing about 50 mph. A motorcycle blew by us at 70, splitting traffic between lanes 1 and 2.

"Jeees!" I said.

"Never do that," Joe said.

"Not me," I said.

Joe and I got out of the car at the Jules Stein Eye Institute, UCLA. I held his hand through the parking lot toward the building.

"The air is so fresh, today," I said, walking with him arm-in-arm toward the building. "A hint of Volkswagen, I think."

"Surprised you're not sure."

"I'm sure I don't smell as well as I could."

"That's true."

"*Joe!*"

"I'm just funnin' ya!"

With all his genius, he wasn't sure half the time if I got his jokes.

"I know." I held him close and talked to him like he was a puppy. "Him such a good boy."

In a darkened room, Joe put his head in the brace and waited.

The eye doctor pressed the button, and a laser dried a tiny bit of his retina.

1982

Christine Jorgensen stood with me on the sidewalk of a club in Hollywood. I was amazed to meet her, and more amazed still that she took the time to talk with me. We had spent about an hour together, talking—mostly about me, I'm sorry to say. Such an opportunity to get her wisdom, and I was missing it.

Thankfully, she didn't.

She was at an age and time in transition, then, about where I am now—her 50s and 30+ years in role—and I'm certain she could see right through me, see what I needed, even if I couldn't see it for myself.

I'd switched recently, and I was fresh out of the gate, rough around the edges. Sometimes when we are new in transition, talking can help. I had gotten onto the university lecture circuit around southern California, trying to explain. I was eager, exploring, enthused, enthralled, enamored, sometimes exuberant. I knew names, dates, places, hormones, surgeries, social acceptances or rejections, what it was like. I could report to classes how my subcutaneous fat had formed and subtly shifted, what it was like to discard all my earthly possessions and enter the world anew. I could talk to them about how people treated me differently, both as female, and also as transsexual. Everything was different, even how I should walk through a doorway, if the person waiting with me was male or female.

I thought I knew what I was talking about, and I did, as far as it went. But I had no depth. I knew all the facts and I had a good presentation, I thought, but subtlety was as yet missing. There was more to know than what I knew, and I know now, there always is.

Christine talked to me as well as she could, reflecting, interjecting, giving me opinions, and I'm sure I understood less than half of what she had to share. I found her manner to be dignified, graceful. She was a charm. I really liked her.

Why didn't I ask what was it like being transsexual when people knew so little? The 50s? 60s? 70s? To whom could you go when you were down? How could you keep your spirits up when you walked down the street, or every time you were on stage, when you knew many people regarded you negatively? Surely sometimes celebrity was pleasant, but sometimes people can be—mean. Why didn't I listen to whatever she had to say and consider what was in her heart?

She was positive with me, didn't dwell on pain. But she had to have had a difficult life. "I don't care what other people think" doesn't work in the long run, because you live with the emotional consequences, the relative social isolation, the loneliness. It can't all be *up* for a club act or play, however public relations may have felt it important to appear. She was a person. She had emotions. It was an earlier time, even less accommodating, in this regard. Likely, a million things had happened in her life that had hurt, where people had done something wrong to her. How had she lived with it?

In thinking back, I did sense some sadness in her at the time. Why didn't I think more to see through her charm and comfort her? Why was I focused on myself?

Because I was young in age and new in transition.

In time, near the end of our talk, she held up her hand, halting me, asking me to listen.

Thankfully, I did.

"The most important thing," she said with uncanny intensity, "is to be yourself, but you first have to know who you are."

I didn't realize, at that time, she was telling me I was seeing myself and my life through rose colored glasses. I wasn't being realistic about myself. It would be years before I understood.

1986

Typical grad student, I had no money. I was living in a tiny, one-room apartment on Fountain, in Hollywood, by the cul-de-sac a block southeast of Sunset and Van Ness. At the time it was immediately behind KTTV Channel 11, owned at some point by Rupert Murdock's News Corporation, which later became Fox Television Stations—very conservative.

So not me.

I have to smile.

My tiny apartment had no room for a washer or dryer, and I couldn't have afforded them, anyway, so I spent an afternoon at the laundromat.

Taking my clothes out of the dryer, I heard noise out on the sidewalk.

Everyone turned to look.

An LAPD officer was shouting at the top of his lungs, publicly degrading a then-termed transvestite for existing. "What the fuck are you doing!? *What the fuck are you!?*"

The lady reeled from the cop, and I went over for a closer look, stepped out the door of the laundromat to stand on the sidewalk not far away.

The cop turned on me. *"Back the fuck off!"*

I stopped advancing, but I did not leave. Instead, I stared at him, alert, unmoving, watching everything.

The TV began to leave, but the cop stopped her.

"Where you think you're going! You're a disgrace, you know that?"

She looked scared. "I'm sorry—"

"You're a *fucking* disgrace! You're a *man*, for Christ's sake. And you're wearing a fucking skirt! You got panties under there?"

"I—" She began to cry.

"I should haul your ass in, but what would I fucking *do with you*—sick pervert!" The cop looked at people watching him, turned suddenly and left.

I took a step toward the TV, but she ran away.

I gathered my clothes in shaking hands, went home to my Commodore 64 computer, where I did my term papers, and typed a letter through angry tears to Mayor Tom Bradley, venting my frustration in unholy manner.

"… How *dare* he, Mayor? We hire police to protect and to *serve* us, not to espouse their own bigoted brand of badge-heavy bullshit on law-abiding citizens! You don't think she has enough on her shoulders? The hell she faces daily in her life? Without having someone—*who is supposed to help her*—degrade her, instead? *In public in front of everybody?* What you want her to do, commit suicide some day? God knows, there's enough pressure without people like your cops making it worse…"

A couple of weeks later, the Hollywood police station called and left a message for me on my answering machine. I hadn't included my phone number in my letter. They told me to come down to the station.

Oh shit.

Anyone who was different knew the LAPD at that time took a hardline approach to law enforcement, and, frankly I was scared of the police. If they called me, I feared I'd be arrested for something.

But they told me to come down, so I did.

I drove up, parked, went inside, introduced myself to the sergeant at the desk.

"This way," he said.

I followed him through a large room of desks to the back of the squad room, where we entered someone's office.

One cop sat behind the desk.

"Have a seat," he said.

I did.

Maybe I went too far?

The sergeant closed the door and stood behind me.

The man at the desk spoke. "We got your letter."

Shit!

My throat was dry and my palms were wet.

"And we'd like to apologize to you."

What?

"Me?" I was relieved, but still worried.

He nodded. "We're sorry for the way we treated the young lady on the street."

My marbles rattled around a bit before I responded. "What about *her*?"

1992

Joe and I sat in a booth in a restaurant in Santa Monica, sipping ice water, waiting. A beautiful, petite young woman in a minidress walked to our table, early 20s, Filipina—a week-old, large bruise on her left cheek, a cut on her left lower lip, and fading bruises in a ring around her neck. Her eyes were red. She'd cried recently.

"Jesus, Jane!" I jumped out of the booth to examine her. "What happened?"

"Hello." Her words were a little clipped. English was her second language.

I guided her into the booth opposite Joe and sat beside her.

"I saw him at the party. He your father?" Jane asked.

"No, no. We're good friends. But, Jane," I pleaded. "What happened to you?"

Tears formed in her eyes. She didn't answer.

"Why he has those big sunglasses?" They were freaking her out.

Joe took them off for a second to show her and put them back on. "My eye doctor wants me to wear them for another couple of hours."

A waitress came to the table and immediately asked about Jane. I intervened for her and ordered three salads for us. "Don't hurry," I said.

I looked at Jane's wounds more closely. It looked like at least two punches, and the bruises around her neck indicated choking.

"Jane." I captured her attention with a serious look and demanded more forcefully, "Are you in pain?"

She shook her head.

I didn't believe her.

"Tell me what happened."

Over several minutes, she shared she'd gone out on a date with a guy from college, just over a week ago, and he'd gotten violent when making out in his car.

"I trangenderis—" She reached for her knees with her hands, rocked back and forth a little.

I touched her arm in support. "Did he know that beforehand?" I asked.

"Tina said to ask you SRS."

"Why?" I asked her. My question was not rhetorical.

"Maybe I should!"

"Why?" I asked her again.

She began to cry and more of her story blurted out.

"I—think I change schools. He—" She stopped to cry some more.

I held her hands for strength.

"When he got here—" she glanced down for a fraction of a second. "He got mad."

"He didn't know?"

"I couldn't get out of car!"

"Darling, do you have bruises anywhere else?"

She didn't answer.

"Tell me what all he did!" I ordered. "What did he do?"

She looked away and a new tear fell down her cheek.

"Goddamnit!" I said as quietly as I could.

I glanced to Joe for help. His head was lowered in sadness for her.

"Did you go to the police?" I asked her.

She wiped her nose gently with a napkin that was on the table.

"Jane, did you tell the police!"

She shook her head.

"Jane."

I put my arms around her.

She laid her head on my shoulder and began to accept sympathy, but after a few moments, she broke it off, withdrawing into herself.

"Jane, why didn't you go to the police? You still can."

"Will you forget it?" she asked.

"I'll go with you—"

"Nobody know about me at college. I am *secret*. Whole school get it." She turned in the booth to face me more squarely. "But I get SRS, then there nothing to tell."

Some people regarded SRS almost magically, as if it cured things it didn't. Discussion about her needs, her desires, what SRS meant, what it would and would not do, went on for several minutes, until I thought I'd summarize a little for her.

"Jane, if I may?" I motioned between us, and indicated I could give her my thinking.

"Sure."

"Okay," I said. "Prejudice is a problem we all deal with. Sometimes it's life and death. And here it's about how to date safely, how to find a guy who will love you as yourself." I looked for recognition, but she wasn't following.

"Dating can be done," I said, "with caution. But I think you pass so well that you're actually at *more* risk to surprise-violence than most. A guy may not know about you until you're making love, if you don't say something ahead of time. I hate to say it, but you might want to be less of a secret, at least some times, so you can tell who likes you for yourself."

"It shouldn't matter."

"He may have been expecting something different," I said. "You know? A lot of guys really do care about that. Frankly, that risk goes for us, too."

"But you—"

I interrupted her. "SRS is no vaccination against violence. We get it, too."

"But they can't tell about you."

I have always been sad when someone said that to me, honestly, because, to me, it means they don't get it. I had many tells on me back then, even more than in recent years because I had not yet had Facial Feminizing Surgery (FFS), but some tells will continue through life. Some of them even become more noticeable with age.

"People can tell about me," I said. "All of us. Sometimes they don't, but they certainly can and do."

She objected.

"It hurts, inside, but it's true," I said.

"So SRS not help me?"

"SRS can help with femaliform genitalia, but it can't protect you from prejudice."

"If I get it, he won't know. He think I born female."

Still not there.

If I'm not clear with her, she may make a mistake she'll regret.

"Some might not know. Sometimes. But listen to what I'm saying: *some will,* anyway."

Jane looked confused.

"Jane, I need to ask you something. Do you mind if I ask you something?"

She shook her head.

"When you have sex, do you like to have your—" I didn't say the last word, for her modesty. I just raised my eyebrows, knowingly.

She nodded. "Yes. It me."

"Alright." I felt I needed to state the obvious for her. "But if you have SRS, it would be gone. You know that."

She nodded.

"So then, if you had SRS, sex would only be as female. You wouldn't have it anymore."

She wrinkled her brow slightly, stared unfocused at her lap.

"The only path to happiness is to be who you really are, inside." I pointed to her heart, for emphasis. "Don't try to be something else, for some other reason. You'll give yourself a world of heartache."

She nodded, but I felt she didn't quite understand.

"Maybe it would be good to go over this with someone who can help you work it through?"

I tried to comfort her and referred her to a couple of therapists with experience in the area.

Trans people suffer hardships literally untold. No one knows how many. We've learned that hate crimes against trans people are a not-so-quiet national pastime. Regarding sexual violence alone, the Office for Victims of Crime, U.S. Department of Justice, reports:

> "*One in two* transgender individuals are sexually abused or assaulted at some point in their lives, some reports estimate

that transgender survivors may experience rates of sexual assault up to 66 percent, often coupled with physical assaults or abuse. This indicates that *the majority of transgender individuals are living with the aftermath of trauma and the fear of possible repeat victimization"* [italics mine].

What can others do for us? Give us deference, compassion, acceptance, and help. Where laws help, follow the laws, yet we also ask—consider in your heart—who among us deserves respect?

7

Heaven

1993

ISRAEL AND EGYPT had beckoned for a long time.

I had been working as a clinical social worker for several years, and I still was. But in addition to that, Joe and I had been "working hard" for years, at one project or another, growing together, and we needed to get away.

I had become a Bat Mitzvah, could read a little Hebrew, and ancient Egypt had been a passion of mine for a long time—looking not only at ancient sites but also origins of western thought, seeds of ideas that blossomed later into western law and religion.

I've always searched for a larger picture—a problem because I only have 2 brain cells, and I need 3. Had there been a dynastic clan that moved in to the area of the Nile, a more advanced people who coalesced ancient groups into one culture that morphed into religion with successors who didn't understand the science?

It was not serious study for me. It was get-away-from-it-all relaxation, refreshing. There was nothing I planned to do with it. But ancient Israel and Egypt felt like re-connecting with myself, discovering who I was, in part. There was something old there, something from the past, closer to the origin of my being that drew me. It felt like coming home to a family long lost.

One day in the spring of 1993, Joe surprised me with tickets for a 16-day trip to Israel and Egypt.

My eyes totally bulged. The cost of that trip was too much. I couldn't—but he was persuasive, and I couldn't refuse.

When it came time to go, the trip became more than wondrous. It became restorative, as we had experienced earlier that summer a tragic loss that was hurting us: the sudden death of a child. I had not been close with my family for a long time, but that has no bearing on my love of life and my sorrow at his loss.

The trust Joe and I had in each other was automatic. Going through other countries with him, even the Middle East with security concerns, having our luggage rifled by Israeli security, never occurred to me to be a problem. We flew to Heathrow, then to Tel Aviv, and took a cab to Jerusalem.

We stayed in a hotel very near old Jerusalem, which seemed fine in concept but didn't work out well. We had horrible jet lag, and we couldn't sleep, made worse by mosquitoes coming in the open window. No screen.

After one night in Jerusalem, we couldn't sleep and bugged out. We took our meager two bags and left for the bus station. There, I read the signs in Hebrew, and got us on a bus to Tel Aviv, where we checked into a reasonable hotel across the street from the beach—that had an air of peace about it.

Maybe it was distance from life back home. Maybe it was the trust exercise of the trip together. Or maybe it was something that clicked between us, but in Tel Aviv, I gave myself to Joe for the first time.

It had been four years since I'd known him. I'd travelled locally with him, met all his friends, family. We'd flown with each other in sun and clouds, day and night. I'd boated with him on Pacific coastal waters, around the Channel Islands. We lived together, and it finally came together.

Afterward, lying there beside him in bed, under his right arm, my head on his shoulder, I played with his little patch of chest hair.

"What was I waiting for?" I asked.

His expression seemed to suggest he understood.

"There's something different about you, Joe," I said.

"You noticed."

"I don't mean from yesterday. I mean—there is something I'm not getting."

He said nothing, just rubbed my shoulder with his hand.

"I'm trying to place you in my frame of reference for humanity."

"I wouldn't worry about it."

"I want to know who you are. You're so humble. You don't tell me much. It took me, like, a year before I learned you were

Skunk Works. Then another year to connect the dots—and I know there's more."

"Well, I was born in the room over the living room—"

"You know what I mean, don't you? But you won't tell me? Don't be so humble. Fess up."

It didn't work.

Maybe he didn't see himself as amazing. Maybe he thought it was wrong to share his great qualities?

I thought more about him, and then myself. Why did it happen that I was now interested in him?

Wrong idea: I'd always been interested in him. I just hadn't been willing to let him in—my own issues, but also— I thought about it.

I'd been such an *age bigot*.

When you get to know someone as a person, they cease being an adjective. I no longer saw him as an old man at the airport. He was a man, and an extremely good man. He cared about me. He loved me and had said so many times. He was intelligent, honest, considerate, conservative of manner yet liberal in respecting people, such as me. He didn't even drink or smoke. He occupied my thoughts day in and day out. All I wanted to do was be with him. I cared about him. I loved—

I stopped playing with his chest hair for a minute.

"What's the matter?" he asked.

"I love you, Joe," I finally said to him.

"I love you, too, Jenna." He caressed my right shoulder.

I was surprised at myself. I'd been worried at times about people not accepting me because of my sex difference, and there I had been, not accepting him because of our age difference. In the span of time—think ancient Egypt—the 40.6 years between us was miniscule. There was nothing inappropriate; our age had no bearing on us as human beings. We were both who we were, and we both needed love.

I had been so foolish, I realized, keeping him at bay—but no more. Love is so rare in this world, how can anyone deny it? Why would anyone want to?

Never was there a more complete feeling for me in life, than being with him. It was the only time I ever felt emotionally whole. Transition hadn't given me everything I needed. It brought me to a starting place—similar, if late, to where most people begin.

For the next couple of days, we did nothing outside the room but go to the beach, across the street, and lounge on the edge of the Mediterranean. I felt so free. I even wore a swimming suit—one of the few times I ever would. My figure has never been close to adequate for me, but social media hadn't yet been invented, I was several thousand miles away from anyone else I knew, and Joe had already seen me with nothing on, so—

I sunned on the beach in a one-piece. No one seemed to care. I was letting my hair down.

Practicing my Hebrew, I read the menu on the wall of a small restaurant nearby, which turned out to be a transliteration for "Milk Shake." I broke out laughing.

Joe looking at me funny—again.

In the two weeks that followed, we did about as much as any two people could in any part of the world, and we did it all holding hands or arm-in-arm. The entire trip was something of a honeymoon for us, though we had not yet married.

We bussed over to Jerusalem on a day trip, to the Western Wall. We were both unaware of local customs, and I was unfamiliar enough with tradition that I led us into it wrongly—to the women's part, it turned out. Fortunately, they were gentle with us. A woman kindly escorted Joe back, and I thanked God for our life together. We went to Masada on another trip—*massive*, significant. I could feel the history. We floated in the Dead Sea—standing straight up, head out of the water. The salty water stung our mosquito bites. And we toured the Church of the Holy Sepulcre.

The land was beautiful everywhere we went, the whole area, so stark, clean, and tan.

Joe wanted to see Bethlehem, so we took a taxi—sort of. We found a cab in Jerusalem, but he only took us half way to Bethlehem. The driver said it was in an Arab area, and it was 1993. The Intifada had raged for years. Half way there, he stopped the car and gave us to an Arab cab that took us the rest of the way, where we saw the Basilica of the Nativity, traditional site of Jesus' birth, we were told.

People in Bethlehem were very nice and said that when we were ready to return to Jerusalem, we should cab back, not to take the bus, because it was too risky. They said the Israeli Army would search the bus, and there could be trouble.

So we took the bus.

Half way back to Jerusalem—sure enough—the Israeli Army stopped us and came on the bus with automatic weapons, searched, but there was no trouble, and the bus was allowed to go on its way.

A tortured, deep stealth transsexual who I'd come to know years ago had begged of me, in pain: "Why do we have to suffer this!? What's the value of a life where you can never truly be yourself?" She meant, simply, to be biologically female, genuine down to chromosomes and pregnancy, not just female mentally and anatomically. I didn't have an answer for her at the time, but I think this is one of many things not yet perceived: variance is a cause of stress in societies, but it also teaches variance as an essential element of our lives and the importance of respect with difference.

I think we humans are at a point in our development where these concepts are difficult for us to grasp. So few people are even willing to try.

After our whirlwind week in Israel, Joe and I walked together along the shore in Yaffo. I was hanging on his arm, leaning in to him. We were slowing down before the move to Egypt.

Joe was ancient, I felt. There was something in him that went back thousands of years— In me, too but nothing wise like he. Where in ancient days he may have been a thinker, planner, analyst, a leader, I certainly would have carried water, cleaned clothes and looked in wonder.

"Joe," I asked. "Why do people have to die?"

Joe knew my question wasn't rhetorical, but I also sensed he felt the issue laid beyond words. I got no answer from him.

"I mean, look at where we are," I said. "People have been worried about this area for thousands of years. Well known historic figures have walked by this shore, like we are, right now. You—"

I stopped to turn toward Joe and look at his face. "You have probably known me in other lives, thousands of years ago. You probably saw me 4,000 years ago and completely disregarded me—riding by on a chariot, fine robes, with me on my knees filling a bucket with something. I'm sure I was impressed with you. Don't you think about stuff like that?"

"Uh," he said. "I don't know."

"So, why do you think the cosmos gives us this magnificent thing called life, and then takes it away, requires all of us, sooner or later, to die?"

I was pressing, even though I knew that line of thought was not his.

"You're Christian," I said.

He nodded.

"You don't believe in heaven and hell?" I asked.

"Uh," he looked like he didn't want me to press, but offered, "Not exactly."

I never could get him to answer that question, but after several years, I came to sense that his vision of the cosmos incorporated a glimpse of realities that were beyond my ability to see. Maybe that was something this agnostic guessed as people's interpretation of God.

"Where do we go when we die?" I asked him. "Do we continue in some way? Or is it nothing, without even knowing it's nothing?"

I remember it well, his response. He seemed to be willing to answer, but the answer was not found in words, so anything he said would be wrong.

Finally and nonetheless, he simply said, "Heaven."

No judgment. No decisions. No Osiris to see if your heart is lighter than the feather of truth. No book of life. No pearly gates. Just "Heaven," as if it were a natural progression. And it never seemed to me, from him, to be anthropomorphized, never the child's image of marble halls and streets lined with gold.

I stopped pressing that line because I got the sense he meant the message to be understood, rather than shared, that speaking lessened it.

I enjoyed the feel of his left arm in my right as we walked, and I reached up with my left hand to feel his arm even more.

Where had he been, beyond my awareness?

How many times had our paths crossed—only now to share?

How had I ever lived without him?

After a week in Israel, we flew in an airliner to Cairo—which was a shaky adventure. It's funny, now, but at the time, it was scary. The approach felt like a training flight, as if the pilot was a first-timer in the cockpit who had previously flown hang gliders. We were all over the sky, the wing dipping, thrust varying. Once we touched down—with a plop—people applauded throughout the cabin, as if it had been a comedy act. I let out my breath—which was where my heart reached out to embrace the land.

Egypt!

It was magical, even impossible—starting with taxicabs.

Apparently, in Cairo, two cars can occupy the same space at the same time—without swapping paint—and Egyptian drivers were experts at knowing both the position and velocity of all atoms involved. Uncertainty had nothing to do with it, in principle. The distance between atoms—between nuclei and electrons, for that matter—is immense, so why waste it? I swear we drove through two cars and one building before leaving the airport. Yelling and honking were obviously effective means of inter-driver communication, but road signs were decoration for tourists. You drive four or five abreast in three lanes. You turn when you get there. You brake for fun.

I didn't feel totally helpless; gripping the seat helped immensely.

I told Joe, "Why be worried if steel can pass right through you without harm? They've got their own physics, here— Well, it's *Egypt!* Maybe it's not the same universe! This could be an alternate reality!"

Joe laughed at me.

What is it with him!?

We got to the Mena House Hotel in Giza—somehow in one piece—at the north side of the pyramids, just west of the Nile, where President Carter, President Sadat and Prime Minister Begin met in 1979 for the Mena House Conference, pre Camp David.

"You want go somewhere?" the cab driver told us, "You ask Omar. Omar take you."

I got out of the cab, looked at it. Fenders, quarter sections, bumpers...

Joe got out after me.

I leaned over to him and semi-whispered in his ear, "No dents," confirming everything I'd said.

"I drive in Cairo many years," Omar said. "I take you."

I couldn't help but smile at him—I mean, the guy was magical and reminded me of Sallah in "Raiders of the Lost Ark."

We checked in to the hotel. Our room was nice, and our balcony had the most excellent view of the pyramids. Thankfully, we weren't jet lagged, like we had been in Israel; we were ready to go.

Figure 7.1. Joe on balcony of our room, Mena House Hotel.

The next day, we went to the pyramids for the first time in what felt like 3,500 years.

Omar met us out front, as if he'd planned it that way. "You want go somewhere? Omar take you."

"Okay," Joe said to him, getting into Omar's cab. Brave soul, all business. Joe wore his old, gold Ray Bans from Lockheed, religiously, and it was another hot day, August in the Sahara.

We were both dressed in light, tan/whitish travel clothes with sunglasses and large, straw sun hats, little purses strapped to our waist for things like sunscreen and tissues, my camera and tiny tripod. We were ready for the sites.

"To the pyramids?" Omar asked.

I got in the cab beside Joe.

Omar took us the short distance to the pyramids, which were right behind the hotel, perhaps a third of a mile and up a grade.

"Short ride okay for Omar. You call me again? Omar help you."

We got there, and we had to park.

"Sign say 'No Parking.' Omar say 'Park.'"

He parked.

"Won't they get mad at you?" I asked.

"They know me. They worry people steal, but they know I won't."

Frankly, we hadn't known Omar very long, but I believed him. He seemed genuine, like a man of good character.

We walked closer to Khufu's massive pyramid. Joe stopped after a bit to stare at it, and I stopped with him. It was the largest thing I'd ever seen, other than the moon. Or the other planets. Or the sun. Or billions of stars. I mean, it was the largest thing I'd ever seen on Earth, other than the earth, itself. Or a mountain.

"Look at this," I said walking Joe closer to the pyramid.

White limestone siding, that hadn't been removed in antiquity, fit together so closely you couldn't get a razor blade between the stones, yet ancient chisel marks were obvious on core stones—which had their own amazement. The core stones were roughly hewn, but looking down the length of them, across a face of the pyramid, they were absolutely level and straight. After 4,500 years.

I reached out my right hand and felt the stones, leaving my hand to rest on them. "I've been here before, Joe. I know it."

Joe's smile to me was pleasant but patronizing. I think.

"Hold my hand?"

He did.

With my right hand on Khufu's pyramid, and my left holding Joe's, I closed my eyes and verbalized, "Ommmmmmmmm—"

Joe took his hand back.

"Just in case," I said, a slight, teasing smile on my face.

Joe walked on, examining the stones.

That gag didn't work.

Joe examined the blocks from his precise engineering standpoint. He ran his hand over casing stones, then over adjacent core stones, leaned his head back to stare up the 51-1/2 degree slope toward the top.

I did, too.

I was sure no one could stand there without appreciating that.

"The closest I ever came to engineering," I said, "was at JPL. One summer I worked there in Personnel, while in college."

"That must have been interesting."

"It was. I used to argue speed of light problems with some of the engineers, for fun."

He glanced at me.

"I was at a disadvantage, but only because they knew what they were talking about."

He returned his attention to the pyramid.

"My reasoning was more in the area of extrapolation. They had science that said we couldn't go faster than light, but I countered with what I felt was humanity's current state of unawareness. I mean, we're amoeba, compared to whatever Great Knowledge must be out there. I told 'em, 'Travel was by foot; then we invented the wheel. The speed of sound was impossible to crack; now we do it every day. So now we think the speed of light is the limit? We'll crack it when we learn how.' It was hard for 'em to win that one."

"How do you think they built the pyramids?" Joe asked, looking back up the slope.

"Taxi drivers."

"Really."

"I know I sound like it, but I'm not an engineer."

Joe didn't skip a beat. "You could be."

We walked toward the opening in the north face, the entrance we could use to enter.

I thought about the area, suddenly serious again.

"I don't know how, but somehow, I feel as if I know what it was like to be here, years ago. I feel I have memories here—one of them, specifically, south of here, looking back north to the pyramids. Sometime after the three were up, or maybe just after this one and Khafre's were up. I don't really know. I have trouble remembering what I did last week, let alone 4,000 years ago."

"What name was that?" he asked.

"This one is Khufu's pyramid," I explained to him, patting it. "The Great Pyramid of Cheops, according to the Greeks, but Khufu would probably disagree." I turned around. "That one there is Khafre's, the 2nd largest. He was Khufu's son, which means Khufu probably had sex at least once."

"Okay."

"I'm not making that up," I said to him, implying he may have doubted me.

Strangely, the feeling I have of being south of there, looking north to the pyramids, felt—like I loved them, but I was emotionally distanced because it felt there had been something wrong, there—as if I learned Pharoah had been great, but not perfect.

Joe was looking at the construction.

"You think you were really here?" he asked.

"I don't know," I told him seriously. "I really don't know. More likely, I connect for other reasons, and it just *seems* as if I were."

We met with the gatekeeper who charged us as tourists to enter the great pyramid, and we made our way toward the hole in the north face.

"But you're an engineer," I said to Joe.

He nodded.

"So you may identify with Imhotep," I said. "He was the engineer who taught this culture how to build pyramids."

Joe glanced at me as we walked.

That got his attention.

"Imhotep was a commoner, but brilliant." We ascended into the pyramid and took the tunnel inside to the Grand Gallery within, that lead up to the King's Chamber.

"He must have wowed them, because he wound up in charge."

Then I continued for Joe. "You remember Joseph in the Bible?"

"Yes."

"Maybe like that, but minus the brothers and plus the engineering."

Joe stopped to look at the Grand Gallery from the bottom. We were the only two people in there. "Someone did well with this," he said.

I, too, stopped to stare. I was struck with the magnificence of the place and the honor to be in there, where only honored ones were allowed, in antiquity. I reached out to touch the walls *again*—this time from the inside.

In spite of my chatter, I couldn't have been more impressed and amazed. Whatever timeline or projection I felt, I was certain I'd never been inside before. Mentally, I asked Pharaoh for permission, but I continued my story for Joe's appreciation.

"Joseph was a commoner, a slave, even, who rose to become Vizier of Egypt—think #2 in the whole land, right under the Pharaoh. And Imhotep was one of those, Vizier for Pharoah Djoser, about 2600 B.C. This guy—probably not illiterate, like me, if I was there—"

"Don't bet on it," Joe said.

"You were probably Imhotep, himself," I said, half in humor.

He shook his head.

"But this guy, Imhotep, was a polymath, a guy who knew many sciences—probably an alien from outer space, like you."

I teased Joe a lot, but his glance to me said I was pushing it.

"I wonder how they did this," I said, touching the stones. They were tight and straight. "They would have needed a saw. No chisel did that."

Joe fingered the seam between two of the stones of the Grand Gallery and examined it closely. We began to ascend the steps, one at a time, toward the King's Chamber at the top of the steps.

I suddenly cringed—pain in my left shoulder. Immediately, I grabbed my left hand with my right and raised it above my head.

"What's the matter?" he asked.

"Nothing. It's okay. Gravity does the trick—and I don't even know what gravity is."

He looked at me. "How are your knees with this?" He pointed to my right knee.

"They're okay." I raised both of my big arms a few times to flex the muscles, tighten them up a little. Muscle tension helped. "For ankles and knees, I need to keep my joints straight. In engineering terms—in honor of Joe and Imhotep?" I smiled at him. "It helps to keep the longitudinal axis of my foot inline with the load on my leg, so my ankle won't collapse and the knees won't torque."

"How often do you need to think about that?" he asked.

"Only when I'm on my feet."

He looked at me, wondering.

"I'm used to it. It's normal for me."

He put his arms around me. "I love you, honey."

He kissed me briefly on the lips, and hugged me, before returning to our ascent in the Grand Gallery.

He buzzed my mind.

"You probably say that to all the archaeologists," I said.

"I do."

"You better watch out, yourself," I said. "How's your hip doing?"

"No problem," he said.

I watched him climb the steps within the Grand Gallery, and his hip replacement was unnoticeable.

"I'm so glad Indiana Jones isn't here, just now," I said, changing the subject, "or a giant boulder might roll down at us."

We stood alone in the King's Chamber, looked in awe at the giant granite blocks, the empty sarcophagus.

The actual King's Chamber—

Neither of us spoke for a long while. No assessments from him; no quips from me. It was absolutely quiet, other than our own breathing. The walls were thicker than anything I'd ever experienced, yet I felt as if I could see out over the Egyptian plain for miles.

Joe walked up to some of the seams between the giant stones of the chamber and felt them, as he had before in the Gallery and outside. They, also, were perfect.

For a long time, we remained where we were, appreciating.

"You want to lie down in the sarcophagus?" I asked him.

"Uh, I don't think so." I took a photo of him giving it thumbs down.

Figure 7.2. King's Chamber, Khufu's pyramid, Joe giving thumbs down to death.

"I think I'd like to," I said.

There was no sign that said not to, and there was no way I was going to damage it.

I went over to it and climbed in. My skin started to tingle, as it did when I walked into the corn at Dyersville, Iowa, per "Field of Dreams." Then I lay down in the sarcophagus—its stone sides all around me, inches from my shoulders—and looked to the ceiling above. I could suddenly see the weight of tons of granite and limestone above us. I instantly felt buried, like they were going to shut the lid on me. It felt wrong, even scary, so I got right back out. I wasn't in there more than ten seconds.

I looked at him, eyes wide and rubbed my arms with my hands.

He laughed at me—

"You knew that'd scare me!"

"I thought you were spiritual," he teased.

"I want to stay in the body!"

We stayed in the King's Chamber for quite a while, absorbing it. I admired Khufu's pyramid, especially from the inside. I let it become part of my soul. It wasn't that it was famous; it was that it was so *magnificent*. This was *the place*, I felt. I knew.

We also got Omar to take us to the Sphinx, as well as Saqqara—

We stared at the crumbling Step Pyramid.

"This is the one Imhotep started with."

"Yes, I see that," he said.

After a few days, we traveled down to southern Egypt, Abydos, Dendera, the Valley of the Kings...

Inside King Tut's tomb, I asked him, "Why do you suppose they put gold and jewels into the tombs" I asked Joe. "I think it may have been a wealth re-distribution program they could sell the king. They used to rob them all the time."

When we were walking through Karnak, I suddenly stopped and asked. "Joe! What does this place remind you of?"

He looked to see where I was indicating.

I answered my own question. "Look," I said to him. "Giant statues to dead kings. Obelisks, like they needed a big phallus."

He seemed to like my non sequitur.

"Hatshepsut put that one there—" I leaned into him and whispered, conspiratorially, as if I were going to say something risqué, then pulled away as if I never meant to.

He laughed at me more—a big laugh.

"And the giant, rectangular pool. See all that? It's Washington, D.C. That is no coincidence. Somebody in U.S. history liked this place."

"Yeah."

"Masons?"

With Joe, it was hard to tell, sometimes, if he knew something and didn't want to elaborate on it, if he suspected something and didn't want to say, if he didn't think we should so inquire, or if he thought I was looney.

Figure 7.3. By the Sphinx.

When we returned to Giza and the Mena House, we wanted to see the pyramids from the south side—where I'd "remembered" being 3 or 4 thousand years before—beyond the Solar Boat, but Omar told us that south area was too far to walk and was not safe alone. There had been strife for a long time. He said he knew where we could get some horses and reliable guides. We shared our plans with the Mena House, and they approved of Omar, so we trusted him to help us get where we were trying to go.

Omar took us into Giza to a family's home he knew. He negotiated a fee, which seemed reasonable, and from there, a man and his son guided us on horses where we wanted to go.

Joe and I rode the horses; the man and his son walked ahead of the horses. We followed them, and the whole time, we felt safe. Omar was a good man; they were good people.

And the photos I got from there were stunning, particularly one of Joe on his horse, with the pyramids behind him. One of the most impressive photos I ever took of him. He looked majestic.

Figure 7.4. South of Khufu's pyramid.

That spot, looking at the pyramids from there—I couldn't move. When he got off his horse, I stood with him, hand in hand, staring for the longest time.

I'm here with Joe this time!

Later that evening after dinner, in the Mena House Hotel by the Nile, we sat in the piano lounge and held hands to the music.

Rubbing the hair on the back of his hand with my thumb, listening to a man play "Claire de Lune," so soft and dreamy, lovingly. I imagined—

I leaned over to whisper into Joe's ear, so as not to disturb the other guests. "I can see Hatshepsut gliding down the Nile on her royal barge. Can you imagine that?"

He nodded.

"She's reclining on deck, on a bed, there. Someone's fanning her, and she's very happy. Content." I smiled at him. "You know why?"

He looked at me, questioningly.

"Egypt has the world's biggest erections."

A laugh escaped him before he could stifle it.

"Joe!" I whispered, acting serious. "*Be quiet!* This place is dignified."

8

Marriage

2015

"BROCCOLI ICE CREAM, please. Two *big* scoops." My smile was broad, my intentions clear, I thought. I held my hands wide to show the cast member how large.

The ice cream parlor on Disneyland's Main Street was noisy, packed with eager patrons. The lady behind the counter looked at me in confusion.

Ellen beside me complained. "You need to lose eight pounds!"

"She's off her meds," I told the cast member about Ellen. "Ana is it? I've explained to her that it really is made of broccoli—"

Ana's face indicated doubt.

"It's *very healthy*—"

Ana started to say something, so I headed her off.

"—but it looks and tastes exactly like—"

She caught on with a smile.

"—Cookies and Cream ice cream. Better make that three scoops."

"*Three!*" Ellen complained.

"Just in case they run out!" I defended. "Relax: There are no calories in Disneyland."

"What would you like it in?" Ana asked.

"My mouth."

Ellen and I walked up Main St. toward "the hub," the center roundabout in Disneyland. It was a beautiful day. Thousands of people milled about, on their way to the next adventure. Stylized music, "The Wells Fargo Wagon" from "Oklahoma," played over hidden speakers. Sleeping Beauty's Magic Castle framed Walt's statue, perfectly, as if they had planned it that way.

"Nobody calls him 'Mr. Disney,'" I explained.

"How do you know?" Ellen asked.

"Watch 'Saving Mr. Banks.'"

Ellen took a small bite of her cone. She only had half a scoop. "So Joe knew about you?"

"Yes." I answered as well as I could. "Sorry. I have to lick this fast." Some of it was getting on my fingers. "I don't always lick my best."

"You don't take enough care with your appearance," Ellen said.

"My jeans are clean," I said.

We turned left at the hub and entered Frontierland.

"You under-rate yourself," she said. "You look pretty well. You could dress nicer, is all."

"I don't have the figure for it," I said. "This," I indicated my jeans and long-sleeved shirt, "may be too casual for most things, but it'll have to do."

"How did Joe know about you?"

"He could tell. He knew things. I was obvious. We talked about it. I introduced him to other trans—"

"Who told whom first?"

The fingers of my left hand were covered in melting broccoli.

"I don't know. At first, I used to pour it out to him. And later—sometimes you mention it. It was just a normal part of conversation, sometimes. Like being Jewish."

I smiled to Ellen. She was born Jewish; I was after-market.

"So when he married you?" she asked.

"What about when you married your husband?" I asked Ellen.

"I didn't. He was my boyfriend. After we married, he was my husband."

"Smartass," I said with a cheeky grin.

"I met him at Berkeley."

"You switched young and married in college." I already knew, but I still found it wonderful. "Lucky." I bit the rim of my waffle cone.

Ellen removed the paper wrapper from the bottom of her cone and put it into a trashcan, in front of the Golden Horseshoe Saloon.

"You're stealth—pretty deep stealth, actually," I said. Her husband was such a hunk. The wedding ring on her finger could sink my boat. "No ripples from other people around you in your life?"

She seemed to ignore that question from me, finished her cone with no drips to her fingers.

I smiled knowingly. "I must be from another planet."

My cone still had a way to go, and Mark Twain's riverboat loomed. Hopefully there'd be a little bit of a line— No. No line yet. It didn't matter. I could eat broccoli on the boat.

Ellen re-directed to me. "After you two got married, what all happened? I know it was bad."

I focused on my cone. "You know I'm not going there."

"It was something, Jen. I can tell."

I knew. "It hurt and it shows."

"I mean, Joe died. You left all your groups. You rarely do anything with anyone. You don't have any friends any more—"

"Some!" I asserted.

"Two?"

"I have people with whom I am 'friendly,'" I defended, "but not so much I would think of as real friends. I have to admit."

"That's not normal."

"Neither am I."

We walked onto the Mark Twain and had a seat on two of the cushioned steel bow chairs, near old-fashioned hemp ropes that would have operated a cargo crane. Tom Sawyer's Island was on our right across the Rivers of America. I leaned over to her so others would be less likely to hear.

"You've led an overtly charmed life, Ellie—on the surface, since adulthood. This marriage you're in? So open and accepting, loving, but so closed everywhere else. You have a great figure. You socialize just like your cis women friends. You project that cis personality for them—which isn't really you, but you're happy with the outcome—"

"It *is* me," she said.

"You are trans, sweetie. Seriously." We'd had that argument before.

"That's not my mindset."

"Yes it is," I said. "Partly. You're just living a dual life with it. What have we been talking about this whole time?"

She frowned.

"But you're the best you can be," I said. "You're living your dream."

"You can, too," Ellen said.

So gently I could barely feel it move, the Mark Twain began its serene trip around Tom Sawyer's Island.

"But I'm not sure I should try to 'just live,' any more," I said. "There's a lot of pain involved, that most of us feel—from people leaving us out of things they do and faking friendships, keeping us away from their cis friends for fear they'll they think they're friends with us, character defamation, false assumptions or accusations, gossip and back-stabbing. We can put on a happy face. We can pretend it doesn't hurt—that's what you do—"

"It's not happening with me," she said. "You're being so negative. Smile and be happy!"

"Denial. You know it does," I said. "It hurts to admit things—because it says you're not totally in the dream. But the truth is, after most of a life with it, it weighs on you, anyway."

The Mark Twain's whistle blew. We passed New Orleans Square and the Haunted Mansion, to head north on the river. Anamatronic critters moved in the trees.

I continued. "And people say to me, 'Why are you so distrusting?' as if prejudice isn't there because they, themselves, aren't doing anything obvious.

"There's a little game that gets played," I said to her. "I hesitate to say, 'Not always' because you'll think your life is the exception, but what happens a lot is people say, 'We're not prejudiced. What we say or do is for *good reason*'; and we dance to a different tune, right there in the same room, as if we're in unison, saying, 'They're not doing anything to me. They accept me as a woman.'"

"Maybe you're exaggerating," Ellen said.

"So you enter a dual dance of denial with them. They get to live in prejudice. You get to live in fantasy. And you both pretend to get along."

1995

Joe and I sat together in chairs at a conference table.

LAWYER 1: "Can you marry? I'm not sure. Let me look into that. My secretary will have a fee structure—"
"How much?" I asked.
"I don't know. But I charge by the hour."

LAWYER 2: "You could marry, but I don't know if it would be legal. For a fee, over an unspecified number of hours, I can research that for you—"

LAWYER 3: "Of course you can marry, as much as any other couple."
What does that mean? What about gays? Legally, am I even female or not for this purpose?

LAWYER 4: "I've looked into this already, and yes, you can marry. Just make sure you confirm that he knows you're transsexual," he said to the both of us sitting there, "against the possibility of him, or anyone else, later, suggesting claim of fraudulent representation. You'll need two lawyers, one for him and one for you, to advise you on all this."
"Why two?"
"Law suits, I think. Possibly," the lawyer said.
"Law suits!?" I was stunned. "For what?"
Joe sat there with his head down.
The lawyer explained. "For anything. What about a divorce?"
"We're never getting a divorce," I knew. I asked Joe, "What could ever separate us?"
Joe's nod seemed to confirm.
"You never know," the lawyer said. "Or someone else might sue you if you two married."
"Why?" I still didn't get it.
"Your sex, maybe," the lawyer said to me. "Maybe his age. Is everyone on board with this marriage? People sometimes face trouble in mixed marriages."

I looked at Joe, too. His shoulders were dismissive of the concern.

"Would you be willing to fight in the courts for your inheritance?" the lawyer asked.

"I'm not marrying him for his money," I said. "If I did—What do they call it? For taking his money?"

"They might sue for undue influence," the lawyer said, "to get at the money."

"If I got sued," I looked at Joe, "my transsexuality could be all over the TV. The ABC Movie of the Week: 'Young Transsexual Democrat Marries Lockheed Big-Shot Republican Old Enough to Be Her Grandfather.' Grocery store tabloids would have a party. I couldn't have that. Maybe we should consider a pre-marital agreement."

Both then and now, I believe Joe's family loved him for himself. He really was wonderful. But I also think that if I had not suggested/signed a premarital agreement, it's possible that could have created a problem that did not exist. I'm not casting aspersions; it's just a guess. Nonetheless, if I weren't concerned for my privacy, I'd have never mentioned a premarital. Joe wasn't worried about it. I believe my stealth concern was a direct result of conflict from others, both as a child and as an adult. Absent those conflicts and those stealth issues, I would have just married him, and if I got sued, I'd have fought and dealt with it. It was a real marriage.

It's been estimated I gave up about five million dollars when we signed the premarital.

It was as if Joe and I were already married. We'd been together for 6 years, living together for 2 years. We were frank with each other, like an old married couple. So we set up the marriage at his church with his pastor to marry us, with friends, one Saturday morning in June. We married. We kissed. We cried. We ate cake. We went home and changed our clothes and went—where else—to Camarillo Airport, to attend our plane on a ramp display. No fanfare; just marriage.

That night, at the airport, in a large room filled with people having dinner, you could see recognition move through the room, literally like a crowd's wave at Dodger Stadium. Heads popped up in succession as word spread.

1996

I flew our 1937 Stinson "Gullwing" Reliant over Encino, heading east, getting Flight Following over Burbank's airspace. Airliners talked back and forth with SoCal Approach, on their way to landing.

Figure 8.2. Our 1937 Stinson Reliant.

The plane was packed to the gills for our intended camping at Oshkosh, Wisconsin.

Joe was folding a chart in the right seat.

ATC called me on the radio: "Gullwing One Five Four, say type aircraft."

I answered easily. "One Five Four is an SR-9B."

Airliners talked about their approach. ATC answered.

We made our way through the area.

ATC called me again: "One Five four, say type aircraft again?"

I pressed the push-to-talk switch on the round, wooden yoke in the antique airplane. "One Five Four is a Sierra Romeo Niner Bravo," as if that clarified anything. I chuckled to myself.

"Jenna," Joe said.

An airliner was cleared to contact Burbank tower.

"One Five Four, uh," ATC paused a sec then asked in a familiar tone: "What's that?"

By now every airliner in the area was listening to our exchange.

I glanced at Joe with that look in my eye.

"Jenna," Joe cautioned again.

"He's probably yakking about it with the guy next to him." I pressed the push-to-talk switch. "You know what an SR-71 is?"

"Yes," ATC answered.

"Same thing, only a little slower."

There were chuckles on the radio and a double click.

Even Joe smiled at that.

"One five four, say air speed?" ATC asked in fun.

I pressed the switch. "Zero point one eight mach."

Near Santa Maria, Joe and I took part in a Star Dusters picnic, an organization for Lockheed retirees and spouses. The setting was a beautiful, pastoral, open area surround by sturdy oak and eucalyptus trees. Our plates were full with hamburgers and potato salad.

Joe was happy to see old friends there.

Figure 8.3. Jack Real, Willis Hawkins, and Joe Ware at a Star Dusters picnic.

"Gill!" Joe said on greeting, shaking hands with them all. "Willis! Jack!"

They all shared their version of, "Joe, it's good to see you."

"This," he said to them, "is my wife, Jenna."

They greeted me with smiles.

"Jenna," Joe said, "This is Gil Cefaratt."

"Hi Gil," I said. He shook my hand. Gil had been an engineer and tech rep at Lockheed, technical writer, who would later write the book *Lockheed: The People Behind the Story*.

"Good to meet you, Jenna—Jenna, is it?"

"Yes," I said. "It's Jennifer, but Joe's from Va-GIN-ya, and doesn't know how to say 'Jennifer.'" The three men teased Joe.

"This is Willis Hawkins," Joe said to me. Willis had been a Vice-President at Lockheed.

"Hello, Willis," I said with a smile.

"It's good to meet you," Willis said.

"And this is Jack Real," Joe said, a tall and slim man with a broad smile. [Jack was not smiling for the photo, but he was quite charming in reality.] Jack had worked with Joe at one time, but Howard Hughes took a shine to him and he became President of Hughes Helicopter and Howard's "last best friend."

"A pleasure to meet you," Jack said. From his friendly manner, I thought he might kiss my hand, if I didn't watch out— Too late. He simultaneously raised my hand and lowered his lips to kiss it.

That was a new one!

Feeling kinship with our ancestors who participated in our country's history, Joe and I joined the Single Action Shooting Society, SASS.

Figure 8.4. Joe firing Gatling gun at End of Trail, SASS

Figure 8.5. Joe enjoying a shooting match.

Shadow Life | 105

Figure 8.6. I was best with the rifle.

We cuddled in adjacent sleeping bags, in the middle of the night, on the tarmac at a Merced fly-in, looking up past the cloth-covered wing of the antique Gullwing, to stars more distant than they seemed.

I lay on his right side, my head on his shoulder. His right arm was around my shoulders, and his left hand was in my right.

"Do you think we could ever travel to those stars, Joe?"

"Oh, yeah," he said. "Someone will work it out."

"But in our life-time?" I asked.

There was a slight pause. "You feel connected with the past?" he asked.

I nodded a little.

"Then feel connected to the future, too. But be where we are, right now."

Figure 8.7. Joe at breakfast, during Merced fly-in.

Joe and I sat in his church for the Christmas Eve candle light service. The choir was caring, people were nice.

"All rise," we were instructed.

There was the bustle of a couple of hundred people standing. I pulled the hymnal out of the pew in front of us, stood with Joe and opened the hymnal to the proper page. I showed support by holding the book, together, with Joe, as he sang with the congregation:

"Oh little town of Bethlehem,
How still we see thee lie…"

Christianity was still not my religion. I'd suffered at their hands, every time someone made a comment against gays or anything not "proper," like me, but I was thankful for kindness when people shared it.

After service, Joe and I greeted friends who shared the warm, Christmas spirit, and shook the preacher's hand in the narthex.
"Merry Christmas," the preacher said to us both.
"Merry Christmas," Joe said back to him with a smile.
"Thank you for the information," I said to the preacher.

The night air was chilly, but there was no wind. Tiny droplets of mist formed on the leaves of trees. We needed to hurry, or we'd get caught in a coming rain.
I peeked around the corner to the apartment across the building's courtyard, to eye the door of the place we had in mind. It was late enough they seemed to be home, early enough the parents still seemed to be up, yet late enough no one else was walking about.
There was an area of bushes across the courtyard to the west that should protect us.
I trotted back to the car. "The coast is clear," I whispered to Joe.
In our best cat burglar clothes—dark jackets and pants—Joe and I crept across the courtyard. My heart was pounding, because—I confess—we were not really cat burglars. I didn't want anyone to come out of an apartment and catch us red-handed, didn't want anything to give us away.
I scanned other apartments. No one.
I listened for dogs. None.

I looked at Joe, beside me, and he seemed fine.
Doesn't he ever worry!

Joe rolled a girl's bicycle onto the apartment's porch and stood it on its kickstand, blocking the doorway. I sat a frozen turkey beside it on the welcome mat.

I rang the doorbell—and we hurried behind the bushes.

After a few seconds, the door opened, and a man stood on his stoop looking at the gifts.

Joe and I crouched, looking at him through the leaves—to make sure he received as intended.

The man looked around, but no one was in view. He put his hands to his face, then picked up the turkey, handed it to someone behind him, and rolled the bicycle inside, gently closing the door.

Joe and I waited for a few moments to make sure the coast was clear. No one re-emerged. The curtains did not open.

It seemed safe. We walked like normal, back to the car.

We didn't know who they were.

9

Ware Lab, Virginia Tech

1997

WE WALKED across the huge, grass drill field in the center of what we then called VPI, now called Virginia Tech. The field was as large as the Grinder in boot camp, a place for troops to march.

"It was my first job," Joe said.

"Skipping school?" I asked.

"Bucket washing the plane." Joe chuckled at himself. "It was 1927 or '28, I think. I heard the Sister Ship to the Spirit of St. Louis was going to be here, so I left school that day and went to the airport."

We were walking southwest through the field, in front of Burruss Hall—ornate in Hokie Stone, the blocks quarried nearby for many of the buildings on campus.

"At the time," he said, "there were no fences. You just walked over."

"You played hookie? I'm so ashamed," I teased. He was charmed at being there, in Blacksburg, at VPI, and I had been egging him on all morning—teasing him, mock-doubting him, getting him to talk.

He chuckled more to himself and looked fondly around. "I went there and found the plane, and I asked them if I could have a ride, and they said I could if I washed the plane, so I washed it. And then I got a ride, and I heard later, from someone else at school, that the teacher had called my name for role, and I didn't answer. So the teacher asked where I was. It happened that at that time, the engine noise from the Spirit Sister Ship was heard in the class room, and one of my classmates pointed up and said, 'There he is, right now!'"

"My husband, the Hookie Hokie."

"Uh, well." He seemed to be having fun, admitting to a little embarrassment.

I confessed with him. "I used to skip all the time, in high school. I couldn't stand to be there. I couldn't stand to be anywhere."

When I'd say something like that, referring to my past, Joe would look at his feet in contemplation, empathizing but not responding. It's not that he disliked the issue; I think he felt silence was the most respectful, letting someone talk. A humble man, he responded to a lot of things that way.

"So this drill field," I asked, "was where Divel Saunders used to land his plane?"

Joe brightened again. "Uh, yeah. It was just an open field, and sometimes he'd come to visit, and I'd run out here to see the plane."

"He'd land right here on campus, on the grass."

"Yeah. It was the '30s. Nobody thought anything of it. But it was something to see. I'd hear him come in and run to the field."

"Where is this 'Solitaire' you mentioned before?"

"'Solitude,'" Joe corrected me. "That big house up there." He pointed ahead, as we walked southwest toward the duck pond. "Divel used to go there, too."

We walked over to the duck pond and sat on a bench by the water's edge, talking forever about his childhood in Blacksburg.

Stories floated out of Joe about early relatives that took me back to the Revolutionary War with General Nathanael Greene and Giles Thomas, to William Thomas who founded the Presbyterian Church in Blacksburg, which is now a restaurant, through the Civil War with John Montgomery Thomas, and to Joe's grandfather or great-grandfather, I'm not remembering which, who was Chief Engineer at Ft. Monroe, VA. He told me how Jefferson Davis, President of the Confederate States of America, after the Civil War, had been imprisoned at Ft. Monroe, how Joe's great-grandfather had given Jefferson Davis a chair to sit on. Joe's father had become a colonel in the U.S. Army, had been the Commandant of the Corps of Cadets at VPI, and a professor of military science there.

Joe loved Virginia and his family's history, and he could relate stories in detail going back those 220 years. His stories of his family's history affected me greatly.

"You have great ancestors," I told him.

"He's your Uncle Heath," he'd tell me, referring to Heath Robinson, an oil finder, or "He's your Uncle Ben Dennis," he'd say, referring to his uncle, a physician and Rear Admiral in the Navy who ran hospitals.

"You mean *your* uncle," I'd tell him.

But he'd correct me: "Your uncle, now. We're married. You say 'Uncle Heath' or 'Uncle Ben.' Not 'your.'"

"Okay." I started doing so. Belonging was something still, and I think always, new to me.

Listening to him, I could reach out and touch the uniform on General Greene, feel the perspiration on his horse.

Later, walking with Joe through West View cemetery in Blacksburg, half a mile east of the Virginia Tech campus, I could see gravestones of some of his ancestors. They came alive to me. I videoed him there, talking about them. All the stones were degrading, toppling, they were so old, barely readable, so in time I had the stones redone, made new, and added that they were the ancestors of Joseph F. Ware, Jr.

We bought future funeral services for ourselves at McCoy Funeral Home, there. I bought a plot in West View, and Joe bought the headstone for us. In time, I will lay with him there, at his right shoulder, as in life. That was the way we slept.

Joe was born and raised in Blacksburg, Virginia, in the stone blockhouse at 404 Clay St., two blocks from the campus of Virginia Polytechnic and State University. By the time we got there, he was feeling so nostalgic, stories were flowing out of him. We stood in front of the house, on the sidewalk, and talked. He showed me, "I was born in the 'room over the living room'—"

Figure 9.1. 404 Clay St., Blacksburg, VA, where Joe was born and raised.

"Your mother's bedroom?"

"Right. Susie Robinson. That's what we called it. To the left of the porch, there."

"But that's not your room."

"No. Mine was the room over the kitchen, behind there."

I was acting like I didn't get it, and he knew I was playing with him. "But I thought you said that you were born in the room over the living room?"

"Yes, but that was my mom's room. It wasn't my room."

"Why didn't she have you in your own room?"

"Oh, uh—"

"To get in up there," I asked, "you'd go up the stairs—the stairs were just in front of the front door, there?"

"Yes."

"I mean *behind* the front door?"

"Yes."

"Which one?"

"Behind—just beyond the front door."

"So you'd go up the stairs—creaky stairs?"

"No, they were pretty good stairs."

"So you'd go up the stairs and turn right around to your room, you said. The room over the kitchen?"

"No."

"But you said that front room, there, was your mother's."

"Yeah, that one." He pointed to the front of the house, the left window. "That was Mom's room."

"And she had you there."

"Yes."

"But if your room was at the top of the stairs, then that was *your* room, not hers!"

He looked at me as if I were nuts. "No, her room was to the left of mine."

"Not at the top of the stairs?"

"No, the stairs didn't do a left 180 at the landing, half way up. They did a left 90."

"So her room was left of the top of the stairs and your room was right off the stairs." I'd pushed that one as far as it would go.

"My mother, Susie Robinson, and I lived with her mother, Nellie Robinson, and I was, um, maybe a little ornery as a child."

"How?"

"Oh, nothing much—"

"Come on." I encouraged.

"Oh, I got into a few things." As he relived his memories, he became very wistful, even tearful, as if it were painful to recall such loved times, knowing they were gone forever.

"Like what?"

"Well, when I was ten, 1926, I wanted a radio transmitter, and I didn't have any money, so I built one up in the attic, out of parts I scrounged around." His face radiated when he talked about it. "It was the Blacksburg Broadcasting System, I called it." He laughed at himself. "I'd be up there in the attic, talking on it as if anyone listened."

"What did you use for programming?" I asked.

"Oh, anything."

"Static?"

"Just about. I'd play music sometimes, or I'd get the news from somewhere and read it to the town. I needed a better antenna for it, so I strung a wire by all the chimneys on the houses up the block," he showed me by pointing to neighboring houses, "which worked fine, until there was this storm, and it pulled our chimney off the roof and landed it in the front yard."

"Right there?" I pointed in the yard in front of the house.

"By the porch, yeah."

"Joe! Your momma got mad?"

He laughed at himself. "A little. It scraped down the front of the roof and landed with a thud right there, and Grandma came out front to look at it, staring!

"And this one time, I needed a little programming, so I— Well, I put a microphone in Mother's parlor, so when the ladies came over to play Bridge, I could hear them up in the attic."

"You put a bug in your mother's bridge game and aired it on the BBS all over town!"

His face showed bittersweet memories. "Well—"

"Did your mother know?"

"She caught me."

"How?"

"I don't know. But I heard her say, 'Where's my son?' and she walked up the stairs and opened the attic door and saw me sitting there, with my headphones on. *'What are you doing!?'*" Joe was animated, imitating her, and was actually laughing at himself on this one. "She said, 'What are you doing?' 'Oh,' I said, 'Nothing much. I'm just—listening—' *'Listening to what?'* She went over to me, yanked the ear phones off my head and heard her friends talking."

"About what?"

"Oh, I don't know. Who did what. What was going on. And then she ran back downstairs and yelled to all her friends: 'Everyone *be quiet*! My son has got a *hidden microphone in here!*'"

"You Dennis the Menace! You 10-year-old skank!"

Joe laughed at himself because he couldn't disagree.

Someone popped her head out the front door of the house and looked at us. I guess we were being loud. "Can I help you?" she asked.

"Uh," I said to her. "He used live here—he was born up there," I dutifully pointed to the room over the living room, "and he was raised here, so we're talking about it."

"You want to come in and look around?"

God!

Joe wasn't surprised by much, but he was surprised by that.

"Sure!" I said, taking her up on it.

And she took us in and walked us around the house.

My head was spinning, imagining the young boy there, as a child, in the winter—say—living, running in and out the front door, growing up, stoking the fire place—

"Yeah, I broke that grate around the fireplace," Joe said inside. "That chip there? I did that. Sorry."

The lady smiled at him, seemed to think that was cute. "I noticed it there, but I had no idea."

Joe walked us around and told us stories. Apparently Joe's grandmother had added the east, wooden room onto the stone block house, so she'd have a place to show off her nice things to other ladies when they'd come over.

After the tour, we stepped back outside the blockhouse, The joy and pain of being back, of those precious times in life that meant so much, of people he loved who were gone, brought him simultaneously to smiles of love and to tears at their loss. He so needed to embrace those times and people, yet—

It was the love of life and the pain at its loss.

I knew it at the time. It was obvious. All I could do was be there for him. But I've learned this, for myself, so much, now, with his loss, that I wish I could have been more than I was.

Figure 9.2. Joe, nostalgic on Virginia Tech campus.

After a time, we wandered through Virginia Tech to see other old haunts.

We walked into an empty classroom on the second floor of Holden Hall, near its eastern end. "This is where I taught math."

It was the room over the entrance, next to Dr. Clark's office. He talked about it and felt the walls, touched a desk, to bring back memories.

"When was that?"

"Oh, about 1940, '41."

Later, in 2007, in Norris Hall, contiguous with Holden Hall to the left, the Virginia Tech shooting occurred, which would leave us hurting for the victims.

The college of engineering was in the northern area of the campus at VPI. We'd been there before, so we walked over and said hello. Joe wanted to see more this trip, and some faculty there were kind enough to show us around, including but not limited to Hayden Griffin, Ph.D., Charlie Reinholtz, Ph.D., and Walter O'Brien, Ph.D. They were very courteous and informative. There were young students working with dedication at engineering projects of their own design: an autonomous seeking robot, a Baja car—several projects.

Most of what I understood as science came from *The Hitchhiker's Guide to the Galaxy* or "Star Trek," so the students took the time to explain things to me, and they put up with me as well as they could. "Maybe add an improbability drive?"

I spent enough time with one student on the autonomous vehicle to ask about its vision. "How do you—" My mind was racing trying to keep up with the students. "How do you actually teach the robot to tell Arthur Dent from Spock?"

The student seemed pleased with my questions and tried to answer, but I wasn't able to keep up with him.

Smart.

I'd been so spoiled by Joe, sharing with me. I'd had no courses, ever, in engineering, and Joe explained things to me with that understanding. I got the ideas, and I could use them in things I did—like flying—but I was simply nothing like an engineer. I referred to myself as a "nerd without the math, so I'm a groupie."

In truth, Joe also taught me, later, that I *could* do the math, but I didn't know that before I met him, when I was in school.

I also brought up the subject, with the student, of where they were working: in the basements of buildings. I got the impression he was success-oriented and was grateful for any space he could get his hands on, but I told him, "You need somewhere—your own shop, where you can keep your tools."

Colonial Williamsburg, Virginia was fascinating to me. We followed the drum and bugle corps down the main street toward the Governor's mansion, then toured the mansion. I bought a fife, which I learned to play.

Ft. Monroe, Virginia— We found the chair that Joe's ancestor had given to Jefferson Davis in the Casemate Museum, there. It was in a glass case with an explanation on it. I took photos of it for his family.

Washington, D.C., the National Mall. Abraham Lincoln was Joe's favorite president, and we spent quite a bit of time at the Lincoln Memorial. I stood with him at the top of the steps, in front of the President's huge statue, and read the Gettysburg Address to him from the wall, line by line. For people as patriotic as we were, that was priceless. We were allowed into the upper gallery of the Congress to watch some proceedings. We toured the National Air and Space Museum, and walked along the length of the National Mall, admiring freedoms this country stands for—freedoms, without which I could not have existed and we could not have married.

I found a cherry blossom that had fallen from a tree and held it in my right hand, reaching out to hold Joe's in my left. My eyes teared, and he held me for the longest time. Us, doing nothing else but feeling.

That was what I had needed, long before.

Ft. Meade was north of us, through the trees, out of sight, but not out of mind.

After we got home to the Harbor House in Mandalay Bay, Oxnard, I was talking with Joe and told him I thought the students at VPI needed more to work with.

"What they need is a Skunk Works," I told him.

"That's for sure." He launched into talking about his old Skunk Works at Lockheed.

"I'm not being rhetorical. They really do need a Skunk Works."

I sat down and drew up plans for their lab. I tried to keep the cost down, because it was my idea that it would be entirely funded by Joe for VPI. As I conceived it, it was one large room with tools and workbenches along the walls, a large truck-sized door in one end that could receive a flat bed truck if needed, with an overhead crane in the room to pick up heavy objects and place them on or take them off the truck. I assumed they could share the space with other student projects.

To my surprise, Joe went for it, and to my greater surprise, VPI also went for it. If I get this right, Hayden Griffin, there, already had an interest in developing a lab for the students, but it hadn't come together yet, so it was a marriage of ideas. The College of Engineering accepted the idea and set about vetting Joe. We supplied them with information, and they began a background check on him to verify he was who we said.

Self-revelation was not Joe's forté. He wouldn't talk about his achievements in life; fortunately, it was hard to shut me up. I dubbed myself V.P. of Joe Public Relations.

We made another trip back to VPI out of curiosity—when we learned VPI preferred in modern times to be called "Virginia Tech"—to see where they intended to put the lab, renovating a large area in the Military Building. I think someone said it was the old laundry. And we went back again in 1998 to be there for the Lab's opening.

"You're a Hokie, you know," Joe would tell me.

"I didn't go to school here. I'm a Trojan, from USC. We know football and John Wayne."

He'd chuckle at me. "You're a Hokie by marriage," he'd say, so I guess I was, complete with genuine, bookstore-bought paraphernalia.

Figure 9.3. Joe giving speech at Ware Lab opening.

I made up about 30 ball caps in Hokie colors to give out at the lab opening that said "Virginia Tech, WARE LAB, Advanced Engineering" on the front. The name of the Lab is "Joseph F. Ware, Jr. Advanced Engineering Laboratory," but it became known as "the Ware Lab" or just "the Lab."

At the opening, Joe gave a speech that was well received, and everyone got a tour. I'd had a bronze plaque made up for the Lab's front, by the door, with Joe's mug in bronze and pictures of the SR-71 and a Connie.

Figure 9.4. Plaque by front door of the Lab.

The Lab was more extraordinary than anything I'd imagined. We were told that once the Lab was established, other entities from Ingersol Rand to General Motors wanted to get a piece of it and had donated money. Apparently, companies were eager to get their hands on young engineers who had proven their ideas in working concepts. Even Lockheed said they'd hire students who had projects in the Ware Lab.

I was so proud of Virginia Tech and Joe.

10

So What Went Wrong?

1998

JOE AND I stood in line at the movies to buy tickets for "Titanic," wearing big, orange life jackets.

The guy behind us tapped me on the shoulder. "Nice."

I smiled.

When we got to the ticket window, I made a peace sign through the glass. "Two, please."

The clerk looked confused. "Which movie?"

2015

The Griffith Observatory planetarium is one of the nicest in the world, I'm sure, with a state of the art, 75' dome, Zeiss projector, and 290 seats.

Inside the Observatory, before entering the planetarium, Ellen and I could hear a hundred people talking about exhibits, stars, cosmology and the sciences. Inside the planetarium, even with the door still open, there was a hushed silence, almost a reverence for contemplation.

We took seats inside the door to the right, two rows back from the "ant with a thyroid condition" projector in the middle of the room.

Before the show, while people gathered, I leaned into Ellen so we could talk without disturbing anyone else. "Flying was our main gig. It wasn't an avocation for us; we didn't do it for fun."

"Uh, huh," Ellen said, doubting that.

"Really. Flying was a *duty* in life for us, important work, a set of skills worthy of a day's work. And we laughed a lot, too, because things happened that—

"Like, once, Joe and I were flying into March Air Force Base to show the Cessna 120 for static display?"

"I don't know that one."

"A little 1947 spam-can taildragger, two-seater, side-by-side."

"Little?"

I smiled. "Yeah. I think we could carry 50 lbs. behind the seats."

"Little."

"And on left downwind for Runway 32, March Tower asked me to start doing right 360s, so I did. Turning little circles in the air beside the runway. Okay, why? I had no idea. No one ever asked me to do that before."

People slowly entered the planetarium.

Ellen turned in her seat to watch me more closely.

"And then this B-1B heavy bomber flew into the pattern out of nowhere and started doing touch-and-goes right around us in left closed pattern, blasting his afterburners, loud as thunder. Here we are going, 'p-p-p-p-p-p-p-p-p-p-p-p-p' with our O-200, and it was going, *'ROOOOOOOOOAAAAAARRR'* with huge jets!"

"Why?" Ellen asked.

"I—don't know." I spread my hands in wonderment. "Advertising the airshow? He was making the devil's own noise. So after about three go-arounds, he was ready to land, and he referred to himself as 'heavy.'

"Then someone on the radio said, 'That's not heavy.' It turned out a C-5 Galaxy heavy lifter was approaching for a landing from the southeast, long straight-in approach. So the B-1B landed, then the C-5 landed, and *then* Tower cleared me to land—our little, 20-pound C-120 antique/classic taildragger, and—you know what worried us!"

"Supper?"

"Wing tip vortices that would come off his wing tips! Can't see 'em. If we hit one, we'll flip upside down and crash. So I'm all hotshot Jane pilot, 'Don't worry, Joe. I got this. I'm on it. Don't worry. I know about this—' 'Maybe we should decline the clearance?' Joe asks, but I reassure him I know what I'm doing."

"Oh, no," Ellen said. "You didn't."

I nodded. "You know vortices, sink down, maybe outside, maybe drift with the wind— So I told Joe all about it on my way down, thinking out loud. I came in high, above the C-5's glide path, slipped it down, and landed well beyond the spot where his nose gear touched down—after, supposedly, where it should be safe. I was all on it, and sure enough, it worked out. On rollout, I said, 'See there, Joe? *I did it!* No problem.'"

Ellen looked relieved.

"Then I exited the runway—*it turned out I used the same taxiway as the C-5!*"

"Oh, my God!"

"I know! *Dumb airhead me!* I was so busy congratulating myself for my flying mastery that I didn't think about the taxi! We we're looking up at the monster on the ramp in front of us, and I said, 'Oh, shit,' to Joe, then 'March ground, One Three November is right behind the C-5, worried about jet blast.'"

"They could blow you back across the runway," Ellen said.

"—and turn us into a little, Joe-and-Jen-stuffed aluminum matzo ball. But everybody noticed, including the cockpit of the C-5. So when they began their taxi, they used other engines."

"And they were probably complaining about the dumb broad in the little taildragger."

"I'm sure. Mind the medium through which you move. I forgot to think!"

I sat back in my planetarium seat, wistful.

"It was stuff like that all the time! Things we shared in life that no one would ever know about, things we were sharing together that *we* cared about. One thing after another. Camping. Sleeping under the wing, looking up at the stars together. Sitting in the car through the rain at the harbor, listening to Nat King Cole's 'Stardust.' Traveling. Teasing people."

"You do that a lot."

"Never! But I did tease those guys from the C-5. Later that night at Sally's Alley—the watering hole at March—everyone was standing around in their flight suits having a drink, when I noticed some were from the C-5 and some other guys were from a C-130 that flew in. They asked, 'What did you fly in?' I answered, 'C-120.' Joe laughed again."

"He seems to have done that a lot."

"God knows why. The guys in the C-5 stood there in their flight suits and said. 'What's a C-120?' I told 'em, 'It's kind of like a C-130, only a little smaller.' Not one of 'em was willing to admit he didn't know what a C-120 was."

"You kept Joe entertained."

"We kept each other entertained. And it was all because we loved being together."

I looked at the perfect dome above us.

It is so peaceful in the planetarium.

"Alright, so if everything's so great, what was it with all the trouble you had?" Ellen asked.

LATTER 1990s

LAWYER 6: "You got off light. You're lucky that's all they did. People don't like you to be married!" He pointed at me with a stiff finger. "But the problem you could have is if you are ever charged with a felony."

"What for!?" I was astonished. I looked at Joe to defend me.

Joe looked disappointed in the lawyer for mentioning that.

LAWYER 7: "You're an easy target—your age and sexuality. It's the '90s, but some people think it's the 50s. In California, everything with an elder is a felony. If someone thinks you delve into his finances too much, or get too much money from him, or if he's ever injured and if it's blamed on you— An otherwise normal marital quarrel could be taken as emotional elder abuse. Or if he needs a doctor and you don't take him, or if someone thinks you're using a doctor to manipulate him, or someone thinks you don't feed him enough—neglect can also be a felony."

"Jesus!" He was scaring the shit out of me.

The lawyer nodded. "You're transsexual, he's older. If someone thinks the sky should not be blue over your head, they'll make it rain—anybody: a nurse, a doctor, someone at the airport, a cop in the mall. You're in a hostile environment. In short, if he wears plaid with stripes, you could wind up in jail."

I'd been recently learning about some opposition to us in our life that had existed since about 1990. It had been kept from me; Joe had been running interference.

I had mounting fears that if there were ever a problem with others, I would not be believed. Joe, I wasn't worried about. But I'd not done so well with many others, through the years. I was becoming aware that I was having increasing difficulty with doctors or others who thought my joint pains might not be real, issues easy to internalize and generalize. I would complain about pain for which people could see no cause, which people may have attributed to clumsiness or malingering.

In a related manner, there are trust issues many trans people also feel. People can't look into our mind. They see us from the outside and interpret us as they wish. Many do not validate a real cause, a real sex identity that matches our claims, and, instead, fill in blanks with assumptions, or someone else's story. I knew my appearance was not where I wished it was, and with that, I think many people assume that if you don't look very female on the outside, you're not very female on the inside.

I'd learned through the previous 40 years that my transsexuality was something that upset a lot of people and set some of them off even more so, that people would disregard law and humanity to hurt me, believing they were doing the right thing, or sometimes not even caring. I knew some people would feel it horribly wrong for Joe and I to be together, that drastic steps must be taken to drive me away for his benefit, to protect an image of whom a decent man should love. I was told Joe would have to be gay to be with me. So, if Joe was, instead, an honorable straight guy, I must be taking advantage of him, manipulating him in the marriage.

An irrationally negative view of me was not in everyone's heart, but I also knew, from hard reality, that it was true for many people—and in any process of law, there would be many people involved. Some people there might be determined to be fair with me, but all it took, I was sure, was one person to ruin me. And some people had proven to me they would.

I thought it unlikely I would prevail if others came after me.

By the latter '90s, things being done that focused on our marriage, or me, to drive me away, became more obvious, as if I wasn't getting the message—which I literally wasn't, at first.

Little things I'd overlooked or didn't want to know about were becoming harder to ignore. Put on a happy face, enjoy life, had been my approach. Overlook things. But I could not miss more blatant problems, which developed.

I began to feel like a target waiting to happen, a prey animal, where some others bared their fangs and salivated. I felt I could not fight back, because it would require me to name the problem, out loud, and—stealth—I couldn't do that in my heart. I was sure I wouldn't be believed for the instant issue, anyway. I felt helpless, as if my own front door could not keep them out, that my meager funds were not safe, that *I* was not safe as a person, even physically.

I won't name the problems. That's not what this is about. It's about how I mishandled my own life issues—living private about something that wasn't even a secret. How could anything be more schizophrenic?

But I would not leave Joe, regardless. Damn them all to hell, I would die first.

So if I would not leave Joe, we had to move.

The harbor house, which had been our honeymoon cottage for several years, became a frightening place to me. I could feel their presence, every moment, everywhere I went in our home. I felt unsafe, but more, I feared what I couldn't imagine. It's hard to know the mind of people who don't share.

That's when I got our little girl, an English Springer Spaniel, whom Joe and I named Counselor Troi, after the brunette "bombshell" Joe had loved on "Star Trek: TNG," Deanna Troi, the one who I pretended had sent Joe his get well card in '92, for his hip replacement. She was bouncy, lively, which was quite positive, but it was not enough. The attacks were traumatic for me, with lasting effect.

So we sold out of our beloved honeymoon cottage in Mandalay Bay, in about 1999, and moved into a development in town. The River Ridge house had no dock for a boat, but they were quality houses, and there was a solid front door. Mostly, I think it was just not the harbor house.

We settled in and adjusted as well as we could. Troi matured. I trained a few tricks with her. We continued to take planes to air shows, went boating—but everything was subdued. I think we both felt alone, even when we were together.

We struggled to rebuild our lives.

So what to build?

Our first year there, I built a "rocket ship," and we held a party, a Bosco Rasche Invitational, for several people wherein we intended to put a beer mug in orbit in honor of Joe's favorite professor of old at then VPI. At the party, I played "Also Sprach Zarathustra" from "2001: A Space Odyssey," and worked the rocket ship with a remote control. It smoked like it meant business—then fell over on the patio (per design).

Watching a documentary on the TV with Joe one day about how the pyramids may have been built, it occurred to me that the ramp idea was wrong for most of the core and casing stones. A ramp may have well been used to the level of the King's Chamber for the megaliths within, but above there, they didn't make sense. The ramps would be too massive.

Better, I thought, was to use two "pivot points," like a fixed, granite pulley, and a rope. Build a wooden plank up the side of the building pyramid, to protect it from abrasion and so you can grease the plank with lard, have a pivot point up on the highest level, another one at the back side of that level. Tie a rope onto the block of stone being raised, string it over both pivot points to waiting people on the ground on the other side, enough so they're only pulling 30 pounds each, or so. Then have the people walk away at normal walking speed. They'd have a mechanical advantage, as they're not walking in line with the rope, and the stone would zip up the side of the pyramid in seconds. Low cost. Easy and fast. Minimal effort to construct. And you could have several of those working at one time on a pyramid. It would be harder to get the blocks TO the pyramid than it would be to get them UP the pyramid.

Joe was always excited to see me try to learn something, so in our Skunk Works in the garage, I built a scale pyramid in plywood, and I tested the pull strengths on the patio with a scale inline on the rope. It worked. This was easy.

I contacted Dr. Wendrich, professor at UCLA, and she said I should look in Professor Mark Lehner's book, *The Complete Pyramids* on page 211. I bought the book, and there, on page 211, was a picture of my pivot points, described as "the mysterious tool." They'd been found in the vicinity of the pyramids.

I reached out to Dr. Mark Lehner, but he never responded. I also talked with Dr. Zahi Hawass on the phone, who was nearby in Marina Del Rey at the time. He was very nice to me, said to send him my papers, which I did, but he never got back to me.

But Joe was proud of me for getting in there with a project.

And Troi was excited about everything, always adding joy to our life.

1999

Joe and I sat in a surgeon's office. The doctor explained to Joe what would be involved in his knee replacement. "So it'll take a couple days in the hospital. Jenna knows how to rehab you, it seems. Remember to get that 110-degree bend on the knee, Jenna. You got that?"

"Yes. And one more thing, Doc."

"What?"

I reached out and put a little piece of metal in his hand.

"A grease Zerk?" the surgeon asked.

Feeling very mechanical, the next year Joe and I built an ornithopter in our Skunk Works garage—flapped its wings like a bird—built with 2x4s, hemp rope and rubber bands. It looked like something Fred Flintstone would love.

Figure 10.1. Ornithopter being "test flown" by a guest in our back yard.

We held another Bosco Rasche Invitational that year, getting 54 people over, wherein I demonstrated the amazing flying qualities of this little hummer. I put on a leather flying helmet with goggles, sat on it, drove it a few feet across the large patio—Troi barking at the unnatural thing—and, with the loud compressor motor running on back, I shouted to the crowd, "You want to see me get the nose gear off the ground?"

"Sure!"

"Okay!"

"I mean *really* off the ground?" I asked.

"Yeah! Do it!"

"Okay!" I yelled.

I revved it up to the max, the thing making the devil's own noise, wings flapping, shaking everything apart, my head bouncing up and down with the wings, and then yelled to everyone, "You ready?"

I'm sure the neighbors thought I'd lost it.

"Yes!" everyone said.

Then I'd let go of the throttle and grab the 2x4 brake lever, pulling it back, levering the nose gear up about an inch.

Joe had paid for the trip in 1993 to Israel and Egypt, so this time, I paid for us to go to England, Scotland, and Ireland, where we toured everything. After we landed in Shannon, Ireland, the first order of the day was to drive on the other side of the road. The second order of the day was not to wreck while doing it.

"So, Joe, when I turn left, do I turn right? Is left right over here?"

"Jenna!"

"But I'm driving on the right side of the car which is right, but on the left side of the road which is also right…"

"Jenna!"

Near Cork, Ireland, he kissed the Blarney stone once; I kissed it twice.

In Scotland, we boated on Loch Lomond and Loch Ness—I told people, "We saw something in Loch Ness! It was a bird, sitting on the water, but *we saw something*!" We watched a bagpiper play "Amazing Grace" at Urquhart Castle, ate haggis neeps and tatties at Drumnadrochit, bought our own Ancient Weir tartans in Inverness, watched the sun set over the river, toured other castles, went to Stonehenge down in England, Leeds Castle, went to 221 B Baker Street, where Joe played Sherlock and I played the distraught client who needed his help—overall, had a marvelous time. We even took the Chunnel over to Paris for a quick look, but mostly the trip was for the Isles.

Figure 10.2. J2 as Sherlock Holmes and distraught client, 221B Baker St., London.

2001

Joe and I always woke early.

9-11, 2001, I woke as usual and turned on the TV with the remote. The news showed the north tower of the World Trade Center in New York burning, smoke filling the sky.

I woke Joe immediately. He could see the TV, but it was small and on the other side of the room, so I described the detail. We sat up in bed and watched, wondering how such a tragedy could have occurred.

I called a couple friends and told them to get on the TV, then returned my attention to Joe.

We watched in horror as another airliner flew into the picture and dove into the south tower. A short while later, both towers fell to the ground in an unbelievably large cloud of dust. Thousands were killed under falling concrete and steel.

We were all stunned, it was so massive. Terrorism. How anyone could be so cruel—

The world, I knew, had to learn to accept the idea of respecting difference—physical difference, nationalities, sexualities, but also ideologies. That basic concept came at me from so many directions in life. "I can only accept you if you're like I understand" was impossible.

Years before, when I was new in Navy uniform, someone bought my ticket into the movies simply because I was in uniform. So, beginning that day in mid September, and several times afterward, I coordinated with Sondra, manager at the Waypoint Café, Camarillo Airport. I'd slip her $100 and suggest, "Everyone in uniform in here, gets a free lunch. Okay? 'On the house,' not from me. Let me know how much else I owe you afterward."

She was pleased to help.

We were saying "illegitimi non carborundum" to the world: Don't let the bastards get you down. Never give up. Adapt. Do something to make it work. Overcome. We will never give up.

At Oshkosh, I stood beside Joe, in front of Richard Bach, at the author's table. I had devoured his books and thought of myself, personally, as Jennifer Livingston Seagull. Barely any joke there. I handed my copy to one of my greatest heroes.

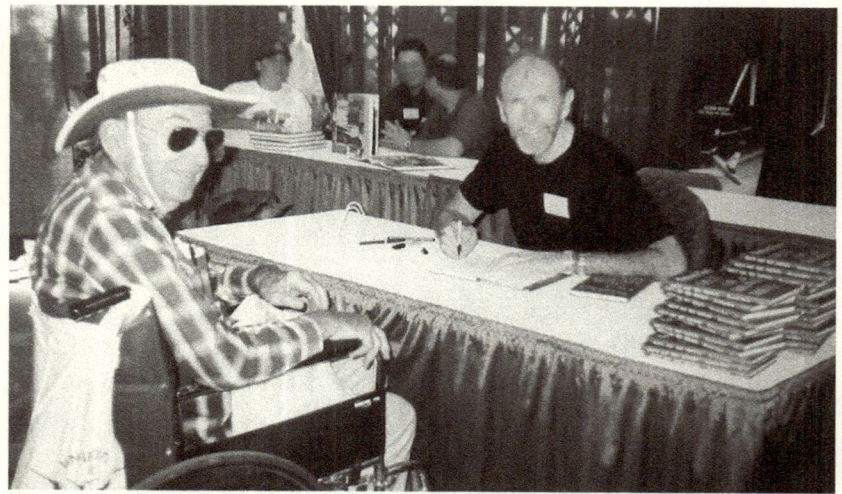
Figure 10.3. Joe with Richard Bach at Oshkosh.

Richard accepted it from me and asked, "What would you like me to write?"

I glanced at Joe, leaned onto Richard's table with my elbows, got close to him, and spoke the first half of one of his famous quotes: "You're never given a wish—" My smile made my request clear.

Richard smiled at me and finished his own quote. "—without also being given the power to make it true."

Joe and I were starting to make life work again. We were finding our footing again, proving we were a couple, that we wouldn't give up, either.

One evening, when Joe went out for his evening walk in Connolly Park, there was a knock at our door. My guard was down. We'd had no trouble for a while. I answered it. A man stepped in through our sturdy front door and made it clear I hadn't been paying attention.

I'm really not very physically able. My frame is robust in appearance. It seems strong because of my size, and is in some ways, yet that is deceptive. I cannot defend myself well in real life, because I cannot move my limbs fast enough, without subluxing my shoulders or wrists, a quality the man did not seem to share.

In the coming weeks, we thought about who was behind it.
I didn't know.
Report to the police?
Never. I could not.
We didn't know what to do or where to go. But I believed we couldn't stay there, again.

I did some rapid research, probably drove a few more lawyers crazy, and I decided we needed to move away from the area, to distance from trouble. Neither of us wanted to move, but staying together was at the top of our list.

It may not make sense to some people, but I felt helpless against unknown people who had repeatedly hurt me, and who seemed to have friends willing to do the same. I had little in the way of anyone to look to for guidance or insight.

Even then, I was longer-term in transition than most, at 21 years. Prejudice and hate crimes were publicly known as concepts, but not very well with these particulars. Joe was a conservative icon, and I was an abomination. I was at a loss.

How could it affect us?
What did things mean?
How might the problem progress?
What rights did I really have?
If I were to choose to act for my defense, what could I do?

How can I assert myself when it seemed that I was disbelieved in the most basic assertions about myself? When others made it so clear I was less than human? When they could enter my home at will and hurt me?

Being with Joe since 1989, dating him/living with him in the early '90s, aroused concern. The dragon raised his head. Marrying Joe seems to have been too much. The dragon fought. We made it work, anyway. The dragon fought harder.

I've worried about how to relate my story without focusing on the actions of others. I don't want speak harshly of anyone, so I'm purposefully leaving out some detail. I hope that doesn't compromise me as my own narrator, but I'll take that risk. My focus is on what I did that made our life harder than it needed to be, not on the details of what others did.

Please let it suffice to say that we sold that house in late 2002 and moved to relative safety, we thought, as far away as we could, into a different state of mind—a "castle," literally with a moat: a house on San Juan Island, in the Puget Sound, a thousand miles away, where, coincidentally, Sandra Bullock had filmed "Practical Magic."

It was a beautiful house in a field near Friday Harbor. The scenery was beautiful, haunting. I named the property Madrona Faire because there were so many Madrona trees on it.

I hoped it could be a place for our family: Joe, Troi, and me.

Until we got a letter, about a month later, from part of our problem back home, telling us we'd moved into an area they happened to frequent, and that they had friends on the island who would be stopping by.

PART 3

SEEMING ECCENTRIC

"Why do we keep making the same mistakes, over and over?"

Halle Berry as Luisa Rey
Movie "Cloud Atlas"

11

Woodhaven

2003

THE LETTER hit our home like a bomb.

I shopped for a new home feverishly, all over the mainland—anywhere away from the island, away from trouble—and I found a place that seemed, hopefully okay, on 10 acres of land—except the house was junk. It had been a foreclosure and appeared to have been gutted. There was nothing in it. Even the sinks were gone. How could I move the three of us in there with only one working toilet, no working shower, no working kitchen?

Hello Joe: If I can understand it, I can fix it.

One month later, at the close of escrow, Joe, Troi and I showed up at our new home, which I dubbed "Woodhaven," north of Gig Harbor, with our Ford minivan packed to the gills. A mover was to arrive with the rest of our things that afternoon.

Driving through the trees, it was easy to get the impression the area was more secluded than it actually was. Trees were everywhere.

"I think God must have planted them," I said. The place was gorgeous, could have easily doubled as a national park.

Troi jumped between the seats of the minivan onto Joe's lap and stared out the windows. She was excited.

"Whoa," Joe told her. "Slow down."

The tunnel of trees ended several feet onto the property and opened up to a wide pasture big enough to land a gyroplane, a small barn, the house, and then more yard to the west big enough to land another gyroplane.

The property was more stunning than any I've ever seen. Trees lined the perimeter and most of the western edge: Madrona, Cedar, Pine—and the pasture area opened to reveal neighboring homes to the south and the Puget Sound, with Mount Rainier in the distance.

On opening the door to the minivan, Troi shot out to inspect the property. She always seemed a little psychic. She knew things, and in that instance, she seemed to realize that was our new home.

Joe got out of his side of the minivan and walked closer to the house, glancing at me out the side of his eyes.

I took his hand and moseyed around the place.

"It is pretty," he said.

"The land," I said. "The house is a wreck."

Joe was a quiet man. Humble by nature, he never presupposed someone needed his opinion. He assessed things, sometimes speaking when needed.

Troi disappeared to the west.

"Troi!" I called to the empty field. "Get back here!" Nothing. *"Troi!"*

She came running back into view, to bounce off my legs at 90 miles an hour, happy.

I petted her. "Good girl. Stick around," I ordered. "We do this together." I gave her a couple of hand signals that seemed to indicate, "Stay close and walk with me."

Her look to me was clear: "Oh! Why?!"

"Stick around," I said to her again. I mean it."

She began to move away. *"Troi!"*

She looked at me sideways, as she did sometimes, but she stayed with us.

I held Joe's hand and wandered toward the house. "Why do you want her so close?" Joe asked.

"I don't know."

The front screen door to the old farm house creaked, but the lock in the main door worked as expected, and the three of us began to examine our new home. The floors were a mess. Carpets were ruined. Appliances were all ripped out. Only one toilet remained. Some electrical outlets were gone.

Upstairs was no different.

"We don't go up there," I said. "Never. Okay? I don't think stairs are safe for either of us."

I knew he didn't like me telling him what to do, but he agreed.

"You're still scared," he said.

I frowned, still looking the house over. "Yes, I am."

I backed the minivan to the front door of the house. I found a folding chair in the back seat and took it inside for Joe to sit on—to supervise—and I began to unload the minivan, putting things haphazardly in the living room for the moment.

Joe sat in his chair and watched me. "You think we can make it work here?"

I knew he didn't like the house.

I stood by him and kissed him briefly, hugged him to my stomach.

"I don't know," I said. "But we can try."

I carried more things in from the car, put them on the pile.

"Troi?" She gave me her attention immediately, alert, looking for a command. "Love Daddy?"

Her face softened.

"Give Daddy a kiss."

She looked happy, and she jumped up on her daddy's lap, licking him in the face. Joe hugged her, I think primarily so she would stop licking him. The two of them sat for a few seconds until Troi jumped off his lap halfway across the living room.

"Stick around, Troi," I said, so she wouldn't run out the door. Her memory was only good for a few seconds, by desire, I was sure. It was as if I could read her bouncy mind.

I took out a small pad of paper and pen, laid a tape measure on the empty counter. Standing in the gutted kitchen, I began to make notes with measurements.

> Stove—electric
> Sink
> Dishwasher
> Refrigerator…

"How you gonna get a fridge in here?" Joe asked.

"I'll get a hand truck from Home Depot. Looks like a solo trip for the fridge. Lay it on its back in the minivan. They'll load it for us. I'll push it out of the van with my feet, teeter it on the bumper, stand it up outside, put it on the hand truck and bring it in. Then just plug it in."

"You can do all that?" Joe asked me.

"You taught me how to look at it. I'll work it out." I kissed him on top the head. "One way or another. Come on, guys," I said, motioning toward the car.

Troi ran and jumped inside the minivan, as its back door was still wide open. Joe got up and began walking toward the car.

"Lets get some lunch and then get on over to Home Depot. Most of this stuff is plug-in. I'll have it up and running by tonight. The dishwasher is tomorrow."

I drove us off the property to the east.

What were we going to do with the place?
Clean it up. Rebuild our lives once again.

Rapidly, within about 30 hours, I had the major issues in the house functioning. Joe's job was supervisory, I did the work, and Troi's job was to run all over the place.

With a place to eat, sleep, and shower, with TV to watch and music to hear, we began to address the rest of the property.

There was an automobile garage on the west side of the house that seemed to double as kindling, leaning over— I immediately urged everyone to stay away from it and took it down. I tied a rope onto a support beam, tied the other end to the minivan, tensioned it slightly, cut a couple of beams on the back side with a Sawzall, and it fell over onto the ground behind the minivan. A handyman took it away as rubble.

One of my early projects was to have the entire 10 acres enclosed in chain link fence, and to add an electric steel gate at the front of the property. No visitors without admittance.

To the northwest of the house was the "shed." It was made of steel at—my guess—40 feet wide by 90 feet long, and the interior was full of torn up drywall, broken glass, 2x4s, scattered or crushed everywhere. I'd been told it had been a recording studio, at one time. It was completely unusable as it was—we couldn't even walk through it—so I got a crew to gut it, which made the largest storage shed either of us had ever had, with a broad expanse of concrete flooring, and a kitchen and bath on one end.

I had difficulty finding doctors for Joe up there. Sometimes it was money—they didn't want Medicare patients. I'd call places to ask for an appointment, and they'd ask about his insurance. I'd tell them he had Medicare, and they'd refuse him.

And sometimes it was me. A couple of times when I was able to get him in the door (passing the Medicare check), they told us on the spot that we were unwelcome. It was before my FFS, facial feminizing surgery, and I was more noticeable. Once, we made it all the way into an exam room, before the doctor told us we would need to seek Joe's care somewhere else—which reinforced my understanding of prejudice. Some people would refuse medical attention to an elder, to avoid having me around. A few times, though Joe's complaint was minor, we found ourselves waiting in an emergency room of a hospital until 3:00 in the morning.

Moved in, fenced in, the shed gutted and made usable, a master bedroom added on the main floor, we began to settle into life. I even added a wood burning stove to both the shed and the master bedroom, for use if electricity went out in a storm.

The place, and our lives, were coming together.

No one sent us any letters that scared us.

No one threatened us.

No one intruded.

I began to wonder if, perhaps, things might work out.

The two of us sat in his new church, 2nd pew back from the front.

"All rise," the pastor said from the bimah.

Joe stood with the congregation and began singing.

In a few seconds, I rose and sang with him.

"A mighty fortress is our God
A bulwark never failing…"

We sat in a movie theatre and watched "Pirates of the Caribbean."

Some neighbors came over to make smores with us at a fire pit in our back yard.

"Here, Joe," I said, handing him a new one I'd made.

He took it and snacked.

"You're up from California?" Sheri asked.

"If you don't count San Juan Island," I said.

"You moved to San Juan and then left it?" She was trying to figure it out.

"We're from California," I said, covering.

Maybe we can rebuild our lives here, instead.

"Alright, Joe." I yelled into his ear so he could hear me over the baseball stadium crowd. "It's the bottom of the third. The Mariners have a guy on 2nd—"

"What's it mean, 'bottom of the third'?" Joe knew better. He was doing to me what I sometimes did to him.

"It means it's not as good as the top, but it costs less, so we don't care—"

One of the guys in front of us seemed annoyed. "What?"

"Don't' listen to her," Joe told him.

The guy looked like he wondered what I was doing.

"He can see the players," I told the guy up front, "but he can't tell just what they're doing. His eyes. Macular degeneration."

"Oh, okay." The guy went back to the game.

I continued to narrate loudly into Joe's ear.

"And the guy's at the plate. He's—burly. Probably good in bed."

Joe laughed, as did two of the guys in front of us.

"What is she?" the guy asked.

"His bat is stiff," I continued into Joe's ear. "He leans to the right—his hips are swinging, and the tip of the bat is wobbling back and forth, like—you know."

The guy in front of us almost spilled his beer.

"AND HE SWINGS!" I yelled to Joe.

CRACK, we could hear the bat!

Half the crowd jumped to their feet.

"The ball went wide to left field," I had to shout to be heard over the crowd, "and he's *running for first*—the guy on 2nd is ramming for 3rd—the ball is gonna be caught by that outfielder—NO!—the guy dove for it, but it BOUNCED, and then he caught it—but he flubbed it! He's going back for it!—our guy is on FIRST BASE, and he's heading for 2nd!—and our

other guy has rounded third! *THE COACH IS TELLING HIM TO RUN FOR IT! He's running for it! THE GUY OUT THERE IN CANADA THROWS THE BALL! The man is still RUNNING—"*

The crowd screamed its delight.

"HE MADE A *TOUCH DOWN*, Joe! HE DID IT!"

We were at the home of a gal named Leah, who was having a few friends over. We sat on the couch with a couple who were sipping champagne.

Joe and I had diet cokes.

Sylvia asked, "You two fly a plane?"

"Yes," I said. "It's a cute little Cessna 120."

Her lover, Paula, asked, "Isn't that hard?"

"Yes," I said, "but the air is very soft."

Paula looked confused.

"I used to fly," Sylvia said.

I looked at her carefully. She looked a little depressed.

"Not any more?" I asked.

Sylvia shook her head.

Paula spoke up for her. "She's down again. It happens."

"Why?" I directed my question to Sylvia, even though it was Paula who spoke.

Sylvia didn't answer.

Paula spoke for her. "She flew in the Air Force, but they kicked her out. It still bothers her. She switched after she got out."

"So did I," I said.

"You were in?" she asked.

I wanted to be supportive. "Navy."

I noticed a cross dresser across the room sneaking my picture with a small camera.

"I wish that lady wouldn't take my picture," I mentioned to Paula.

"Why?"

I shook my head a little as if I didn't want to talk about it. "I'm stealth."

"We're all out of the closet, honey," Paula said.

"Not me. I've had trouble. So could you ask her?"

"It's probably not a problem," Paula said. "Don't worry about it."

My look of concern didn't fade.

"Where?" Sylvia asked me.

"Ft. Meade."

I hoped Paula was right about the pictures.

"A spook?" Sylvia asked.

"I guess."

"What did you do?" she asked

"Smoke signals," I said. "You know: damp blankets over the camp fire? Where were you?"

I looked to Paula with questions in my eyes.

"She had a hard row," Paula said. "She lost her girlfriend last year, after two years."

Most trans people had difficult love lives, on top of everything else.

"I thought you two were together?"

"We are, now," Paula said, "but she doesn't trust me." She leaned over and gave Sylvia a brief kiss on the cheek, then lay in her arms on the couch. "I told her I'm here, and I won't leave."

"What did you fly in the Air Force?" Joe asked Sylvia.

"C-130s."

"Oh, for crying out loud," I said. "Joe was a flight test engineer on the C-130."

"No kidding?" Sylvia took a bit of an interest.

Joe sat upright more on the couch and started talking with her. Get him on airplanes, and he had a subject.

Sylvia sat on the examination table, and I sat on the little chair beside it.

The doctor stood, waiting for her to speak.

"Go ahead, Sylvia," I said. "Tell him what you told me."

"I'm fine," Sylvia said.

"What's the matter?" the doctor asked.

"Nothing," Sylvia said.

I noted Sylvia had invited me to join her in there, and she hadn't asked me to leave. "I'll tell him if you don't," I said.

Sylvia looked away from me.

The doc looked to me. "I have other patients."

"She's had some depression and suicidal ideation—"

Sylvia lowered her head a little.

"Ah," the doctor said, looking harder at Sylvia. "How have you been feeling?"

Sylvia said nothing.

"Life's hard for us," I continued. "She's also on Prozac, so I thought you should see her."

The doctor's office smelled of cleaner.

I felt the pressure of the speculum, inside me.

"Are you sure, doc? Why is the Pap smear so important?"

"Gotta check for cancer," the doctor said. "Female parts."

I wondered what— "You mean just because tissue is up there?"

It would be years before another doctor broke ranks and told me what was probably going on.

Joe and I drove north of Gig Harbor, toward Woodhaven, in our 4x4 SUV, with two alpacas lying in the back. Though they'd seemed comfortable until then, for the entire 30-minute drive, one of them decided it was time for a change.

"Holy shit?" I said, looking into the rear view mirror. It was full of cute, white, furry alpaca face.

Joe turned around to look.

The alpaca was nosing us, sniffing the front seats, the back of our heads and shoulders.

"Joe, see if you can get him to lay back down?"

"Lay down!" Joe told him.

The alpaca nosed further into the front seat.

Joe pushed on his face, trying to keep him back. Without regard to Joe, the alpaca walked into the front seat like a dog might, except he was twice as large as any German Shepherd could have been.

"Whoa! Hold him back!" I yelled, "What the hell!"

Joe tried, but the alpaca out-sized us both, and there was very little we could do.

In seconds, he was in the front seat area with both of us, his butt on me, his head by Joe.

Looking over alpaca wool, I applied the brakes and brought us to a stop beside the road.

"Joe! You alright?"

"I'm fine!"

We didn't know what to do; we'd only been alpaca ranchers for about 30 minutes.

"Turn his head back to the back," I said, "Maybe he'll go back there."

Joe did, but the alpaca stood up, instead, pressed his back against the windshield and bowed it out. Cracks splintered from one side to the other.

"Shit! Joe!?"

"There's nothing I can do!"

The alpaca turned around and sat on Joe's lap, his head on mine, and made himself at home. That was obviously a good spot.

"Did you get the car in park?" Joe asked.

"Stand by."

I reached around the front side of the alpaca, through piles of wool, down toward the center console area, but all I got was a hand full of alpaca penis.

"Ugh!" We were on level ground, so we wouldn't roll. I turned the engine off.

"You okay?" I asked again.

"Yeah."

The alpaca's face was near mine. "You don't suppose?" I thumbed for him to move to the rear.

Nothing. He was happy right there.

The other one was happy in the back, thank God.

I got out of the car and went around to Joe's side, opened his door and helped him out from under the warm pile of wool.

The alpaca stayed where he was.

My heart was racing. "Are you hurt? Are you bruised?" I bent over to brush his pants off.

"No. I'm fine," he said again.

"How could that be?"

I checked my cell phone, but there was no signal there.

"Now what?" I asked.

The windshield was pushed out. Alpacas fore and aft. I couldn't drive the car.

A fire truck happened to work its way up the road, non-emergency, on the way to somewhere else. I flagged it down in distress—nothing firemen enjoy more.

"Guys! Do you have a radio?"

"What's the matter?"

We took a little teasing while they assessed the situation.

One of the firemen tried to coax the alpaca out of the car, but it didn't work. He pushed, he pulled, he yelled at it, but the alpaca wouldn't budge, so he shut the door and left it in there.

"I hope he doesn't shit on your seat. How far you going?"

"Only about two miles."

He smiled. "Easy."

They had a radio and called us a tow truck, blocked the road with cones to divert traffic while we waited for it.

In the end, Joe and I rode in the tow truck, while both alpacas rode in our car.

"Why don't you drive right into the pasture," I told the driver.

He did.

We opened the car doors of our busted SUV, and both alpacas walked right out like it was Sunday.

My insecurities mounted through years of fears.

I spoke on the phone to the same lawyer I'd used down in California for a while.

"You have a problem up there," Angie said. "You don't have a good doctor for Joe—"

"I don't have one for him down there, any more, either. His old doctor retired."

"But you've had trouble finding a doctor up there, for him. You've shared the culture is quietly less accepting of you."

"True. I don't know who's going to do what next—"

"I think—"

"But the worst part of it is," she said, "out there on Woodhaven, you're isolated."

"Just to keep trouble the hell away—"

"So, it's a shallow moat for a paper castle. You may feel good to keep people at bay, but that also opens you to potential criticism."

"Angie—"

"You know I'm right. Some of the people who have hounded you? You really think they're going to think, 'Oh, well, now that I *can't see what's going on,* everything's okay?"

"Where is Kelly," I asked Wendy, walking into her backyard near the charbroiler. Wendy was tall and fit, hair down her back, very out, with an air of comfort about herself. She laid a few more burgers on the grill. They sizzled. Smoke rose past an awning toward gray clouds overhead.

Joe took a seat on a lawn chair.

Other people milled about in Wendy's back yard. Some were trans; some were cis friends.

"I don't see her," Wendy said.

Wendy's girlfriend, Kim, walked up to me. Her manner didn't seem friendly. "Jenna, why do you look so familiar?"

"I don't know. Maybe you've seen me in the movies."

Both Kim and Wendy's ears perked up.

I smiled. "I go about twice a week."

Joe chuckled.

"Oh, Jees!" Wendy smiled at the joke.

"Oh," Kim said, finally getting it. "I don't know if you should be here."

"Why not?" I asked, looking at Wendy. It was her home.

"You think you're better than us," Kim said.

"Oh, for God's sake," I said.

"We're using 'transgender' as an umbrella term over everyone," Wendy said. There were a growing number of them who were adamant about that.

I looked at them both.

Should I assert myself?

We're at a bar-b-que—

I tried. "You shouldn't use your term for us. Transsexualism and transgenderism are different things—"

"Don't say that!" Kim said.

"Why not? It's the truth. It has been since SRS made the different ways clear—"

"Old school!"

"Mixing sex and gender is *older* school."

Kim was adamant. "It shouldn't matter what genitals someone has!"

I looked to Wendy for rescue, but she didn't help. I had to answer on my own. "It shouldn't be a *problem* on a social level, but it damn sure does matter. It matters to me, and it matters to you, too. Like having sex—"

"It's none of your business how I have sex!"

"I don't care, on a personal level—"

"You don't care about us?" Kim was turning red.

"I didn't say that—"

"No!" Kim blew her top. "And I heard you don't think Bailey is an asshole!" She was referring to condemnation of his book, *The Man Who Would Be Queen.*

"I don't know the guy!" I said, beginning to take a stand. "I disagree with much of what he says, also, but it's wrong to say some of the shit that gets said about him. You don't like his research, so you make up lies? Ad hominem attacks? It makes us look like whackos!"

Kim asked Wendy, "'Ad' *what*?"

Wendy had invited us to the barbeque, but she stood back and let the fuming Kim have her way.

"You don't accept you're with us."

Joe dropped his gaze, a little. The look on his face told the tale.

Use ourselves as an example?

"We don't have to look at all this the same way. Can't a Jew and a Christian be friends—"

Kim crossed her arms. "We want to be accepted as *female* because we're *women*!"

"You know those are different things—"

"Get the fuck out!" Kim said.

I knew what I wanted, a minivan, like the one I had before, tan, no extras. It would work well at Woodhaven and give me the room I needed inside to carry bales of hay for the alpacas.

"Hi," I said to the salesman. "I'm interested in that one."

The sales man's look to me was disapproving.

My heart sunk.

"It's not for sale," he said.

I looked at it again, then back to him. "Yeah, it is."

"Not today."

Maybe he didn't understand. "I'm a cash customer. I'll just pay you for it." I walked over to it and checked the window sticker.

"You better leave," he said.

99s, the International Organization of Women Pilots, sat around the table and talked about flying. I had been a member for 15 years or so. It seemed like a good group of women pilots. Friendliness was the order of the day—except for the way one of them looked at me.

It was evening. Lights from the housing development south of us subtly illuminated snow-covered fields to give the area soft glow. Snowflakes drifted down from unseen clouds and settled softly in the field, on trees and fence posts. The alpacas, I knew, were in the barn. I'd checked them earlier with Troi.

We'd had a nice dinner. Joe sat in the living room watching "Touched by an Angel" on TV. Troi sat in his recliner with him, her soft head on his lap.

I sat in my "office," in the dark, looking over the fields, remembering when I'd done the same thing at Christmas in my troubled youth.

Where is my mom? I wish she could help.

I don't want to fight, I argued with myself.

But I still need to talk with her.

My doubting self was resolute. I knew we fought, though neither of us wanted to. If I called her, it could become another battle. But if I didn't try, I'd be cutting myself off from her, further.

I lifted the handset on the desktop phone and dialed her number.

Any chance it was snowing in Kansas, too?

I heard the line make the connections.

A woman answered. "Hello?"

"Hello. Mom?" I asked. "It's Jenna."

The line was silent for a few seconds. "No, I'm not coming out there for Christmas," she answered, evidently continuing the same conversation we'd had the last time.

We had never gotten along, but on some level, we both refused to call it quits, talked about things that were so light they were fake. Weather, health and food—shallow.

It was wearing on me that she wouldn't address me by name. "You still can't even say my name?" I finally said. "It's been a long time."

"I'll get used to it."

"It's been—what—23 years? I don't know if I should ask, but are you still using my name wrong when you talk with other people?"

"I'm your mother, and I love you."

Not "You're my daughter."

"Yes, but my name's 'Jenna.'"

After a few moments, she eeked out, "Don't push."

"I'm not pushing, Mom. I've been patient. How long is it supposed to take?"

"I gave you your name when you were born."

"You didn't know me very well, then. Hell, you don't know me very well, now." I stopped to think for a second. "I think something else is going on, there."

"How would you know. You're never here. You wrote us all off, years ago."

"I don't come around because there's hate for me there. You know that."

"No one has said anything to you."

"Yes, they have."

She was quiet again.

"Mom, does someone near you whisper sweet hatreds into your ear about me? Who won't admit it?"

"Don't start with this."

"Does someone dis me to you?"

"What is that?"

"Does someone put me down to you? Do they use a wrong name for me when I'm not around? Put me down? Or refuse to mention me?"

She got upset. "Don't call me up and start! I don't know if I can take this any more. Don't you know how—"

I could finish her sentence for her, but I didn't. "Sick" was the word she was looking for.

"I don't want to talk about this," she said.

"We have to sometime, Mom. Ever since I was a child—"

"You're bringing that up again?"

"It's been 40 years without it, so yes. I need to."

"That is ancient history."

"You've never once talked with me about it."

Mom started to cry. "You're so hateful."

"I don't mean to hurt your feelings but we've put it off forever. You're 70. If we don't talk soon, when will we? There's trouble here, Mom! People make life hard, and I have a husband—"

"A man!" She had a way of acting like she was a steam kettle about to blow, and I could hear her lid rattle.

"I love him! He's a truly great man—"

"We're done with this."

"Mom—" I tried to calm my tone. "Sometimes, you know—I need you. This life isn't easy. I could use your help—"

"Then don't be that way!"

She started to cry and hung up.

I lowered my hand to my desk in defeat, put the handset back in its cradle.

A wind blew some snow around the field, and cold crept in though the window.

The next morning was bright with snow-reflected sunlight. Joe still slept in our king-sized bed. Troi walked over the quilt to get closer to me, snuggled between us for some love.

I kissed her on the forehead and got up to go to the bathroom—when I noticed the most beautiful scene out the windows.

Be positive!

"Hey Joe!" I told him. "Get up. It's beautiful out there! Look at that." It was a little cold in the house. I started the wood burning stove in the master bedroom, with the propane tank outside.

"What?" He roused and looked. "It's snow."

"Oh, shit. I thought it was cocaine," I teased. "And there must have been a shooting war, because power lines are down. There's no electricity at all. I'll start the generator."

Troi jumped off the bed and got excited at the window.

"There's people out there," Joe said.

I looked more closely. "The neighbors, sledding down the west hill. Get around, okay? We gotta take this in."

Joe got into the shower while I got the house warmed.

There was a knock at the west door, and I answered it.

The neighbor lady stood there in a winter coat, earmuffs and mittens, like Norman Rockwell.

Troi jumped all over her as usual.

"Are you two up yet?" she asked, petting Troi.

Her husband and their kids were still on the hill.

"Good morning! Give her a break, Troi. What is all this white stuff?" I acted like I didn't get it.

"You don't have snow in LA?"

"They snort it before it hits the ground. It's hard on traffic, either way."

"Is it okay if we sled down your hill?" she asked.

They already were.

"You won't get hurt?"

"Never." She was a good mom, and I respected her judgment.

"Tell you what, I'll make some hot chocolate and bring it out to you in a few minutes?"

She smiled greatly. "Thanks!" She turned and ran back to her family.

"Go help them, Troi! Go on." The happy dog ran out to help the neighbors.

We had our Christmas cards for family and friends, that year, taken with the alpacas, out by the barn.

The day after Christmas, Joe and I stood in the barn.

"Okay, Joe, this is the way to do it, I think. Like I'm an old expert."

Troi nosed around the area, inspecting.

I put a small feed bucket under Joe's arm.

"If you— See, look."

Both alpacas were looking at Joe, because he had the feed.

"If you just hold the bucket, they'll come get some."

He did and they did.

"But if you move your arm to pet them—" Joe did, and both alpacas jumped away. "I think they're prey animals. Like me. And skittish, like I am, any more.

"But if you hold the feed bucket under your arm," I took Joe's other arm and straightened it out in front of him like Frankenstein, "and leave this other arm straight out, they'll come get feed and walk right past your hand. Hold still a minute."

One alpaca came forward and stuck his head in the bucket, leaving Joe's other hand right beside the alpaca's neck.

"Now your fingers are out of his sight. Just move your fingers and pet him."

Joe smiled at me, watching it work.

12

Paris

2004

MY DISCOMFORT grew, the first couple of years in Washington state, with my awareness that the culture, as I was experiencing it, was not very accepting, and in that culture, we were married. I feared people hostile to our marriage. It was little things I'd missed at first. People would smile, but I learned to glance back, after walking away, to see their reaction. The more I did it, I found people had a quiet way of acting pleasant to my face while not actually liking what they saw in me. I confirmed it by watching the reaction of people to other trans.

I can't say that southern California was more accepting as a whole. Los Angeles seemed to be more accepting, but Ventura County was not, where we'd lived. I was sure. Social signals were different around the Puget Sound, though, and I was less and less pleased with it. People up north seemed less direct about their pretense. They were kinder, on the outside. Gentler. But just as disapproving.

Which I believe interfered with Joe's health care, because we were together.

An example was a large squamous cell carcinoma Joe developed over his right ear. I watched it for a while, took him to two doctors up there, who didn't want to treat him. It was too large, we were told.

More and more, I was developing the view that a lot of doctors are egocentric, arrogant asses who can't consider they're wrong, or unkind, or harsh. It's hard enough to know what is going on when people hide their transphobia, without adding things like avoidance of Medicare onto it. I was feeling the need to be a more proactive.

I contacted Joe's old pilot friend and dermatologist in Oxnard, who had treated Joe for many years. I'd taken Joe in to him for treatment dozens of times, over the years, and I liked him also. He also respected my ability to detect skin cancers, saying I had about "an 80% pick rate." I couldn't always tell what kind one was, but I knew when to take him to the doctor.

I emailed him some pictures, and he agreed to treat Joe's squamous, so I booked us on Alaska Airlines, out of Seattle, for the trip.

Through TSA, at SeaTac International in Seattle, a screener was being badge heavy. He had been angry with Joe while wanding him, asking him to hurry up, being rude about it. I stepped in for Joe's defense, and told the screener, loudly enough for others to hear, to take it easy with Joe.

He turned his wrath on me, said I would be under arrest for interfering with him, made me stand in a square, arms wide. The NIS flashed through my mind, but my gut said he was being badge heavy, so I told him over and over, loudly enough for others to hear: "Sir! You were being mean to him! I am complying!" He told me to shut up, but I wanted everyone to hear, so I repeated myself, again loudly. That pissed him off more—then after a few minutes, he abruptly walked away without a word.

The incident scared me. My heart was pounding and I had to work to control my breathing.

We were cleared to proceed, and I wandered in a daze with Joe into the terminal.

What really happened, I don't know. Were I to guess, I'd say he embarrassed himself. Or someone over him told him to stop it.

But it scared me to my socks. This was one of the things I feared: being condemned, not believed. I believed he would have me up for God-knows what federal charge. And if he rolled transphobia into his own embarrassment, I could only imagine what he might say.

Inside the terminal, hands shaking, my heart racing, I made an anonymous phone call to Alaska Airlines and complained about him. He was TSA, not the airline, but I just wanted someone to know. I didn't want my name on it, for fear someone might think I had done something wrong, that it was me, somehow. So I was careful not to identify myself in my complaint.

After we got in the air, in coach, a flight attendant came to us, smiling greatly.

I was still getting adrenaline out of my system.

"What kind of wine would you like?" she asked.

I glanced at Joe. We rarely had wine.

Joe said, "Diet Coke."

I echoed him. "Diet Coke."

"But what kind of wine would you like?" she asked again, as if we were in first class.

"Well," another glance at Joe, who shrugged. I said, "I'd guess red, if I were choosing, but—"

She left and came back with a whole bottle of red wine for us and a gracious apology for our difficulty.

Maybe they watched video from the terminal?

You never know where kindness will rear its beautiful head.

In the spring, to get away, I suggested Joe and I go back to Paris. The single day we'd spent there in 1999, over from London, could in no way do the city justice.

We stayed at the Hotel Lotti, Rue de Castiglione, right near the Jardin des Tuileries, the multi-block-long park located between the Musee du Louvre and the Place de la Concorde, where the Egyptian obelisk exalting the reign of Ramesses II is located.

Joe was still able to walk at the time, but lengthy walks were becoming more difficult. He was 87. Where before we could walk for a couple miles, we were down to a few hundred yards. So I brought a transport chair with us—the kind with four small wheels, because they're lighter.

And Paris!

Figure 12.1. Having lunch inside the Eiffel Tower.

Figure 12.2. Looking up to Joe and the Tower.

Figure 12.3. The plaque on the ramp at Le Bourget said that's where Charles Lindbergh landed, 1927.

We ate on the first floor restaurant (2nd story, as the U.S. would call it) of the Eiffel Tower, visited the site at Le Bourget Airport where Charles Lindberg had landed in 1927 for the first trans-Atlantic flight, did the Moulin Rouge, a cabaret, which did, indeed, have a red windmill. We had dinner in there before the show, and—

"Joe! Look at that!"

The line to the ladies' room was so long, the ladies were actually using the men's room with them. And the men didn't care! Joe got a good laugh out of that.

We ate at a sidewalk café. That's one of the rules in Paris.

Joe and I sat there, chatting, waiting on our meal, when a waiter brought the man at the next table his food. The man stood and exclaimed, "What the hell is this shit!?" and walked away.

We didn't see anything wrong.

The waiter was unruffled, calmly took the man's plate away.

We asked the waiter what happened.

"Ze man? He came to Paris," (pronounced pa-REE), "and ordered a hamburger and fries. He thought zis was McDonalds! But the chef tried to make ze hamburger for him, anyway, so he did. Zen ze man said it was too rare, so I took it back, ze chef cooked it some more—and to make it special, added a ladle of sauce over ze whole thing, and *voila!* Ze you are."

There was a long line of people waiting to get into the Louvre, but because Joe was in a wheelchair, they let us in first. And we toured. We saw the inverted pyramid where Dan Brown has Mary buried. We saw what I call the Grand Gallery of some of the world's greatest paintings. We were in the Louvre the whole day *twice*. There was too much to see, from the Code of Hammurabi, to Rembrandt, to Venus de Milo, the statue of Aphrodite.

And when we went down the long hall to the Mona Lisa—my heart stopped.

I had had great difficulty with my mother, all my life. She had issues—I had issues—and we didn't mix. But one great thing she did have in spades was an appreciation for the arts, which she somehow handed down to me. It was a point of connection between us. I'd always known, she'd always told me, of her desire to one day to go to Paris, eat at a sidewalk café, see great works of art.

And there I was, face-to-face with Leonardo's most famous work.

I really knew where I was. I held Joe's hand in a long silence, as in the King's Chamber, in Egypt, and appreciated being there. Among a large crowd of people standing and staring, we looked and loved.

Yes, of course the Mona Lisa is well done. Everything there was. But it was more, to me; it was a symbol that I'd made it, that an important part of my life was complete.

I squeezed Joe's hand, felt the hair on its back, put my arm around him. "Thank you, God," I said. "Thank you, Joe, too."

We melded into Paris as if we'd been there for years. A taxi driver told us, it is okay if we don't speak French. Virtually everyone there speaks English. But if we at least open anything with "Bonjour," then they know we are making an effort, and it makes all the difference in the world. We always did.

Joe and I married every year in June for our anniversary, whether healthy or ill, without fail, including once with his children in their home. We happened to be in Paris, that year, and the timing was close enough. With Monet and the Mona Lisa in my head, and Joe's hand in mine, the preacher at

American Church married us again, to each other, for the 10th time.

After being there a week, I started to get into the whole Paris attitude frame of mind, myself—speak an attitude directly and be done with it. On the Champs-Elysees, one day, at a sidewalk café—of course—Joe and I went in for some refreshments. We sat at a table, and when the waiter came by, I said to him, bluntly. *"Bonjour. Du coca light, s'il vu plait?"* Because I was tired, I continued in Midwest-country-accented English. "And not with these two little, dinky ice cubes in there. I want a whole glass of ice."

Ooops!

My manner had not been rude, per se, but I'd made no effort to be pleasant.

The waiter did not seem displeased. *What you say is what you say.* He smiled at me and said in return. "Are you from Texas?"

"Yes." I'd lived there, sometimes—close enough as seen from France.

He smiled to me and the other patrons in the area. "Americans!" He left and returned with a smile, our two Diet Cokes, and an entire bucket of ice. He sat them all on the table.

The next day, after touring the Musee du Louvre and staring again so lovingly at the Mona Lisa, Joe and I were walking, while I pushed the empty companion chair, through the large park just west of there, the Jardin des Tuileries, and I noticed two police riding through on their bicycles. I read the patch on their arm—

I raised my hand to flag them down and yelled, "Oh! Oh! Oh!"

They both stopped riding and looked at us.

"Are you the police?" I called to them in English.

"Yes," one of them said.

With my serious face, I asked, "Do you know Chief Inspector Jacques Clouseau of the Sureté?" My joke was about one of France's greatest embarrassments: the Pink Panther movies with Peter Sellers.

There was a slight pause before he smiled broadly at me. "Yes!" he said. "I know him!" The two policemen pedaled away on their bikes, talking about us.

Joe sat with me and studied the park. He had a way of discussing something without talking.

"You said you'd like to go to the beach at Normandy?" I asked him.

"Yeah, I would."

"Well, if we're ever going to, now is the time."

The Hotel Lotti arranged a car for us, a Mercedes, and that night I studied maps of the roads we'd need to take the next day. The concierge swore I should be able to do it, even if I only spoke a little French, and it turned out he was right. Driving there was no problem: 283 km to Omaha Beach, a three-hour drive, if I drove it, myself—or 10 minutes in a Cairo taxi.

Joe and I got out of the car at Omaha Beach, and Joe made his way to the surf line. He was slow going, hunched over from arthritis in his back, but he didn't want to be rolled out there. He walked silently toward the large monument on the beach and stood beside it for a long time, finally starting to cry.

Figure 12.4. Joe crying, saluting fallen veterans at Omaha Beach, Normandy, France.

A local French woman saw us and kept her distance, respectfully. I could tell by the look on her face that she admired

Joe. I got the impression she thought, perhaps, Joe had been there, on the beach, himself, in World War II, but he was not. Joe was in Burbank as flight test engineer on the P-38 Lightning, at the time—itself, a major help to the war effort. But Joe always felt guilty he was not in the military, proper.

With the French woman thanking him from afar, Joe stood there on the beach and cried to the monument. Tears rolling down his face, he saluted the monument for the men who had died there.

I took his photo, holding his salute, because it was a treasure, and went over to hold him, because *he* was a treasure.

Thank you, God, for Joe.

13

Shallow Moat, Paper Castle

2005

TROI WENT BATSHIT at the master bedroom's back door. She was jumping at it, bouncing off, barking madly.

I had just stepped out of the shower and was drying off.

"What's the matter?"

I looked out the window, and saw a large coyote stalking both alpacas. The defenseless creatures were running toward the center of the pasture, to get away from him.

Not my alpacas!

I grabbed my pistol and ran out the door like a shot after the coyote, yelling and screaming at him, noting his closure rate on the alpacas, calculating an angle at which I could shoot him without having a round fly onto a neighbor's property—but Troi was three times faster than I was, and before I had to shoot, Troi was on his heels, viciously attacking. The coyote was twice as large as Troi, but Troi was fearless, with a mad woman on her heels. The coyote turned to dash down the driveway to the east—the wrong way from the coyote's area in the woods to the west.

"Troi! NO! Don't chase him! *Get back here!*"

Naturally, she didn't listen.

I didn't want the coyote to turn on her. I was afraid he'd kill her.

I can't have any bloody Troi!

"TROI!"

Nothing.

It was quiet.

The alpacas were shaken, but fine. I took in the scene. The pasture was free of any other coyotes. Neighbors were to the south. Mt. Rainier was in the distance.

I wondered, *What else might be wrong?*—which was when I realized I was standing outside in the field completely naked—not a stitch—with my gun in my hand.

Shit!

I turned back for the house, when I saw the coyote run back past the house to the west toward his woods, Troi still hot on his heels.

Joe and I sat at the kitchen table. I was in a heated phone call with Angie down in L.A. She'd been helpful a number of times.

"Angie!" I complained to her. "I'm trying to keep my business *PRIVATE!* Keep people out of my business—a losing battle!"

"I remember," she said. "Have they done anything to you directly?" Angie asked.

"I don't know. How would I know?" I said into the phone. "Joe, have they ever done anything to me directly?"

Joe sagged his head.

"I don't know," I said to Angie. "How would I know unless they told me?" Nothing to my face, that I'm aware of—except they have a habit of acting like they're inviting to me to things, but they only invite us to something that doesn't involve other people they know."

"Prejudice," Angie said. "Same as if embarrassed to be friends with a black person."

"I know. And now the bank sent my private statement to them! *My goddamn statement!* If they wanted to know how much I'm worth, they know now! No more questions. They've got the whole damn thing."

"Is that the same bank that was involved in that other business?" Angie asked. She was usually discrete, even when it was just me.

"Yes. Different individuals, I think. I think. And I called the bank on the phone, complaining, '*How the hell can you send them my bank statement!?*' They said it was a mistake, that it wouldn't happen again—which is what they've said before—and that 'deniable' shit is what keeps happening to me. Mistake?

Different name! The address is in a whole 'nother fucking state! How can you make a *mistake* like that!?"

I was more than upset. This had been going on for years.

"Has anything else happened?" Angie asked. "This time. Was the statement all of it?"

"What the fuck, Angie?"

"How did you find out the bank sent your statement to them?"

"Because they sent it to me in the mail."

"Not the bank, the other people?"

"Yes. They up and sent it to me in the mail. That's how I found out."

"Why in God's name would they do that?" Angie asked herself. "If they wanted to deny it, they'd just act like they never got it."

"Outside chance they were being honest?"

"Or were they making sure you knew they knew?" she asked. "We could sue them."

"No! I can't do that."

"Why?"

"That would be public."

In the 16 years Joe and I had been together, to that point, I'd grown increasingly worried about how to live with Joe. At first, life with Joe seemed heavenly, but—as much as I loved him—I began to feel he and I should live separately.

I've been harshly critical of myself my whole life, and in this situation, I made it worse. As I look back over our life together, the idea of living separately— I still wonder if it was needed. Of course, we could have stayed under the same roof, regardless, but just as I have gone back to worry if I made the right choices with the NIS, in the Navy, so, too, I've gone back and worried if I made the best choice in this.

My self-critical inclination is to say that I could have done it better. But I'm also reminded that I was sensing things that I needed to deal with, however difficult. It almost sounds okay, until I also remember that my need to be stealth, private, complicated any thought of standing up for myself. It wasn't all about what I'd experienced elsewhere in life from others; it was also about what I was doing to myself, to us, with it.

Even today, many years later, I criticize myself for aspects of myself that made our life harder than it needed to be. I apologize to Joe in my mind, over and over, for my being trans and for not having better judgment, knowledge, or courage. But I just didn't know what to do. I had no one to ask with as much experience in this area, no one's advice I could get.

Joe knew my struggle. We'd discussed it many times through the years. And on living separately, he'd seen it coming for a long time, before I brought it up.

It was sad for both of us.

"But Joe," I tried to rationalize, "it's just a different place to sleep. You're still welcome here, and I'll still come get you to go places with you of a day. But it will give us something we don't have, now, help me figure myself out. At least for a while."

"What is that?" He seemed resigned, though sad.

"You'll be cared for while I get some down time at night. That's what I need."

I didn't see it well at the time, but I was so raw from so many things that had happened, that it had stacked in my heart. Any little thing that happened, any more, felt large.

It was very emotional when I took him there. His assisted living home was far nicer than our house on Woodhaven, but it wasn't our home, and I fear he felt he was being abandoned.

I'll never forgive myself.

I went to a few gender conferences—not my thing, but I just wanted to touch base and get away. I had to work at not getting laid on my way to the dinner table, the sex was so thick. I met some people I knew, shared a little, learned a little more about current cosmetic surgeries.

Joe and I lifted off the runway in our 40-year-old, new-to-us Cessna Cardinal. Troi inspected the plane from the back seat. Joe inspected the plane from the right seat.

It wasn't much. It was a simple, straight-leg, fixed-pitch, small-engined Cardinal, but it fit the bill.

"I know, it sucks, doesn't it?" I asked Joe.

He glanced at me.

"But you couldn't get into the 120 any more. Small door. The bend at your hips and knees."

Troi laid down in the back seat to nap during the flight, as she had in other airplanes, when the back seat was available.

I banked left and headed up the coast of the Puget Sound, climbing to 5,500 feet.

"This plane," I said, "Has a large door, and no wing strut. You're getting older, you know."

"No!" Joe mocked himself.

"And if I ever need to get you in from a wheelchair, it'll need to be this plane. 'Cause I could wheel you right up to the door."

He nodded.

Joe's response to most things was business-like, practical: what would work; what we needed to do; how things were at the moment.

"You want to fly it?"

"Sure." He took the yoke and maneuvered, banked left and right. The plane responded to him as several others I'd seen him fly: sure and gentle.

"Listen, Joe. I'm considering having some surgeries for a bit."

He glanced at me, made a slow right turn in the plane.

"On my face," I said. "To make me look better."

"You look fine."

I shook my head.

"So people are nicer to you?" he asked.

"It's related, but— Yes, that partly. But also, you know I just need to be myself. You've always known that. I need— I've been all my life, seeing this Neanderthal in the mirror, and I need to see myself. It's called Facial Feminizing Surgery, FFS."

He nodded as he flew.

"Where's the fuel selector?" Joe asked.

"On the floor, between the seats." I showed him. "Right, left, both. But don't select, okay? I don't think you can see it well enough. You might get it between tanks and cut the fuel flow off."

He nodded. "I just wondered." He looked over the panel and touched a knob. "Carb heat?"

"Conventional." I pointed to it and the other two knobs beside it. "Mixture control, throttle. Adjust the throttle as needed."

"I can do the mixture, too," he said. "It's a little rich." He adjusted the mixture a tiny amount. "Makes a big difference."

"Damn, you're good," I said. "I still can't believe I get to go flying with you."

"You think the face work will make that much difference?" he asked.

"It's just a little bit here and there," I said. "But it makes a big difference."

Joe banked and Gig Harbor turned beneath us, a mile below.

"Will I recognize you when you're done?" he asked.

"Yeah," I said. "I'll be the one you married."

I lay under sedation in the hospital bed, my head completely wrapped in gauze, seeping evident in some locations. Two drain bottles were clipped to the gauze, one on each cheek. Tubes ran from inside my cheeks into the bottles. My nose, chin, mandible, forehead, scalp, orbital ridges, upper lip—all were changed to suit a design the surgeon and I had selected, the design I'd prayed for as a child, that I'd needed since birth, that I'd never had.

"What's the matter?" I asked, Caren. She was another long-term, stealth I'd met some time ago through another acquaintance on the Internet. She'd come to Woodhaven from Miami to help me through my recovery.

"I moved to Florida *after* my FFS," she said. "Nobody knows about me."

"Hmm," I said.

She was so secretive, I wasn't even sure she lived in Miami. She probably didn't let anyone close for fear of discovery.

"Not even my boyfriend," she said.

I was going to say that her boyfriend probably knows, anyway, and doesn't want to say, because she doesn't want it said, but I'd catch hell for that, and I was in no mood for a fight.

"I wish you the best with him," I said.

I looked into the mirror in the den, turned my head a little to see my new jawline from a different angle.

"Just a little bit here and there, makes all the difference," she said.

"My God," I said. It was true. My face was immensely better. Much of the swelling had gone down, and I was beginning to see my new self. "If I didn't know it was me, I wouldn't know it was me. I could stare my mom in the face, and she wouldn't recognize me."

"It's wonderful, isn't it?" she asked.

"Amazing."

Caren said, inspecting me. "It looks like he did a fine job." She gingerly touched my cheeks.

"I am amazed." I couldn't believe how much better I looked. "How did I make it through those first 47 years?"

She stepped back and looked at me a little farther. "You're gonna need a face lift, and while you're at it, a few other tweaks."

2015

Ellen and I strolled down Venice Beach. People skated along the concrete walk in swim suits while eating ice cream cones. A few waded into the Pacific. A street magician entertained a small crowd of people at a street corner.

It was a tourist area, and she was a tourist.

"What's that worried look for?" she asked.

We had been discussing TS medical issues. We were both long term enough to have known our share of problems, but our orientations on how we were taken were different. Ellen tended to assume she was not read if people didn't spell it out in iambic pentameter, where I noticed looks that bothered me, and I worried about them.

"I've been guinnea-pigged so many times," I vented to her. "I've even had people I never knew were there, looking at my crotch, on an operating table while I'm out. A doc told me when I asked about it being a teaching facility. I'm so sick of the whole bunch."

"What were they doing looking— How'd that happen?" Ellen stopped to look at me.

Beautiful women strolled by in swimming suits.

"I was told I shouldn't mind. They were students, and they needed to learn."

"So—"

"You can bet I gave them hell over that. I'm in for some other work, and observers are lifting the sheet to look at my crotch." I kept my gaze toward the concrete beneath us, but my disgust was clearly evident.

"And that wasn't even the only one," I said. "These other asshole doctors—"

"Trick you into show and tell?"

2005

Joe and I lunched at a restaurant in Tacoma.

I spoke into my new Motorola Razr flip phone. "What?" I asked Leah.

Joe's look to me was a question.

"Remember Kelly?" I asked him. "We met her at Wendy's once? Before they kicked me out."

Joe could tell by my expression and lowered his head in sorrow.

"She's dead. Overdose."

I listened more to Leah on the phone. "Why?" I asked her.

There were a million possibilities.

I raised my head and spoke to Joe. "Leah thinks it was— Kelly lost another girlfriend." I returned to her on the phone. "If she had any support at all from her family, just *one little bit of support!* She was barren. That's the problem. Emotionally barren."

14

A Drink from the Ohio

2006

    I dumped my feelings all over Angie.

    Joe's health was not as good, which I feared might have related to feeling alone—in assisted living, separate from me, also separated from his family.

    I was afraid to live with him, which was my weakness, but I couldn't stand by to see him fail. I knew he needed his family and his old friends back in the lion's den.

    After much soul searching and discussion with Joe, after three years in Washington, we agreed to move back to Oxnard.

2007

    Joe and I held what I've since referred to as the Big Meeting, attended by his lawyer, my lawyer, Joe's friend who would also later become his Trustee, when Joe could no longer run his own Trust, and a couple of others. Joe's effort was to restructure his affairs and get some things planned as he moved in to older age. A question for me was how could I do the things Joe wished of me, as he aged, if I was a target.

    Joe made it clear he wished me to continue taking him flying, boating, riding on the Harley, movies, church, family gatherings, Disneyland—everything and anything we had done for years—no matter how disabled he might become in the future. If he were severely disabled, continue. If he were so physically disabled he required a team of muscle men to do it, hire them. If he were to become so mentally disabled, such as dementia, that we thought he wasn't even aware of what he was doing, do it anyway, as we couldn't be sure. Why not? he asked. He'd always led an active life. It was what he enjoyed. And who would rather not? His fear, he shared, was to be abandoned in a nursing home, forgotten.

I worried that someone who had hurt me in the past might use my activities with Joe as a reason to do so again with any kind of accusation, to use the legal system in California to hurt me, get me charged with something if anything went wrong. I was worried that even someone disconnected who had the belief that an elderly person should, indeed, sit in a rocking chair the rest of his life and gum his tapioca pudding might accuse me of endangering Joe for trying to take him out so much, bring trouble to get me to stop. In nursing homes, there would be a lot of people over Joe, and I knew I could not stand against them, if it came to that, without some help.

"I don't know how I can do it," I shared in the Big Meeting. But I couldn't turn him down.

From that meeting, and from other meetings as well with doctors and family, Joe codified, in his Trust and elsewhere, his intentions. He gave me explicit powers to do things with him, outlined how the Trust would pay for this and that at my request, for the maintenance of his lifestyle, and so on.

I'm sure I left the meeting pale, a little in shock. I felt like I was agreeing to face a school of sharks, cheered by a group of highly paid lifeguards on shore who had nothing to lose. If something went bad, I'd be the only one eaten.

But it was about life and love, longevity, quality of life—about living vs. dying. What would *any human being* deserve?

Figure 14.1 J2 flying in the Cardinal over Oxnard Plain.

Figure 14.2. Joe driving the boat off Ventura, California.

Figure 14.3. Us out by the breakwater.

I also talked with Angie, later. I made plans. I began to document my activities with Joe on a daily basis, either to my own email or to some of his family, his doctors, and/or to our lawyers, such as taking photos of us doing things and emailing them with descriptions, etc., so that knowledgeable people were in the loop.

For motorcycling, I had ridden off and on since I was 13. I had already had the California Motorcycle Safety Program under my belt. And to further prove myself on the Harley, I rode to Flagstaff, New Mexico and back, one day, verified, to join the Iron Butt Association. The IBA called it the SaddleSore 1000, riding at least 1000 miles in one day— I looked at it like my old flying record: It was about doing my best.

In the airplane, I maintained my Certified Flight Instructor's certificate, and I attained my ATP, Airline Transport Pilot, certificate in both multi- and single-engine aircraft, though I only flew us around in our cardinal. I bought a 4,000 lb.-limit shop crane that would fit under the wing, so I could get him into the airplane if needed.

In boating, Joe had trained me, himself, for years, as he'd been a Commander in the Coast Guard Auxiliary.

I'd had the Red Cross' Advanced Lifesaving back in the Navy, at Ft. Meade, a lifeguard. I could swim like a fish, float without moving a muscle because of my large lungs. Though I would not be taking Joe swimming, it was extra, in the event of some emergency.

I drove carefully in the car, and I outfitted it with numerous supplies as needed to both make outings more comfortable and to help service him as needed.

I obtained season passes at Disneyland, for multiple visits.

Figure 14.4. J2 at Disneyland.

I familiarized myself with a dozen different kinds of places we could visit for outings.

I bought an electric three-wheeler and two different kinds of wheelchairs for him, large wheel and small.

I took him to doctors regularly to make sure his health was as good as it could be for all activities.

Abandoned in a nursing home?

That was not going to happen.

Joe and I walked toward the Athenaeum, the university club at Caltech.

"This is where you went to graduate school, after Virginia Tech?" I asked him.

He nodded. "Uh-hum. I stayed right here, in the Ath. Up stairs."

We moseyed over to the west side and into the patio area. He pointed up to the second floor, to the southeast corner of the patio. "Right up there, room 28, top of the stairs."

"Room 28?"

He nodded.

"And you had a T-28, in hangar 228 at Camarillo."

He smiled.

"Can we get in there?" I asked.

"Oh, I suppose."

We walked in to the front lobby area while he talked about it. The circular stair case rose to the right past busts of Nobel Prize winners Linus Pauling and Albert Einstein, curved up twice to Room 28 at the top, as advertised.

We stood in front of Joe's old door.

"It had a bed in there," he said, "against that wall." He pointed to the left. "A closet. Bathroom, over there," he pointed to the right. "Window." He pointed straight through the door. "And there was a built-in bookcase over there." He pointed a little left.

I saw a lady to our right, cleaning rooms, and I spoke to her a minute, described what we were doing, and asked if she would let us in so we could see this room. "It's where he stayed in 1937-'38, when he went to school here," 70 years before.

She was gracious enough to let us in, and Joe explored the room. "There's the bookcase," he said with a smile, and then with tears in his eyes, "and that looks like my old bed."

"This same one?"

"I don't know, but it looks like it," he said.

As time passed, we sometimes brought a wheel chair. Joe could still walk, and sometimes he'd walk beside the wheelchair, but it helped for longer distances.

Figure 14.5. Joe in main dining hall, Athenaeum, beneath portrait of Executive Council.

The walls were thick in the Ath, lined with real wood paneling—quality old construction throughout. There were six large floor-to-almost-ceiling windows, three on each side, six large lateral interstitial beams across the high ceiling, and 16 smaller beams that ran its length. The buffet table in the Hall of Associates was fit for academic royalty, which, after all the years I'd been with Joe, I was beginning to understand. We ate at a table beneath the large-framed painting of three men on the south wall of the main dining room. I didn't know, yet, who they were.

Joe was a mild-mannered man who didn't share much. It was hard to get him to talk, yet I found the best way to get him to do so was to physically take him places where he'd had experiences, then reminisce.

"You came out here from Virginia?" I asked. "How could you afford it?"

"Oh, I had a little help."

I pried and got vague references to uncles Rear Admiral Dr. Ben Dennis and Heath Robinson.

I was impressed with both Joe and Caltech.

"I have a math question for you, Joe."

"What's that?"

"Do octopuses do math in base 8?"

"Do humans do math in base 4?" he answered without hesitation.

"Okay. But I have a physics question?"

He looked at me like he wasn't sure. "What?"

"How is it I can eat 5 lbs. of ice cream and gain 10 lbs.?"

Joe smiled at me.

"It's molecules," I asserted. "They have to come from somewhere!"

He continued his lunch without comment.

That doesn't rate an answer?

"Playing aside, why did you go here for your master's?" I asked.

"Uh, they had a wind tunnel I wanted to use. Down there at the Guggenheim Lab."

"Down that way?"

He nodded.

"How did you know it was there? It wasn't on the internet."

"Engineers knew."

"You showed up. You lived here, up stairs."

He nodded.

"You'd never been out here before. Were you scared."

He shook his head. There was an air of confidence in him that suggested to me that "scared" never occurred to him, as if he had been aware of his abilities—not cocky, not arrogant, just confident. Aeronautical engineering was something he knew he could do, and he followed a path that allowed him to do it.

He smiled at me. "I got a date with Olivia de Havilland, once."

"What?"

He nodded.

"You had a date with Olivia de Havilland?"

He shook his head. "Not really."

"Make up your mind?"

"I, uh— Well—"

He stumbled through not quite telling me what happened. "I, uh, *got* a date with her—"

"How'd you do that?"

"Someone set us up. I think it was 1938. But I cancelled it."

"Joe!"

He chuckled at himself—at yet something else he'd confessed to me. He didn't seem to mind humor that pointed out embarrassing things he'd done.

"You dropped Olivia de Havilland. The actress."

"Well—yes. I didn't drop her. I just didn't go on the date."

"She was a big actress by then?"

"I think that was before she hit it big."

"So you weren't worried that she was a star?"

He shook his head. "No."

"What then?"

Joe hedged a little before he told me. "I didn't have a car."

"You didn't go out with Olivia de Havilland because you'd have had to go in *her car*?"

He hung his head, slightly, in admission, yet he seemed to enjoy laughing at himself.

"God, Joe. If I were she, I'd have come in here and got you anyway. I bet the car was nothing to her. She may have been excited she got a date with one of the geniuses here at Caltech."

Figure 14.6. J2 behind, just west, of the Athenaeum.

We left the Ath through the patio area and rolled west down the brick sidewalk toward what Joe called the "Guggenheim Lab."

"They have a cannon there?" I asked. "It's got a heavy chain on it."

Joe didn't seem to know why, so I flagged someone down, a professor-looking guy, and asked. "Excuse me, are you afraid this cannon will wander off?"

"It did, actually," the guy said with a growing smile. "That's the Fleming House Cannon. MIT 'stole' it once, in fun."

"MIT? Never heard of it."

The guy got an evil grin. He knew better. "We've been going at it for years." He shared a couple of stories. Apparently, playful and reciprocated—even traditional—intercollegiate rivalry between MIT and Caltech is legendary.

We walked on to the Guggenheim Lab and Joe showed me the place. They had an A-12 wind tunnel model in a window—precursor to the SR-71, which Joe managed for flight test.

"Little genius made good," I told him.

2008

As difficult as they had been, the years of struggle with Mom began to see a change in her approach to me. I don't know if it was because of her courses in psychology, time, a change in interpersonal dynamics back in Kansas, or experience in her latest, and apparently good, marriage, but she softened toward me, and it was very well received. She was 73; I'd been in transition 27 years.

Seeing her in person with her latest husband, and talking with them on the phone, over a time, I began to feel the urge to share with Mom the joy I had felt in Paris, talked with her about going, herself. But Paris is a city for lovers, so I had to talk her husband into going, also.

After some months of discussion, they both wound up agreeing, and I bought them airline tickets and a week's stay at our old haunt, Hotel Lotti.

"Why would you do this," Mom asked.

"Just to say thank you," I said, "for accepting me. And I love you."

"But this is so expensive."

"It's—one of the important things in life. You're the reason I wanted to go with Joe, and it meant so much." I told her stories about it.

"But what about..." this or that problem that could arise? She talked as if it might not be civilized.

"Mom, you kidding me? It's Paris, France—I mean, *the* Paris, France!"

"What do you want out of it," she asked.

"I'd really enjoy it if you stood for a while and stared at the Mona Lisa in the Louvre and had at least one good meal on the Champs-Élysées, at a sidewalk café. I'd love pictures. Just enjoy. Anything else is extra: get pregnant, get arrested. Tease the cops—they love that over there, the more the merrier."

One of Mom's greater attributes was her sense of humor. I know that from experience. Once she and I came together, our relationship improved dramatically. She also told me she would do playful stuff with her mother, back in Minneola, like send her a case of toilet paper while she played the organ at church.

I wonder where I got my sense of humor.

Mom and her husband did go to Paris. I know it meant a lot to her, and I've always felt it helped put a positive cap on our relationship.

2008

Every time we moved, every time we had to uproot our lives, we tried to get it back together again. It was my nature to play with him, enjoy things, wear costumes to movies, or stretch my Flintstone-era engineering, so we did it again with another Bosco Rasche Invitational—this time using my pyramid building technique as a curiosity.

Figure 14.7. Joe with family and friends, Bosco Rasche Invitational, pyramid building mock-up.

Figure 14.8. Guests in the back yard demonstrating how to lift stones up Khufu's pyramid.

Four elderly people walked easily through our back yard, and a stone was pulled up a slope equal to the angle of Khufu's pyramid in Egypt.

"It works!" one of them said to me with a big smile.

"Of course it works," I said. "I've been sleeping with Joe for 15 years! It soaked in through the pillow."

The back yard was full of people enjoying Sunday afternoon. I'd served burgers and potato salad to people in the area, trying to get them over—and oh, while here, why not pull a 120lb stone up a slope?

I built a scaffolding with a slope of 51-1/2 degrees, 15 feet high, which meant, as usual, a little borrowed math, trips to Home Depot and other places to get supplies. This was the idea I'd earlier contacted Dr. Wendrich about at UCLA, 6 years before. The "pulley" at the top was fixed in place, so it could not turn, to act like a pivot point as I'd described in ancient Egypt, and the line was greased with lard.

It was easy for our guests. I put the stone on the ground at the bottom edge of the pyramid slope, a line tied to it, draped over the top of the pyramid through a pivot point, then down to people on the other side, a 2x4 tied to it there. The people laid the 2x4 against the front of their hips, leaned forward a little, and walked.

If ancient Egypt had a Home Depot, raising stones was no problem.

Joe sat with his youngest son on the patio under an umbrella while people worked on the project. They'd pull the stone up the slope, laugh, let it back down, and then another group would pull the stone up.

I plopped in a chair near Joe. "Did you ever have to rest when you were Imhotep?"

Joe and I wore brown leather flight jackets into the theatre to see "Indiana Jones and the Kingdom of the Crystal Skull." Joe also wore a fedora hat, like Indie, but my jacket had Yeager beer in it, a talisman against evil.

At a 99s Section Meeting in Santa Maria, I won my third Spot Landing contest. I was in the Cardinal, this time. It was a windy/gusty day, and I had a student in the plane with me, but it seemed we did okay. I brought her up front with me to accept the award. She was part of the flight.

"Wait here for me a couple minutes, okay?" I asked Joe. "Let me take some stuff down to the boat first. I'll be right back."

"Okay," he acknowledged.

I gave him a brief kiss. "It's a beautiful day. Warm, no wind. Nice day. We'll have fun."

I got out of the driver's side of the car.

"Come on, Troi," I told her.

She jumped out of the car and started running toward the docks.

"Get back here!"

She ran back to me, her tongue hanging out of her mouth.

"I know. That was fun!" I pet her on the head, back and ribs, got some nice dog slobbers on my wrist. "But stay here with me."

Like, maybe she'll listen?

I sensed she was about to run off again. "Stay with me!"

She seemed to get it.

"Good girl."

I opened the back of the Ford Minivan—Troi jumped in.

"Out!"

She jumped out.

"Good girl."

I began lifting out tools, equipment, and a sack lunch for Joe and me.

"Be right back, Joe."

I shut the back door of the van and headed for the boat. Troi followed me, then she led me.

"You know where we're going! Smart girl!"

She started to run.

"Stay here with me!"

Aw, mommy!

"I'm supposed to have you on a leash, so don't push it."

Troi spied another boater on an adjacent dock and ran to him for some well received love.

"Troi! I'm sorry, guy. She's everybody's girl."

"I used to have one like her," he said, delighted with her attention.

"Get back here, sweetie."

She returned again.

I pointed up ahead. "Go get on our own boat," I told her. "Go ahead. Go to the boat."

She looked at me curiously, and then the light came on. She ran to it and jumped right over the gunwale into the aft deck, then turned around and put her front paws on the gunwale to see me coming.

"Good girl."

I opened the side door to the minivan and lifted out Joe's walker.

Troi jumped into the minivan.

"Yes, I know," I said. I found her leash and put it on her. The slightest tug, and she knew to jump back out of the van for another outing.

I got Joes walker off the back seat, placed it on the ground and opened Joe's front passenger door.

"You ready to go down to the boat?"

"You betsky," he said, turning to get out.

"I've got the place stocked. We have food. We have water. And we have work to do."

He put his feet on the ground, and I set his walker in front of him.

He took a few steps.

I closed his door and locked the car.

Troi was tugging on her leash.

"It's a beautiful day, and it's all three of us: You, Troi, and me. All of us together."

"Yup."

Joe's eyes weren't as good as they used to be. He could still read, but he needed his magnifiers to do it, which we didn't use when out on adventure. He wasn't very stable on his feet, any more, either, so "off roading," outside, I tended to keep a hand on him.

Troi jumped on the boat again and turned around to watch Mommy and Daddy get on after her.

"Stand right here," I told Joe, placing his walker on the dock beside the boat. "Sit on the gunwale—that's right. And," I held both his waist and his legs, "swing your legs over onto the deck. Easy."

"Yup."

"Like it was made for us. Well, I bought it because it fit us! So same thing."

"Nobody's bleedin'," he said, quoting Fish again.

"Nobody's bleedin'," I repeated. "You sit right here in this deck chair, under the overhead. You're in the shade." I set a bottle of water beside him on the captain's chair. "And you can watch me work—we have a big job to do on the boat today. We need to *work*." I said it like it was a duty, something important.

"Yup. You think you can manage it?" he asked.

"I had you to teach me," I said.

"Smell that 20.5 oxygen," he said, taking a full lung of harbor air.

I was sure half of it was waste or dead and rotting marine life, but—honestly—it did feel refreshing.

I opened the sack lunch and pulled out some sandwiches, laid them on the captain's chair beside him. "And you have food right here. See this stuff?"

"Yeah."

"Great. And let me get to work."

I began to arrange the stuff on the back deck, which included my tools, the dog, the crane I'd bought, stuff that went with the crane, the dog again—

"Troi, why don't you get up here?" I patted the passenger seat beside Daddy.

She jumped up there then back down again.

Joe laughed.

"You wouldn't think she's 10. Troi, get back up there."

She did.

"Now, stay!" I held out my hand, palm out, in the stop/stay motion, right in front of her face, and she stayed, that time. Then she looked at our food.

"I know what you're thinking!"

"You bring her anything?"

"I sure did." I opened the companion way and went below to get her bowl and some water and dog food, and while I was down there, I put on a little Glenn Miller. "Moonlight Serenade" softly filled the air around us. Food and water on the floor beside Troi's chair, she happily lapped and sat.

"Okay. Now stay there?" I both ordered and asked Troi.

"That'll last two minutes," Joe said.

"If we're lucky. If you see her move, will you tell her to stay?"

"For all the good it'll do."

True. She tended to mind me, not him.

"Nice music," Joe said.

"You're a good dancer, too," I told him.

He reached up and turned his ball cap slightly to the side. When I looked at him, he smiled and said, "It's jaunty."

I gave him a hug and got things organized, lifted the engine hatch.

"How's it look?" Joe asked.

"Actually, it's probably the prettiest engine in the harbor."

I'd bought the boat new in Washington, for our retirement, and we'd literally been all over the Puget Sound in it. It was stable and agile, ran well.

"You remember when I got it, I coated the engine in sealant? I'm not gonna have any rust on this engine."

"That's my Jenna."

"Thhhhhank you," I said sounding like Groucho Marks."

"What's that crane rated for?" he asked.

"A thousand pounds."

"How'd you make out with the salesman?"

"I didn't make out with the salesman, Joe. I'm married."

"No! I mean the price!"

"He didn't pay me nothin'?" I looked at him like I didn't understand.

Troi jumped off her chair, and I reached for her. "Okay. I'm gonna have to— You want to hold her leash?"

"Sure. Come here, Troi."

She loved her daddy and jumped up on his lap to kiss him in the face.

I went down into the engine compartment to look at the area. Lying down inside the engine compartment, beside the engine on the port side, I could see up into the cavity under the gunwale. It was about 4 inches wide and a couple of feet up there. I could reach it, like I had thought I could. There was room. The fiberglass bulkhead thickness there was more than adequate. The stainless steel bolts I had were of a good length— a little long, actually, but they'd stick out inside the cavity, not where they could snag anyone, so it was fine.

I got out and closed the engine hatch, because I needed to sit on top of it for a minute.

Troi watched Joe snack importantly on a sandwich. He gave her some.

I shook my head.

I held the white, steel crane mount on the side of the boat, vertically, over the area I'd just cleared.

"Make sure you get the holes in the right place," Joe said.

"Now, who would worry about drilling holes in a boat?" I used a marker to draw circles inside the holes on the mount.

I picked up the drill. I'd pre-installed the proper bit at home for the size bolts that came with the crane.

"This is what every boat owner dreams of." I squeezed the trigger and heard the buzz of the motor. "I just hope this is the right bulkhead. It might be the hull."

His smile showed his trust in me. With his arms, he patted Troi's ribs to keep her still.

The cordless drill make short work of the holes—safely into the air inside the cavity.

I stuck my fingers in side. "Well, no water coming in. What are we gonna do?"

"Good, good."

"I knew I could learn something."

Installing a crane may sound difficult but if there's already a place in the boat for it, it's a simple matter. You just drill the holes and bolt the bracket on. That's all there is to it.

I was making a big deal out of it because it was our project for the day, an excuse to picnic, play, sit, talk, listen to Glenn Miller, and enjoy some good time together.

"And the crane, itself? You ready for this, Joe?"

He watched. "How does it mount?"

"Well, that's the great thing about this, for boating. It doesn't have to bolt in. It just sits in the mount. I can stow it below, and when we want to use it, I can get it out and stick it in this hole, like this." I picked it up, held it vertical, and slid it down into the mount. "It turns easily by hand, and there's this winch on the side that will raise and lower you."

I was using a transport chair for Joe on most days for our outings, and Disneyland was very good with people in wheelchairs.

As usual, on entering the park, we stopped by to see our beloved President Lincoln, without whom, I fear, we would not have the nation we know and love.

Like everything in Disneyland, the theatre is well appointed, the doors opened to Mr. Lincoln's show, and we rolled in to the center.

I leaned over to Joe before it began and told him. "This show always reminds me of Blacksburg. Your family history—"

He looked at me.

"—*our* family history," I corrected myself. "You had people there."

"*We* had people there," he reminded me. "We're married."

I hugged him. "God, I love you, Joe."

The curtain rose.

Background stories ensued.

Then another curtain parted, and there was Abraham Lincoln, played by Walt's animatronics and the exquisite voice of Royal Dano—as perfect as any such thing could be—reading a compendium of statements President Lincoln actually made over time.

Mr. Lincoln talked to eager listeners about the unity of the nation, how no one outside of ourselves could ever ruin us, that destruction, if it ever happened, must come from within.

For me, President Lincoln was talking about the strength to stand against forces that could drive us apart. It felt very close to home, as I felt, rather continuously, as if we were circled by wolves, waiting for any sign of weakness, to hurt me, to hurt *us*:

> ...At what point shall we expect the approach of danger? By what means shall we fortify against it? Shall we expect some trans-Atlantic military giant to step the ocean and crush us at a blow? *Never!* All the armies of Europe, Asia, and Africa combined could not, by force, take a drink from the Ohio or make a track on the Blue Ridge in a trial of a thousand years. At what point, then, is the approach of danger to be expected? I answer, if it ever reach us, it must spring from amongst us; it cannot come from abroad. If destruction be our lot, we be author and finisher...
>
> Neither let us be slandered from our duty by false accusations against us, nor frightened from it by menaces of destruction...

What could make us stop, if we chose to overcome?

I wished I felt as confident in my heart.

PART 4

LIVING WITH DEATH

"Being deeply loved by someone else gives you strength, while loving someone deeply gives you courage."

Lao Tzu

15

Fear and Prayer

2009

MY HEART POUNDING, I parked the minivan in the hospital lot, pulled the lever for the parking brake, turned off the ignition, unplugged the phone from the power port, and— "Sec," I said. I took the phone from my ear and unplugged my ear buds, piled them in the passenger seat beside me— They slid onto the floor. I reached down, picked them up, piled them again onto the passenger seat, and put the phone up to my ear— Hair is in the way! I leaned my head over and put the phone under my hair.

"Yesterday," I said into the phone. "They said it's a Zenker diverticulum. They're supposed to put it in later today—"

I was trying to fill in one of our relatives as well as I could, without losing any time.

I got out of the car and locked it. Still holding the phone to my ear, I walked through the parking lot as fast as I could. "No, that was— He went in for pneumonia, but he *also* has a Zenker diverticulum—"

She wasn't familiar with that.

I stopped for a second to let a car drive by, then looked— the wind blew my hair in my face. I looked between the strands, continued walking without hesitation.

"I think it's a feature that developed in the esophagus that interferes with food going down. It's not a cancer, but it looks like it will require a minor surgery to put in a 'G-tube'— It's a tube in his belly that sticks out—right out through the belly." With the phone to my ear, I looked both ways to make sure the traffic was clear, walked across the street, turned smartly around a pylon toward the front door.

"Plastic and rubber?" I guessed into the phone. "Yes. I mean, who knows, but I think it's supposed to stay in there the rest of his life."

I entered the hospital and moved across the lobby. "If I lose you, I'm getting into an elevator." I waited while she mulled it over. Then I continued. "At his age? He's 92, so yes. It's minor, but it's a concern."

In the elevator, I pushed the button to take me to Joe's floor. Other people got on, the doors closed. "I don't know. The doc said he usually does them on older patients, like Joe, but that some people get these put in younger and live with them for years—like Joe will, too, I'm sure." Some others in the elevator glanced at me. "It's not a matter of nutrition for him; the food will be liquid from a can, but it will be nourishing. I see no option but to do this. He can't eat reliably."

The elevator doors opened. I was the first one off the elevator, turned toward Joe's room. "Okay," I said into the phone. "We're scheduled this morning. I'll call you later."

I hung up the phone at the nurse's station and got someone's ear. "Excuse me."

She walked away.

Another nurse came by.

My smile was quick and forced. "Excuse me! Can I ask how Joe Ware did last night?"

I stepped in to Joe's single hospital room and halted, standing quietly. There, in the darkness, in his bed, across the far wall near the window, I heard him praying. I could tell it was a private time for him, something personal with God. He was going through a mental list of people he knew, asking for God to bless them, each in turn, and to help them with something important.

He prayed for all of his children.

He prayed for me.

He did not pray for himself.

When he finished, I approached him quietly and slipped my hand into his.

"Jenna," he said.

"Joe." I brushed my fingers through his thinning hair.

I waited in recovery for them to wheel him out of surgery, and finally he came.

"It went just fine," the surgeon said. "See this?" He held up Joe's new G-tube for me.

Back in his room, the nurse instructed me. "You've got to learn to do this," she said.

"Me?"

"He's got to eat, doesn't he?"

"Sure, Yeah. Okay."

Joe lay in bed and watched us.

"All it is," she said, "Is this tube—"

"Joe," I interrupted. "You've seen 'Aliens.' You know, 'Aaaaaaaaah'!"

Joe didn't react noticeably to it.

"Stuff goes *in,*" the nurse said, maybe half getting the joke.

"You really going to let me do this, Joe?" I asked.

"Go ahead," he said. He wasn't responding as well. He was very weak from his pneumonia, the surgery. The skin on his face was thin and sagged over bones beneath.

Joe's status was beginning to look to me like what I called "Multiple System Failure," when a number of things would begin to go wrong at the same time. To me, it meant passing could be soon.

Not yet, I swore. *Not my Joe!*

"I use the gravity method," the nurse said. "I just take this big syringe—take out the plunger and throw it away. We're just using the body of the syringe as a funnel. Stick it in the end of his G-tube, like this." She showed me, then laid it down on his stomach. "What works for me is to open both a bottle of water and a can of lunch at the same time—"

"Does that come in pepperoni?" I asked her, keeping it light for Joe.

"Caviar," she said. She opened the water and food, sat them beside him on his bed.

"Do you like caviar pizza, Joe?"

"Sure."

"Well, lets see if we can have some," I said.

"Pick up the syringe about this high," the nurse said, "Unclamp the tube to let any air out, if there is any, and clamp it again. What I do that seems to work for me, is I pour in a little bit of water, about a third of the syringe? And then fill it the rest of the way with food. Then unclamp it, let it flow in. Here. You hold it."

Carefully, I held the large syringe body and let the food/water drain slowly into his stomach.

"If it won't flow in this way, then he might be full."

The syringe was almost empty.

"Now," the nurse told me. "Pour in a touch more water and some more food. 'Till we get the whole can in."

I did.

"And there you go," she said.

During all of 2009 and half of 2010, Joe was extremely ill. It was frightening for all of us. I thought we were going to lose him several times. He was going into the hospital with pneumonia on a fairly regular basis, every 2 or 3 months, each time coming out weaker than before.

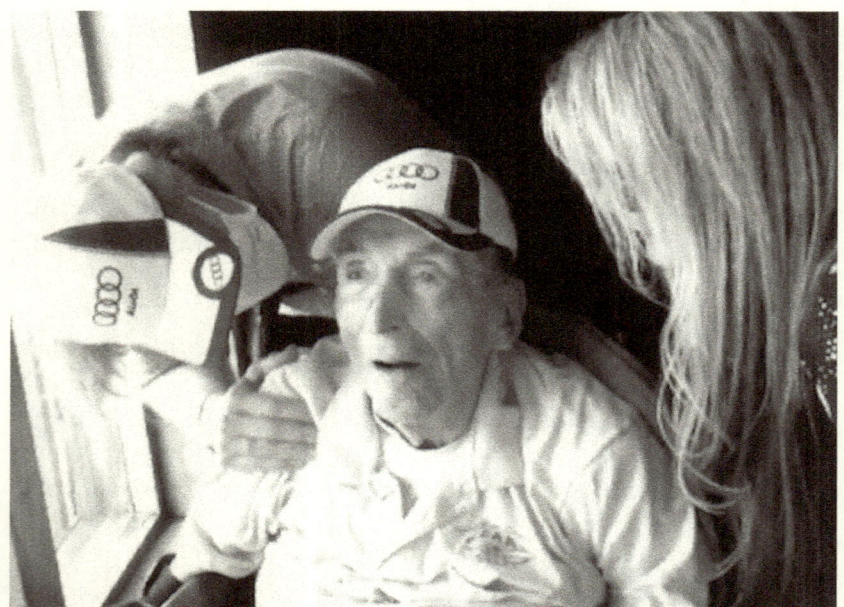

Figure 15.1. Joe with family, weak after several hospitalizations.

It was a hard time for him, and I was searching for ways to help. I was scared out of my mind every day, worrying that something I might overlook would matter. I spent my "free" time scrambling to find medical services for him, gathering health notes to give to an increasing number of doctors and hospitals, interfacing with staff at hospitals and Skilled Nursing Facilities—"SNIFs"—and I coordinated with his family, his doctors, and our lawyers on a regular basis.

I became something of a germophobe, except "phobia" implies an irrational component, and this was not. He became extremely sensitive to infections, and I was determined to protect the both of us: him, because he was so infirm, and me, because if I got ill, I couldn't be around to help him. A simple cold could mean no outings for a week or two, and I'd noticed inactivity made him worse. I developed a devotion to antimicrobial agents, benzalkonium chloride, ethyl alcohol. I'd shield his or my eyes and spray us with Lysol, spray his wheelchair, spray the car. Spray Troi. Give cans of it to the nurses. I'd use hand sanitizers regularly, which made my skin crack. It was not unusual to see me with a Band-Aid or two on my fingertips, treated with a little polysporin. Sometimes I also used surgical gloves and masks.

My stress was through the roof. Acid reflux grew in me. I developed difficulty talking, due to burning in my throat. My sleep was troubled.

But in the mornings, rain or shine, 7 days a week, I would greet Joe in the SNIF, bright and cheerful, to try to convey the clear message that we are together, that we're going to continue to enjoy life just as he wanted, and that he will never be deserted. His primary doctors were excellent, and over time, I discovered they were trusting more and more that I was capable and reliable with him, that I was not going to leave when the going got tough.

I learned to note early onset pneumonia in him. It was a change in his level of energy. Tired because of not sleeping well, that was one thing. Tired because of a medication change, age, or needing a nap, those were others. But a reduction in the amount of energy he had, somehow beneath those things, began to signal to me that it could be pneumonia. I'd call his primaries, they'd begin treatment, confirm the diagnosis, and we were able to decrease his hospitalizations over time.

When we got him on a CPAP machine, it was a major improvement. Normally, people take a few deep breaths per hour, even without noticing it, but with his advancing Parkinson's, he was not doing much of that. He could breathe fine otherwise, but the repeated deep breaths were not happening per norm. I was told the CPAP helped aerate his lungs at night just enough, so that his hospitalizations for pneumonia decreased quite a bit, and slowly, over time, he began to get stronger.

SNIFs took quite a bit of effort to figure out, in part, because I learned you can't judge a good SNIF by it's building, the eloquence of the Director of Nursing, its outreach coordinator, or its balance sheet—any more than you could judge any book by its cover. It seemed to me that some SNIFs were more interested in making things look good on paper than actually working with patients, and that some SNIFs actually cared.

The Director of Nursing, the "DON," stood in front of me, in the hall of the SNIF. "They won't walk him any more," she said, "He's too unstable on his feet. They're afraid he'll fall."

"But he's got to walk," I said, "or he could get blood clots in his legs which could kill him. Doctor's orders. Range of motion sucks by comparison. It's do or die."

"They won't do it."

I looked at my big arms—the ones I'd complained about my whole life—but now, I was thankful for them. I had to talk her into letting me do this, and I wasn't above begging or bragging to do it.

"I can walk Joe of a morning—just a little ways down the sidewalk, outside—flex his leg muscles under load—if you give me a couple of people to help."

She shook her head. "I don't think—"

"With respect," I said, "I've already been doing some of it for a year-and-a-half. Joe and I are both used to it. And I've been trained for this, years ago."

She raised her eyebrows at me, doubting.

"Why should that surprise you?" I asked. "I over train for everything. You've seen the way I help him into the car—and you've seen me walk with him before."

"Yes, but now therapy says he can't walk any more, so that's it."

No!

"Okay," I said, determined. No more diplomacy. "With*out* respect, let me say I've seen the way they walk people, and it's pitiful. You know what they do? They put *one* gait belt on the patient, loose about the middle, and then they walk beside the patient—*maybe* touching the gait belt with a finger, maybe not even that."

I could see she knew what I was saying.

"God only knows why they don't hold on, and I'm thankful I *didn't* have that training. If something happened—if the patient's knee went out, or if he collapsed—he'd drop like a sack of potatoes so fast, staff wouldn't be able to catch him. The patient would get injured. You'd have lawyers two feet up your ass before you could bend over."

I could see my familiar tone was not welcome, but neither were the risks I asserted.

"But they're right on one score," I said. "Joe *can't* do it on his own any more. My training, even though it was years ago, can help him actually walk. Safely."

Over the next several minutes, my tone became a combination of assured strength and confidence, combined with a plea for help. I shared with her my experience in Aikido with Take Sensei, my coordination, my arm strength—and my technique, in specific, right down to the *two* gait belts I'd use, how and where.

To my great surprise, the she took a chance on me, and she didn't even ask me to sign a waiver. *That* is good people. She cared about the patient more than perceived liability.

For the remaining year-and-a-half of Joe's life, I walked him every day, minus only a day away every couple of months for rest.

It was a new morning, and I found Joe sitting in his wheelchair in the lobby of the SNIF, waiting for me. "There's my guy! Good morning, Joe! How you doing?" I began assessing Joe—always for pneumonia and also for the possibility of a walk that morning. A twinkle in his eye, body language, recognition of me, his energy level... Usually, he was up to it, on some level, advanced Parkinson's or not.

I coughed due to my acid reflux.

Joe smiled at me.

I pulled out my iPhone 4S, played a 50s song, "Shake, Rattle and Roll," sat it on his shirt, above his tummy, and did what I called "hand dancing" with him, where I'd hold his hand and dance with it, giving it enough inertia so that he got the feeling we were stand dancing, while he sat in his wheelchair.

I looked like something on a "Saturday Night Live" skit. Other patients laughed with us. Joe brightened.

I got the receptionist's attention. "Where are my two aids? Can you let them know I'm here—Oh, there they are. Hello—" I greeted them by name with a couple of phrases in Spanish. "You two ready?"

They told me they were.

"Great. Come on, Joe. Let's go walk! You ready to get up and walk this morning?"

One rolled Joe out through the front doors onto the sidewalk outside, and the other followed, while I organized the two gait belts I'd use.

Outside, I continued to assess Joe while I put the belts on him, one on top the other, for redundancy. I could do it while he sat in his wheelchair, by scooting him forward about two inches in his seat, using the gap behind his hips. I positioned the belts on his hips, below his tummy, well below his G-tube and more recent colostomy, and synched them tight.

Troi exhausted her meager patience in the car and started barking.

"Troi, that's enough," I told her, giving her a stop motion with my hand. She stopped. "Get in the back seat," I told her.

She did, then hopped back into the front seat.

"She's so cute," one of the recreation therapists said.

"I know. She is." I got in Joe's face so he could see me well. "Doesn't mind for two seconds, but she's our girl. Right, Joe?"

He smiled at me.

I looked with Joe at the sidewalk ahead. "Okay, Joe!" Encouraging smile. "We need to walk down to that corner in the sidewalk—50 feet over there. You think you're ready to do that today? You can do it, I know you can. You do it every day. And then we can love Troi, okay?"

Joe smiled at me.

My aids were experienced with me. They knew the drill. One would walk beside us, maybe put a hand on him to feel him. The other would follow us with the wheelchair. If Joe collapsed, I would hold him up, and the other would put the wheelchair up to him so he could sit down. That only happened once every couple of months, but it was a safety feature to have them there, and it worked.

We always did the same thing, the same way, every day, so Joe's muscle memory would know what to expect.

I stood always on Joe's right side and half squatted beside him, bringing his right shoulder into my chest. I reached down behind Joe's back to the tight gait belts at his hips, and grabbed it mightily in my left hand, lifting slightly, and I put my right hand under his right armpit, for lifting there, as well.

"What do you think? You ready to *get up and walk*?" I was trying to sound excited, induce energy, inspire him. "Are you ready to get up and walk?"

I felt Joe lean forward just a little in his wheelchair. That was him saying, "Yes."

"Here we go!" I said.

I lifted with my left hand on his gait belt at his rump, and with my right hand in his right armpit, to get him into a standing motion—and off he went! Step, step, step, step!

My walk with him was not a normal "walk," but a series of sideways steps as I might have used to advance forward in a technique. He was walking; I was doing technique. I kept his hips near my hips and made one body with four legs. I lifted his armpit some as well, and I could tell by my own legs I was carrying maybe some 30% of his weight to assist. Yet he was going through his morning walk motions on his own.

"That's it!" I said as we walked. "You're great! You're doing it! 20 feet more! You're great! Keep it up, Joe! You can do it!"

He began to sag just a little.

I stopped sidestepping, held him up, and looked at the aid behind me, who brought up the chair. She could see it was time. I sat Joe down into his chair nice and easy.

"You did it, Joe!" I said to him, excited. "You did great! You went about 40 feet today! That's fantastic! *Yea Joe!"*

Joe's smile was broad in accomplishment, and he breathed heavily, while I fawned all over him.

The aid pushed Joe in the wheelchair around to the side of the car, and I took it from there.

I opened the passenger-side door—

Troi jumped into Joe's seat to greet us.

"Get in the back, Troi."

No response. So I used a hand motion and a little clap for emphasis. She did tend to respond well to hand motions. "Get in the back."

She did.

"Stay!" I gave her a stop motion at the same time, along with a stern don't-mess-with-me face.

She stayed.

"Good girl."

"She's so cute," the aids said again.

"Yes," I said to Joe, in his face. "We love Troi, don't we, Joe?"

Joe smiled.

I positioned his wheelchair exactly two inches from the car, right beside the door jam, locked the wheels, and moved his two gait belts from their walking position to their transfer position. I put one around his upper hips, not tight, and another at the bottom of his hips—top of the thighs—also not tight. I could put them both in position while he sat in the wheelchair.

I took a deep breath.

My right wrist, and oddly, my left shoulder, had been tweaking on some of his transfers. His weight may have been 140 lbs. at the time, and that was a problem. I had to make sure I didn't let myself get injured.

I'd learned that if I picked up something heavy, the weight would definitely sublux my right wrist. I was never close to dropping him, but it had hurt. I found that while he was in my arm, if I clenched, not only the muscles to close a fist, but also the muscles to *open* a fist, hard against each other—freeze my hand into a claw around his gait belts—it helped to hold the joint together.

I'd also learned it was important for Joe to NOT help me while I did the transfer. If he sensed that I was helping him transfer, and if he then, halfway through, decided to stand, he could hit his head on the top of the car's door jam as he entered, which wouldn't do.

I spread his knees a little with my shin and stepped in with my right leg, until my knee was against the front of his wheelchair seat. I reached down and grabbed both Joe's gait belts, together, in my right hand, so they formed a sling under his butt for the transfer. I then grabbed his shirt (or vest, or jacket, whatever he wore) together in my left hand.

Do the same thing as always, so he recognizes the cues.

Even say the same thing: "Okay, Joe. We're going to get into the car. Relax, and let me do it. Don't help me. Let me do it."

Whether he understood me or not, that was the cue for both of us.

With a grunt, I stood up—lifting him entirely with my right hand in his sling, using my left only to control his body's angle, *tenkan* to the right—and sat him down in the car seat, then leaned his body in. Still holding his shirt with my left hand for attitude, I put my right hand on his knee and scooted him back into the seat, lifted his feet in and turned him into a forward seated position.

We did 2-8 transfers a day, with a median of probably 4.

I sat on the door jam beside him and buckled him in.

Troi danced in the back seat.

Figure 15.2. Joe and Troi in car, after a wheelchair transfer.

The girls started to take the wheelchair away. "Watch this," I told them with an evil grin.

They looked. "What?"

"Troi?" I asked her.

She was instantly excited to be called.

"Give Daddy a kiss."

Her stubby tail wagged and she stepped in-between the seats and leaned over, licking Joe square on the mouth.

Joe made a face, then smiled even bigger.

"You got a kiss, Joe. Troi gave you a kiss"

The nurses giggled at the sight—"It's the funniest thing!"—and left with the wheelchair to go back inside. I carried his personal wheel chair in the trunk.

With me sitting right there, and Joe in his seat, I didn't have to tell Troi to get back in the back. She stayed near us, half standing on the center console.

"We love Troi," I said to Joe, fussing with his clothes and seat belt, petting Troi on the head.

I smoothed Joe's shirt and held his hand, assessing. My joints were okay. They made it through that one. I rotated my right wrist. It was hurt from a lift a couple weeks ago, but I was babying it, and it was healing.

"Joe, this is Jenna and Troi, here together with you in the car."

He didn't move.

I tugged on his seatbelt to make sure it was securely fastened, reached over to pet Troi, and rubbed Joe's chest.

"I'm sorry, Joe. I'm sorry I'm me. You deserve more."

Joe still didn't move.

Get his motor running.

"You remember the T-28? That we had in Hangar Two Two Eight at Camarillo? God, wasn't he a powerful beast?"

Nothing.

"We could feel that man vibrate through the frame. Couldn't keep it on the ground. He'd climb like a homesick angel. You could see him flying with his tongue hanging out, like your old childhood dog, Fritzie. Remember Fritzie?"

Joe was smiling at me, but it was the same smile he'd had from before, no change. I feared no recognition of what I was saying.

"—Two Eight Fox Echo was so great, Joe. A dream come true. I bet you wanted one ever since they put Wright Cyclones on them, back in 1840, or whenever it was." Maybe teasing would work? "A good choice."

Sitting in the door jam of the car, I held Joe's hand for a moment.

"I love you, Joe." I said, quietly, squeezed his hand.

"I love you, too," Joe said to my surprise, with tears in his eyes.

A lucid moment!

I hugged him deeply and didn't let him see me cry on his shoulder.

He'd said it many times, in years past, but that time sticks in my mind more than any other. It was so special. We were a family. We were together, and nothing could split us apart.

He gave me a big smile.

I faced him. "Joe, always know I love you. Forever."

16

Loving Him

2011

"HEY JOE! Can you say, *'Goooooooooood MORNin'!'?"* I said it with gusto, loud and full of energy, like I was excited, and doing this was FUN, like we were having a great day. My effort was to wake him up and inject some zest for living. I did this every morning in the car, when we loaded to go somewhere.

I coughed, my acid reflux.

Joe's smile went from ear to ear.

I put the car in gear and exited the SNIF parking lot, drove down the street.

I egged him on. "Well, Joe? Can you say it?"

He smiled broadly, obviously happy to have this fun with me. It was a ridiculous thing to say, the way I was doing it, and acting silly was my forté.

I laughed at him and played along. "Ha! Yeah, Joe. I know. It's funny to hear me say it, but can *you say it?*"

"Yup," he said.

"No! No! I don't mean *can* you do it." I stopped for a red light. "I mean, *will* you say it for me? 'Gooooooooood MORNin!' Like that!"

I waited, and then he responded in kind. *"Gooooooooooo MORrnnnnn!"*

I laughed at him heartily. "Yeah, Joe! That's it! You did it! Yeeeaaaaaaa Joe!"

The light was green, so we proceeded.

"Where we going today?" he asked.

"Today, we get to go to the doctor. Oh boy! Lots of fun! A cardiologist."

"Joy."

"Well, hey. We go walking and flying. I want to make sure you're okay for it. Okay?"

"Then what?" he asked.

"Well, then, what about we go fly today? It's nice out. Then hang out with the guys at the airport a while?"

The doctor walked into the room and talked with us about Joe's health.

Joe sat in his wheelchair by the exam table. I sat in a regular chair beside him.

"Here's my wondering, Doc. It's not really a worry, but I thought I should ask."

"Go ahead."

"Okay. Joe walks less well, as these months go on, so he's sitting in some kind of chair the rest of the time, or a bed."

"Okay."

"So it's vital he walk every day to pump fresh blood through his muscles?"

"Oh, yes. He needs to do that. It helps in a number of ways, not just blood clots."

"Okay. I'm on board. He does and we will. But in addition, I take him flying in the airplane?"

His eyebrows went up a little. "How do you do that?"

"I have a Cardinal—big door, no wing strut—and what I do is roll his wheelchair up to the door, use a crane to hoist him up about a foot. 2 hooks on the crane, for redundancy, hooked to some 4 gait belts, spread out—similar to but about 10 times stronger than the bed cranes they use in the hospital—and I raise him still in a sitting posture. Then I just slide the crane forward and lower him into his seat."

The cardiologist looked at Joe with appreciation. "You go flying with her?"

"Yup," Joe said.

"Okay."

"Egress is even easier. I can lift him down into his wheelchair, myself. I just need the crane to help get him in."

"Okay. So what do you need to ask me about it?"

"We have less atmospheric pressure at altitude—about half at 18,000 feet. I don't fly that high. My plane won't even go that high. But at some point, as we climb, I would think his body might slightly expand—"

The doctor finished. "And if there is a clot in his legs, it could break loose—"

"Right. My question is how high can I take him, when we go fly?"

"Uh, oh, well, I don't know, but I don't think the lower altitudes would be a problem."

"Like maybe 4,000 feet in altitude? Camarillo Airport is only 77 feet, so lots of room, there."

The doctor looked like he was considering that.

"4,000," I said, "because of two things. One, if we do a practice IFR approach into Camarillo—something we've always taken as important work, a safety issue—they like for us to do that below 4,000. I guess that's about 86% atmospheric pressure."

"And the other?"

"Well, when we taxi in the car to visit some relatives, it's over the hill into Palmdale, and the crest, there, is about 3,400 feet, and that seems a normal thing to do. And if we go to Vandenberg Air Force Base, the Gorman pass is about 4,000 feet."

"Yeah," the doctor said. "4,000 should be fine."

Joe, Troi and I soared over the Oxnard Plain at 2,800 feet, above Camarillo and Oxnard air space, but low enough so we could maneuver without having to change altitude. I was left seat, Joe was right seat, Troi was back seat, as per norm.

I pulled out my cell phone and took a selfie of all three of us in the cockpit.

"Yep, I got a picture of us," I told Joe through the headset. "I'll send that later to everybody, okay?"

Figure 16.1. The three of us flying in the Cardinal, trying to keep life together.

Joe looked out the window, watched us curve over fields, beside the ocean and the mountains he'd loved most of his adult life.

"Thank you, God, for letting us be here," I said aloud, into the intercom. It was my intention to speak his feelings for him, to help him form his own words, as well as I could, knowing him. "And thank you, God, also, for Joe. He is the greatest person I've ever known."

Joe looked at me, then back out the window.

"Thank you, God, for Troi, because we love her so much. Thank you, God—" I continued, naming each of his three children and other important people in his life.

The sky was the altar at which we prayed.

"We gotta buzz the guys," I told Joe. "There they are, sitting in Abe's hangar."

Joe, Troi, and I taxied by in the Cardinal to see the guys inside sitting on chairs. I stopped the plane and throttled the engine to get their attention.

The three of us sat inside the hangar with six of them, talking about anything and everything, spending the day. One of Joe's old friends, Jack Norris, was there of the Voyager Round the World flight.

We rolled into the theatre to watch "Iron Man 2." I hosed down the theatre's handicap seat with Lysol.

Joe sat there, his empty wheelchair beside him. Our eyes were glued to the screen.

"You think this movie is fiction?" I asked him, inducing some flight test engineering into the film. "I mean, he doesn't look aerodynamic. If you had enough power, you could fly like him, but even moving his head would torque him and institute a yaw about the vertical axis, send him careening off in a new direction, and if he has a power-out, he's gonna glide like a brick."

Joe stared eyes-wide at the screen.

To raise spirits, I took him to quite a variety of places from county faires to airshows with family.

Figure 16.2. J2 playing with hats.

Figure 16.3. Doing our best to duck bird droppings.

Figure 16.4. Flying has always been a major part of life.

Figure 16.5. Picnic on the boat.

Figure 16.6. Joe, his son, Joe, and Troi at Camarillo Air Show under the wing of the Cardinal.

We sat in church, third pew back from the front, right side, in front of the choir. The organist is the one who had inspired us to marry every year on our anniversary.

Joe was sitting in the pew, his wheelchair to the side. I sat beside him, singing the song into his ear, helping him think the old, familiar words.

> "What a friend we have in Jesus,
> all our sins and griefs to bear!
> What a privilege to carry
> everything to God in prayer!"

Out on the patio, after service, his old pastor married us for the 17th time, renewing our vows for our 16th anniversary. I didn't know it would be our last.

"Hey, Joe! We're getting married again. You want to get married again?"

"Sure!"

I cried for both of us.

In previous years, we were known to cry, both of us, renewing our vows—usually in church, once in family's house, and once in the seat of the car, following a hospitalization for pneumonia, because Joe was too weak. The pastor was so helpful. But that year, Joe was just happy to be there.

The boat floated in the water beside the dock. As I cranked the winch on the crane, Joe rose in the sling, and the boat, ever so slightly, tilted to port.

Joe's son steadied Joe enough so he wouldn't yaw as he rose.

"That should do it," I said. "Just high enough so his butt clears the gunwale," the "GUN-nel," the side of the boat.

I stood beside Joe at that point and moved him over the gunwale, setting him down in a chair that I'd placed there for him.

Figure 16.7. Joe riding through harbor on boat, his son driving.

Joe sat on the aft deck, all decked out in his life jacket and ear-to-ear smile.

Sometimes if I wondered if Joe was more there than he seemed, his smile being the only way he could manage to communicate.

His son piloted the boat through the harbor.

"Hey, Joe! Smile!" I took pictures with my phone. "I'll send these to everybody," I said to his son. "Thank you for being here. It means a lot to him."

I found Disneyland increasingly important, because as he withdrew into his Parkinson's, some of their silly antics could get a smile from him. Big, tall, animated characters, or someone singing, or a band playing on the sidewalk. They were always cheerful, even when I felt like crying. They were good with him.

A day at Disneyland was one of our longer trips. I had to ask the SNIF to get him ready for me by 8:00 instead of 9:00, walk him, load him, then drive down to Disneyland, getting there by 11:30 or so, spend 2.5 hours on site, leaving at 2:00 for the return drive to the SNIF, avoiding most afternoon traffic, so he could be back by 4:00 or so.

But those 2.5 hours were golden and gave him a sense of happiness, I think, and love.

Pushing his transport chair up Disney's Main Street, I took a full breath. "Great air, today, Joe! You smell that?"

Joe didn't respond much.

"You smell that air, Joe?"

"Yup," he said.

"Good, old hamburgers, it smells like to me. With a hint of—Aston Martin? You think *James Bond* is around here?"

I smiled into his face so he could see me, and I got a smile back. I don't think he was responding to my joke but to my face in smile.

We could go boating in three places in Disneyland: Mark Twain's river boat, Small World, and also the Jungle Cruise boat on its river. They have a great method on the jungle cruise for wheelchairs that was right up his alley: very mechanical, a treat in itself. The boat would come—almost no waiting in a wheelchair—and they had an electromechanical gangplank that would rise on the boat and turn toward him. They'd roll him on, then it would turn parallel with the longitudinal axis of the boat and lower back into the boat. The Jungle Boat "ship captain" would tell jokes on the tour, and Joe would turn his head looking at everything floating by.

Mostly, what we enjoyed was the experience of being there. We could watch a horse pulling a cart up Main Street, see droves of people having a good time, Watch Great Moments with Mr. Lincoln—always a delight—or go into the Golden Horseshoe to see the 15 minute play—but I was always divided on the play. At the time, it focused on Sally Mae, and had for a long time.

Disneyland does such a good job helping people have a nice day, but that one never made sense to me. I took Joe in because the noise and the "fun" of it got through to him. He enjoyed watching. Usually, he'd have a fun look on his face.

But the play we kept seeing at the Golden Horseshoe, over and over, was some variation on the ugly Major's daughter. Sally Mae was so ugly, they made it clear, that no one wanted her—and to make the point she was ugly, they used a man in a dress. They ridiculed her over and over for her ugliness, and then had to find some sucker and trick him into getting engaged.

It blew my mind that the audience seemed to like that. That was totally not Disneyland, to my way of thinking.

I talked with staff about that a few times, outing myself, anonymously, to them in the process. I didn't want to wear out my welcome, but I thought I should say something.

Every time I told them about this, they seem as though they were listening, concerned.

"You're slamming both ugly women and men in dresses when you do that. Women and trans people."

"But people think it's funny," they'd say. And in truth, the play was an ongoing hit. For years. People did laugh at it.

I'd counter. "That's part of the problem. You're teaching that Disney says it's okay to laugh at that. Disney has some of the best writers in the world. Couldn't you come up with something else to laugh at?"

"That kind of humor is traditional."

"So are women in the kitchen, a lack of education, making fun of gays, bigotry and oppression—but we should learn as we grow, and you could help…"

I arranged for Joe to have a private tour of Vandenberg Air Force Base. I called around up there, shared Joe's history with

Lockheed. Someone remembered him, and they granted us a private tour, drove us around the base in their car and shared all about it.

We toured through Ronald Reagan's Air Force One at the Reagan Library in Simi Valley, CA. It was a Boeing 707.

Joe liked Reagan.

"Joe! Look at this! We're on *Ronald Reagan's Air Force One!* Can you believe it?"

I slowly pushed his wheelchair down the center aisle of the airliner.

"Joe helped make the first two Air Force Ones," I bragged to the docent, "for President Eisenhower."

"He did?" she asked.

"Yes. Columbine II and Columbine III, I think it was. Connie variants, Engineering Flight Test, Lockheed. I'm not the right one to ask—ask Joe, here—but I think the first Columbine was the one Eisenhower had when he was in the Army."

We sat on the lawn outside the dignified Athenaeum at Caltech and got everything organized: Bagpipes, chair, air can, me, some of our family including grandkids.

"You all ready?"

Everyone assured me they were.

"Joe, you ready? I'm gonna play the *bagpipes*." I spelled it out for Joe, because he was severely impaired by then, and I was trying to help him understand. "Hey Joe. We're here at the Ath, and I'm gonna play the *bagpipes*. Okay? We'll *wake 'em all up!*"

Figure 16.8. Jenna playing bagpipes with air can on Caltech campus.

He smiled.

"Yeah, it's fun. But are you ready?"

He smiled bigger.

"You ready, Joe?"

I was hoping to get him to verbalize.

"Yup!" he finally said.

"Great! Here we go!"

The studious air of concentration on campus broke at the first screech from my bagpipes—made worse by the fact that I could not actually play the bagpipes.

In the *Hitchhiker's Guide to the Galaxy*, Vogon poetry was so awful, it was literally gut-wrenching. When I began to "play," something resembling a Vogon's "Amazing Grace" seared through the campus and echoed off buildings at full volume. I think two windows broke. Geniuses in a dozen labs within a half mile of the Ath probably grabbed their heart and scraped their chalk across boards, ruining 10 equations and accidentally creating 2 new ones.

It's probably why we don't have antigrav, today.

Family laughed at the screeching noise, but I think the melody was recognizable.

Unlike Ferris Beuller, I'd actually taken a lesson, but I was a lost cause because I didn't have the strength in my left arm to squeeze the bag. That motion I hadn't trained for. I could lift Joe, but I was weak in the area of pulling my elbow in to my ribs. And no way was I going to spend the time to build up those muscles.

So what can I do? Sleeping with Joe, since the early '90s, came to my rescue. He flowed in through the pillows: engineering by osmosis.

I got an air can from Home Depot—what would our Skunk Works do without Home Depot—pressurized it, and hooked it up to the bagpipes to use for our demo—which worked.

After a few halfway credible bars of the song, the pitch rose, and the pipes began to squeal out of control. No doubt cats in Pasadena arched their back and hissed. The can was over-producing for us, so I had to stop playing for a second, let the pipes play themselves—sounded the same—and reached down with my right hand to adjust the airflow on the can. Then I returned to my masterpiece as if it was the appropriate thing to do.

I sounded a little better when one of the grandsons pitched in to help. He could tell when to turn the valve, to increase or decrease the pressure.

"It's only the Mark One, Joe," I said as I played, referring to the first prototype. "I have a few bugs to work out!"

I had been a member of 99s—think Amelia Earhart—since, 1990 or so, I rarely did much with them other than a few presentations I made. This is not due to any lack of opportunity, not due to the lack of invitations, but due mostly to my own reservations. There had been some looks, and they were a female-only group. I feared they'd kick me out if my sex became an issue. I'd taken more than my share of pushback for being trans in other areas of life, all my life, that said I was not accepted, and once, at a section meeting, there was a trans woman there who was a topic of controversy.

Most stealth are skittish, unwilling to risk focus, and that was my problem.

What rumors are there about me?

What do they know?
What do they think they know?

A look or a comment from someone could send my mind reeling, yet I couldn't ask any of those questions. I couldn't even raise the subject for my own fears.

Do some people know, but don't want to admit they know?
Is it something they're pleased to "forget" if allowed to?
Will the subject turn critical if mentioned?
What about others, if I think they know— It could put them at ease if I'd just mention it, but if I mention it, and they don't actually know, if I've mis-read some signal, then I will have caused my own trouble—

Typical stealth worry.

I was increasingly on edge with them, probably because I was also having more fun with them than ever. The closer I got, the more I feared intrusion rejection.

For the 2008 International Business Meeting, I think it was, I flew commercial airlines—"took the bus"—to Anchorage Alaska for about a day and a half. I didn't feel I could take any more time away from Joe than that, but it was a good trip as far as it goes. And I took some photos while up there. Of people. Buildings. Things. A moose. And I got Martha and Art Phillips to pose for "no reason" sitting in a chair, in profile.

After everyone returned to Oxnard, I asked if I could show my photos at the next chapter meeting, and to my surprise they said okay.

Fools!

I got my PowerPoint up and working, off my laptop, projected onto a screen, presenting about the meeting in Alaska, when I began to slip in phony pictures I'd made, including Art and Martha riding north to Alaska on a moose.

My artwork was sloppy, but I'd discovered Photoshop.

I gave them no warning; I just did it in dry humor, as if it was real.

The look on Martha's face, when she saw them sitting on a moose, was priceless, mouth open.

It went over well, and I was delighted. I think I needed something pleasant to happen, in counterpoint to some other things. I needed it very much.

They asked me if I'd do another PowerPoint presentation for the 2008 Holidays, December VC 99s dinner, and I agreed, gathering up a few hundred candid photos, some real photos that were posed that I could play with, and then some outright made-up photos on Photoshop, putting people's heads on other people's bodies, making it look like they did things that obviously never happened, being silly.

It worked, so for the next year, they asked me to do the same again.

Joe's 2009 was extreme. He was near death several times, in the hospital for pneumonia, and I found I could use the break in thought—rising at about 5:00 a.m., getting ready, working on the presentation from about 6:00 a.m. to about 7:00 a.m., usually. And for the holiday dinner, it worked again, playing about 400 photos in a live presentation, timed to music played at the same time.

They liked it enough to ask me again in the fall of 2010 to do it again.

Will they never learn?

But this year, Joe was getting stronger, so I made the switch from static photos in a PowerPoint to video, which took longer to prepare, but it was easier to show.

Joe's son and daughter-in-law arrived at the presentation dinner with me for the showing. And when the time came, I turned on the video on my laptop and sat back to watch. It was 23 minutes, starting off with the low-quality, Monty Python zaniness typical of my PowerPoints, becoming funny, then slowly improving into sentimentality, including shots of Joe and I in the airplane, climbing through the clouds out of Camarillo.

I also showed Martha as the President of the United States, standing behind the Resolute Desk in the Oval Office. She actually became the President of the Ninety-Nines, Inc., shortly thereafter.

I got a good round of applause, and I was thankful. It was one of the good things that could come from not giving up. I think Joe's family enjoyed it. And I'm thankful for it.

Flying Joe into a major military air show took a few logistics, because of the problems of leaving my car at

Camarillo Airport and not having my shop crane with me at the air show to get him back into the airplane. With help from the U.S. Navy and Sondra at the Waypoint, we worked it out.

Figure 16.9. Flying low over Oxnard Plain.

Pt. Mugu Naval Air Station was only five miles from Camarillo Airport, and they were having a show, so it was a must-do. I called around Mugu, found the petty officer I was to coordinate with for static displays, explained the situation and bragged on Joe. He would be in a wheelchair. We needed no housing or rental car, just permission to land for the weekend, a place on the ramp to show the plane, and some Navy help to get Joe back into the airplane on Sunday afternoon. She felt it was worthy and accepted us.

It was imperative that Joe and I fly in together in the plane—not me fly the plane in and then bring Joe to sit under the wing with me. He needed to be in the cockpit, hear the radio, familiar military protocol. We needed to land there, like we had in the T-28.

Lifting off Runway Two Six, I hit the radio. "Camarillo Tower, Cardinal One Seven Niner, left to Mugu, frequency change."

"Left turn approved, Frequency change. G'day."

"G'day," I said to them.

I already had Mugu weather, so I changed the radio frequency to Mugu Tower.

"Here we go, Joe—just like flying into Edwards. Remember us flying into Edwards? We're flying into Mugu, now!"

Joe was watching out the window, a pleased look on his face. I'm not sure if he understood, or on what level.

I got on the radio without delay. "Mugu Tower, Cessna One Seven Niner, off Camarillo, Static Display, PPR."

"One Seven Niner, Mugu. Say PPR."

I did.

"One Seven Niner, approved. You have the airport in sight?"

"We have Mugu in site. We've been here before."

I looked over at Joe who was still looking out the window.

"One Seven Niner, cleared to land Runway Two One, check gear down."

"One Seven Niner, gear is welded down."

"Okay, Joe! We got the field. You see it up there? Pt. Mugu is approaching." I tended to repeat myself for Joe, to help him hear me, if he could. "We get to land at Pt. Mugu for the air show."

I flew on a couple miles at 1,000 feet. Mugu air base sat right beside the ocean, with the hills of Malibu to the left. Crops were green in checked fields below us.

There wasn't much time to look; the flight was too short.

"There's the runway, Joe. Runway Two One, that's us."

I didn't need to ask Mugu to repeat anything; but I wanted Joe to hear it again."

"Mugu Tower, One Seven Niner. We're cleared to land?"

"One Seven Niner, A-firm. Clear to land."

"Here we go, Joe! Clear to land at Mugu! Carb heat on, power back, glide— Watch for cables, Joe. Remember once we hit a cable in the 120, they had stretched across the runway. Made a terrible bang on our tail gear. Remember that? I don't see any cables…"

We landed.

"Nobody's bleedin', Joe!" I said with a glance to him. "Nobody's bleedin'."

Joe was smiling broadly.

Military ground personnel marshaled us into position on the ramp, and the petty officer, who coordinated us, met us at the airplane.

I got out of the Cardinal and hugged her mightily.

"So this is Joe?" she asked, seeing him in the right seat.

"Yes. And he's been flying around this area since 1941."

"Well, we're glad to have him!"

"And we're glad to be here. Thank you so much."

Joe's transport chair was in the back seat of the Cardinal. I pulled it out, got him into it, and fussed over him.

Some people gathered, and I shared Joe's history—my nature.

At the appointed time, Sondra came to pick us up.

Both Saturday and Sunday, I picked Joe up early at the SNIF and we drove onto Pt. Mugu to take part in the air show—we sat under the wing of the Cardinal, listening to the noise of jets zooming overhead, the smells of hamburgers and jet fuel.

I was excited for us both. "Look at all there is to see, Joe!"

Pushing Joe around the ramp in his transport chair, I listed planes buzzing through the sky overhead, "tying a knot in their tail," and described a hundred planes we saw on the ramp around us.

"And Joe: There's a C-130 over there. You were flight test engineer on the YC-130. Remember that?"

He turned his head to see.

Walking over to the C-130, I found they were letting the public go onboard, so we joined them. I rolled Joe up the ramp in the tail and described everything I could. It was all available for Joe to see, but his vision wasn't as good as it used to be.

I got little reaction from him.

I thought there would be more.

After leaving the C-130, I rolled Joe to the side of the fuselage, near the gear—the main wheels of the airplane—and sitting there, kneeling beside Joe's wheelchair, I began to see the light dawn on him.

He was near one of his old airplanes.

Slowly, he reached out to touch the plane, and I could tell by the look on his face, that he knew what he held.

Figure 16.10. Joe looking into C-130 at Pt. Mugu Air Show.

Figure 16.11. Loving a design he worked on.

2011

For Joe's birthday, in November, I arranged for several people to meet together at the Athenaeum: Joe and I, family, and his old friend who was his accountant and Trustee.

It was a day of celebration of Joe's life.

The maître d'hotel seated us in what I call the Hall of Associates, near the buffet.

The Athenaeum is elegant—not just in its architecture, but in, well, Caltech. Dozens of Nobel Prize winners have been through there. I have seen Kip Thorne there and Stephen Hawking. Einstein had been there, as well as Joseph Fulton Ware, Jr. I am such a groupie.

It was a good day. People ate and talked their way through lunch, told stories about Joe—that was easy to do. He's a family legend. It was non-stop good-times sharing, that day with stories of his growing up in Blacksburg, his old friends, practical jokes at Lockheed, planes he worked on—and, frankly, how he may have saved millions of lives with his work, per the cold war—his family, his natural, humble Christianity, the amazing way he could see simple solutions to complex problems.

How could anyone live a better life?

Afterward, I took them all out on to the patio, as we're not supposed to operate iPads inside the dining area, and I played a 4-minute video I'd made, set to music, of many of the things Joe and I had been doing these last three years. It showed Joe so crushingly ill in '09, then getting stronger in '10, '11, with dozens of different activities.

I gave them each a DVD copy of that movie. It was my gift to them for Joe's birthday, the best thing, along with his continued living, I could imagine.

We had all worked, together, to make it possible.

Joe and I could never have done all the things we did, for his longevity and quality of life, if we'd remained in Washington. Physician cooperation I'd experienced there was slim for us, and vision was absent. It turned out, for us, Ventura County was where we needed to be.

17

Hell

2012

ONE DAY, Joe was called home and entered the hospital for the last time. They ran every test on him for a week. They were good, but they kept telling me there was nothing they could do. He looked fine, as far as could be seen, but he was hooked up to monitors and IVs, and he was intubated. He lay quietly in his bed, unmoving, the entire week, as if he were asleep, his bed sheet perfectly folded by nurses over his chest.

Joe had written in is Medical POA, which the hospital had, that if he were effectively brain dead, that if he were being kept alive by machines, then he must be maintained for one week while tests were run to see if anything could be done, but after a week, if nothing could be done, he was to be disconnected. It was out of my hands. There was nothing I could do. The doctors made it clear.

I checked also with his attorney, but she agreed. There was nothing we could do.

I consulted with his family repeatedly, who came to see him in the hospital and paid their respects, but Joe was already gone, we were all sure.

His doctors scheduled his last day. I asked them to wait until I got there.

At the appointed time, four nurses and I went into his room. The lead nurse explained the process to me, and when I was ready, she began. She disconnected him, and he lay in his clean bed, apparently as peaceful as anyone could, breathing normally.

Over the next hour, however, his breathing became shallow. His heart rate on the monitor became weaker.

No one could have witnessed the scene without crying.

Throughout his last hour, the nurses listened to me intently while I told them stories of his life.

I told them of his childhood as a playful Dennis the Menace, in Blacksburg, a genius little kid who loved practical jokes, bugged his mother's Bridge game. I told them he turned down a date with Olivia de Havilland while he was a student at Caltech, which he always playfully knocked himself for, that he had pretended to put a bolt through a propeller at work to tease a prop rep, how he loved President Eisenhower's Columbine II, that he had been in charge of engineering flight test for the U-2 and the SR-71. Two of the nurses recognized the airplanes; I explained it for the other two, right up to the altitudes flown and the basic aerodynamics of the aircraft. Joe would be so proud I had learned. He helped in his way to win the Cold War with the Soviet Union, promoted its dissolution, because we knew what they were doing, when they had less information on us. He saved countless lives in potential conflicts. They named a laboratory after him at Virginia Tech. He married three times. He fathered three children from his first wife. He taught people, not only engineering and basic principles of science, but also how to be a better person, in themselves.

And I also told them there was not one prejudiced bone in his body. He loved people of all kinds without judgment—a Christian in the truest sense of the Word. God could never have made a better person.

The nurses seemed to believe every word I said, perhaps because it was all true.

Joe had changed my life utterly. He taught me that I mattered—a first, for me—and that everyone matters. I could never be the same. If I live a hundred years, I will be dazed, learning the permutations of his teachings.

Through the hour, Joe's breathing slowed and eventually stopped, with his last breath undetectable.

I melted down, hugged the lead nurse and cried on her shoulder for a long time.

It wasn't possible!

Then they left the room, and I sat on a chair, in the corner. Alone.

The pain I felt was as bad as anything I had felt before— which I would gladly suffer again if he could live.

Let me switch places with him! I cried to God. *He'd do so much more with my life than I! You know it's true!*

But I heard nothing back.

It was wracking, an impossible internal conflict that felt like it would tear my soul apart. *He has to live!* Yet, he no longer could.

Why does life have to end!? God!!?? I screamed in my mind, though I sensed, as if from Joe, it was the wrong demand to make. *Cosmos?? Why do you give us this miracle of life, this amazing consciousness, only to take it away??*

WHAT'S THE FUCKING POINT—

In my mind, I stopped. He wouldn't want me to say that.

What are you doing? I asked the universe as well as I could, but I knew there was more to it than I could fathom.

Joe!

I looked at him lying in his bed, more still than possible, as if asleep without breath. There was no distortion in his body, no facial expression at all, not even a sense of peace. He was simply not there.

I tried to console myself by telling myself that he had been gone for a week, that the man lying in bed, there, was his body, the body he had used. But it did no good.

Time went by, I don't know how long. I felt numb, like my arms were too heavy to move. I needed to fade with him, but my mind had long been trained to work with emergencies, and that part of me took over.

Thumbing on my phone, I sent an email to his family, his Trustee, his lawyer, some friends, even the funeral home in Blacksburg: This great man, who had helped so many in life, who served as an example to all, had passed away. He was 95.

18

Joe!

JOE'S FUNERAL arrangements had already been codified, years ago. There was nothing I had to do—very little I *could* do, even if I wanted. I carried out his wishes as he'd instructed.

He was laid in Blacksburg, in the West View cemetery, in the western corner just outside the drip line of the large tree, not far from our ancestors that stretched all the way back to the Revolutionary War.

It was early May, and it was cold. The funeral home had set his coffin over his grave, and a tent over that, in case it rained. Family were in attendance as well as representatives from his Lab. A minister spoke.

And I was a mess.

I couldn't grieve at the funeral.

I feared trouble would raise a hand again if it believed Joe should not be laid in *our* plot. My name was on the headstone, as well as his. I kept looking at the area around us for someone who may arrive and start a fight. Saying goodbye to him was cerebral, in me, not emotional. I couldn't let myself go.

They opened the coffin for us to look at him. His son's wife and I went forward to look, to confirm he was in there and to affirm, again, that he had, indeed passed on.

I placed some beloved items in his arms—as messed up as I was, I needed him to take these things with him, including something from Troi. He had to always know she loved him, too, so much.

After we sat back down, they prepared the coffin, and we all stayed to see it lowered into the ground and covered.

Still in defensive mode, looking over my shoulder for some problem to erupt, I toured the Lab on campus with family. Staff were so kind to us at Virginia Tech; they always were. And I walked on campus with the family to point out things regarding Joe in summation. Out into the middle of the Drill Field, where

Divel Saunders had landed, I pointed out Joe's life there as well as I could. It was right around there that Joe's life had centered, where he'd been put on track for the great life he'd led: 404 Clay St. was right over there, two blocks, where he was born and raised; his high school was right over there on the edge of campus, now the Architectural building, I think it is; the radio station he'd worked at on campus, in high school, was over there to our south, in addition to the BBS he had in his attic in the block house; the room he taught math in, in the '40s, was Holden Hall, right over there…

We all looked beaten, whipped, tired.

There was nothing else to say.

Joe had always kept his affairs close to his vest, preferring to share with his Trustee, Lawyer, and me, so at lunch, in the restaurant that had been the Presbyterian church, founded by our ancestor William Thomas, I explained a few things to family that helped them know Joe had cared for and loved them, and for which I believe they were thankful.

When I returned to Oxnard, I stopped at the kennel to pick up Troi, aged 14, and took her home. We both hobbled into our quiet house and sat together on the couch.

I had no way to tell her what had happened, but she knew I was hurt and it was important. She comforted me with her head on my lap.

During the next year, again with me doing everything I could for her, she aged, and one year minus two days after her father's death, she passed away at the Vet's. I made sure the last thing she saw was my loving face, right in front of her.

I almost died with her. She was not a dog to me; she was family, deeply emotional, loving and loyal.

I had her cremated. I keep her ashes on the mantle, and I made arrangements for her to be laid with her father and me, in my arms, when that time comes in the distant future, in our plot in Blacksburg.

The house was empty, even with me in it.

Ellen stood with me on the Santa Monica Pier, overlooking the ocean, with a view north, up the beach, toward Malibu. She didn't speak. There was nothing to say.

I've cried many times sharing my story, and I did with her, also. But there was nothing to be done.

"I felt like my life was over," I told her. "I don't mean dead; I mean—I felt my heart was cut out, like the only thing—like, the thing in my life that made me whole was gone, my reason for living was gone. He was my focus, everything. And then Troi dying—"

"And the trouble with your mom."

"Yeah. I'd been back to see her a couple of times during her stay in a SNIF. I made phone calls now and then to see how she's doing. I thought everything was fine with that. Then one day when I called, I was cut off. No information could be given to me. I was not allowed."

"That's what the fight was about?"

"Yeah. I went back and found— You know, in her room, she had a photo album of pictures she took in Paris?"

Ellen nodded.

"I think she loved that trip. I think she loved me. She just had problems of her own. And on a trip, back to see her, I found this one nurse who was particularly nice to me— It was a very Christian area. I've always had a problem with many, in Christianity. Some people seem to say that God is a bigot and doesn't approve of me. So they act to oust me."

Ellen was disgusted along with me.

"I think religion hurts more than it helps, when it sells an ideology that some people aren't worthy." Los Angeles, behind us, responded with increased traffic noise and a hint of car horns. "Yet on the other hand are these saints who walk the earth—like Joe—Christians who live to be kind, who don't judge, who respond with love, who prove it with their life. Special people.

"So I found a good nurse back there, on this one trip, and I got her to help me. I wanted to get a smile out of Mom. I played 'Nessun Dorma' for her, and I got the nurse to video me with my phone."

"What's that?" Ellen asked.

"One of the most popular arias—a song in the opera, 'Turandot.' I know Mom loved it. Pavarotti could *sing*—that man was good. Mom didn't respond, at first. I'm playing 'Nessun Dorma,' talking to Mom about it. No response. I knew it could take several minutes, if ever, for it to soak in that I was there and playing one of her favorites. I waited. No response. So after I played it, I went over to the piano and began to play Beethoven's 'Moonlight Sonata.' All I know is the beginning part of that, but Mom liked what she called 'good music'—and then a big smile suddenly broke out on her face!"

My smile was large to Ellen.

"We did it! We got through to her! Not because of my playing, I'm sure!" I said. "But because 'Nessun Dorma' finally processed."

"And then I gave Mom a big hug. I'm not sure if she knew who she hugged, but I know who hugged her."

19

WV-2

ELLEN AND I SAT in our seats at Dodger Stadium, two hours before the game, working on little plastic baseball hats full of frozen yogurt. The other team were having batting practice on the field.

I ate my frozen yogurt without reservation.

Ellen picked at hers. Her figure was better than mine, too.

"Well?" she asked.

"That's a deep subject."

Ellen persisted. "So do you think I'm a real woman?"

"I am not God. You'll have to ask her."

"Don't dodge this," she said. "I want to know."

"I assume you're asking 'woman,' not 'female'?"

Her retort was pointed: "Fuck!"

"I can't validate people, Ellen. I try to talk in concepts or generalities for that reason. I mean, I could say something. You'd be happy or mad. But what difference would it make what I said?"

"I'm a friend," she said.

"One I cherish."

"And you won't even tell me if I'm a woman or not."

"Right. I can't validate you. If you ask, then you don't believe it, in your heart."

She looked at me hard.

"Like my being a Jew. Some people don't think so, but others do. And I do."

"So how do I know?" she asked.

"Why do you need validation at all? Cisnatal females don't ask for validation."

"Because it's assumed."

"Yes. I see that. Our selves are in question, by others. And so it's hard for us to feel secure in ourselves. Why is this coming up? You've never pestered me for it before."

"Someone on the TV last month," she said. "A bigot. He questioned it, for others."

"All I can say is that self-validation is a growth process. Everyone will handle it differently. It's hard to know yourself, especially when others don't. We all have that problem."

"Thanks," she said, with more than a little sarcasm. She nibbled at some of her frozen yogurt.

"So how do you handle dating?" she asked. Joe had been gone 3 years.

"Easy: I don't."

"None?"

I shook my head. "I'm not on the market. In the year after Joe passed, 6 men at the airport asked me out, but no way. I don't want to. Joe is my husband."

"So what did you do?" she asked. "After he passed."

I stopped working at my yogurt and stared blankly onto the ball field. I didn't want to get into the worst of it. "After several months," I finally said, "I traded in my 45-year-old station wagon airplane for a 4-year-old, 2-seat sports car airplane. I put 2 caps on the back shelf, in the cockpit: one for Joe and the other for me. In the summer of 2013, after Troi's passing, I had to get out, so I flew to Kansas and saw Mom. Then I flew to Blacksburg to see Joe."

"That was hard."

My look to her confirmed. "Then on to Colonial Williamsburg, the church and the Governor's mansion. Joe and I had done those. Then D.C., the Lincoln Memorial. We loved Lincoln."

"Big trip." Ellen sat her empty plastic Dodger cap-yogurt-cup onto the concrete beneath her seat.

"Yeah." I sat my plastic ball cap of yogurt on the concrete floor of the stadium as well, scooted it back under my seat as was the custom. "And then it occurred to me to go to Ft. Meade, my Navy haunt. I hadn't been back there since 1977."

"Oh, they'll be glad to have you back." She smiled.

"I bet they were!" I kidded. "I landed at Tipton Field, no problem, right there beside Ft. Meade. Rented a car, and they let me drive on the base, no problem."

"I doubt that."

"No, they did. They asked me at the gate where I was going, and I said to the church—which was true. And they let me on. It surprised me, but they did. I'd like to have gone to my old barracks, but as I approached the area, there was one little sign that said "NSA PERSONNEL ONLY," from there forward. I was not about to press the issue. I just enjoyed seeing my old church and the PX. I couldn't find the gym where I got my Advanced Lifesaving or used to play racquetball. But the NSA had set up a Cryptologic Museum across a street and through the trees to the north, for both the curious public and also nostalgic people like me—and—"

Ellen looked at me. "What?"

"Guess."

"How would I know?"

"The first thing I encountered when I walked in the door was a whole wall set up to display info and pictures of NSOC—my old operations center—and featuring a WV-2 electronic intelligence gathering version of a Lockheed Constellation, top center—that plane of Joe's that he had a picture of back in the Harbor House. They had many photos there of NSOC from my time and descriptions of how it was a signal intelligence response center."

"Okay," she said, not following me.

"That means at least that much of my old stuff isn't classified any more. And NSOC has been on '60 Minutes' twice, that I know of."

"But you still won't talk about it?"

"Not the mission. I'd like to confirm it's unclassified, if that's okay, beforehand.

"Well, so later I made phone calls to the Navy. Gave them my name, my old station, all of it, asking if it's still classified, but it turns out my old group doesn't exist any more, and it's fractured and changed names a few times. It's something totally different. 'Call the NSA' they said. 'They're the classifying body.' So I call Ft. Meade, ask the Navy there. Nothing, but I did get a phone number to call a Lt. Commander in the building, so I called into there—"

"The building?"

"The NSA. So I called over there and explained the whole thing to him. He took down all my info and contact info, swore someone would call me back, but—black hole. They never called me back. Nothing happened."

"You don't exist," Ellen said. "That's your problem."

"I guess not. So where to check next? I found a member of the House Permanent Select Committee on Intelligence and went over there to ask him if he could look into it for me."

"So he said, 'Okay! It's old news!'" she said.

"No! He wasn't there."

"No surprise."

"But I got an aid—that's all I got at the Senate, back in '77. So I talked to the aid, told him my old unit, and he promised to get back to me."

"Nothing?" Ellen asked.

I nodded. "Nothing. Not a word. No response at all. Even a black hole emits some radiation." I crossed my legs the other way. My hips never take very long in either position. "They don't tell me not to ask. They don't tell me it's okay to ask. Nothing. Hell— Nobody seems to care, but I don't think I'm finding anyone who even knows about it."

"So you can talk?"

"Hell no. Nothing is not permission. They said 10 years, back in '77. But I don't want to mess with them. I could keep trying to check—but where."

"So you still haven't said."

"So I still haven't said."

"Why does it matter to you?" she asked.

"You were never in the military."

"Oh, no. I was crazy with this," she indicated herself, "and the surgeon required I go to this shrink for a letter—who drove me crazy with his ignorant behavior."

"You and I," I said to her, "stealth or no, have been living through society's adjustment process to this whole thing. Hopefully people who follow will have a better time— especially if we ever learn to speak up."

"I—can't speak up." She wiped under her eyes with her middle fingers, careful not to smudge mascara.

"Come on," I said to her. "We have to do something about that."

I got up to climb the stands toward the Loge concession.

She followed dutifully.

We walked up to the concession stand on the Loge level and ordered. "Two chilidogs, please." I turned to Ellen. "It's a rite of passage, here at Dodger Stadium."

While we waited, I continued. "Sometimes, some of us, who were in the military, like to ask others, 'What did you do?' Then we talk about it."

We got our chilidogs and headed back to our seats.

"This is going to do wonders for my figure," Ellen said.

"There are no calories in Dodger Stadium, either," I told her with authority.

We reclaimed our seats. The stadium was about a quarter full so far.

"But I can't do that," I told her. "I can't say what I did. I saw two sailors in Home Depot the other day? We chatted. What do you do? Great! How cool! What, me? Where was I? Ft. Meade. What did I do? 'Stuff.' That's all I said. They smiled, and that's all. I can only say general stuff like 'Ft. Meade' and 'the NSA.' It's not pressing; but it would be nice. If it's not classified any more, then what's the problem? I just—beyond what was on that NSOC wall—I can't confirm it."

In respect for hir non-specific gender, I used non-specific gender pronouns.

Gail and I sat in booth in an Italian restaurant, not far from a movie complex. We were dining at hir request. The food was good. Our conversation was pleasant.

Gail told me about hir FFS, and ze complained about some pitting after electrolysis. Ze had never been on any female hormones, and said ze wasn't sure ze wanted any.

"I express how I feel," ze said, "and it's not the same, day to day. I'm 'Gail,' either way."

Hir manner was tender, soft, feminine, yet, dining with hir, I found usual stereotypic categorizations failed me. It was hard to think of hir as either "man" or "woman."

"So, can you give me passing tips?" ze asked. "Sometimes it's helpful."

"Yes." I thought about hir request. "I can, but let me preface by saying I'm a little reluctant. There are some problems with 'passing.'"

"Why?"

Ze seemed intelligent, thoughtful, friendly though rather closed, unused to sharing hir inner self with others.

"Well," I shared, "one of the problems is because when I've tried to answer that call in the past, people usually get mad at me."

Ze looked at me questioningly.

"Because," I said, "it depends on what someone wants to hear, and, in this case, I don't know you very well. Yet." I smiled. "Hope to. If it's another, highly stealth, deeply integrated person I'm talking with, and she is worried about being read, a passing idea may be seen as a god-send, but more often, ideas shared are taken as an insult, because an idea for passing is also a comment about not passing."

Gail looked at me, clearly thinking about what I was saying. "Even if she's asking for you to say?"

I nodded. "Because a request for ideas to help someone pass is, more often than not, really a request for validation of what she's already doing."

Gail seemed like a thoughtful person. I could see hir mulling my words over.

"What's the other problem?"

I was impressed with hir willingness to listen, so I shared. "I'm not a big fan of passing, regardless."

"But you pass," ze said. "You look very—natural."

I furled my brow at that. I think ze could see I was sharing my inner feelings with hir. "I'm—pleased, truly, when I'm taken as cisnatal-ish, on the one hand, but I'm not pleased to 'pass' on the other hand, because it means that I'm pretending to be something I'm not. I'm just *passing* as one."

"What do you do to try to pass?" ze asked.

"I don't *try* to pass. I'm just me. I mean, I used to not do as well, but I had FFS in 2005, there's ongoing adjustment in role, as it were, and part of it— I'm just being myself. What you see, you see. Actually, as far as 'passing' goes, I make mistakes every day. Did you see the way I teased the server when she brought our food?"

Gail nodded.

"I joked, she got a laugh out of me, I enjoyed talking with her, but I was expressing too much energy if 'passing' were my goal. Don't make light of this," I cautioned hir. "This is key. It's important. My manner was too—strong—if you will. A little less energy is better for passing, for males-to-female. A little of the reverse helps females-to-male."

Hir eyes turned inward, it seemed to me, letting my words reflect off hir inner self.

"How?" ze finally asked.

I tried to think how to share. "I think the inner feeling-intent-energy someone has is one thing, but the *frame* a person has in body can serve to increase or decrease the way inner intent is expressed and received. Cisnatals don't experience that difference in themselves, so much. It's us in the trans world who do, because of our changes."

Ze pondered my thoughts.

"So," I continued. "I have a largely male-shaped frame. Bone structure. If I were trying to pass, I would lower my inner energy, because my frame will exaggerate my intent. A higher *expressed* energy level not only appears a little more masculine but draws attention, and attention invites scrutiny. Stealth maxim: Don't be in the spotlight, because people will find tells. I'd want to appear pleasant, with no issues or concerns, such that someone leaving an encounter with me wouldn't give me a thought. Some people call that 'secret agent stuff.' For me, it's called hiding, or making myself small."

"I see."

"I don't think you have an energy problem as much as I do, but you do some. You're softer than I am, smaller boned, more delicate—and you're only in transition a little." I smiled at hir again. "Some people have all the luck."

I discussed a few other points, in specific, that I thought might answer hir questions, and I was pleased that ze took them well.

"Maybe that'll help," ze said.

"By this point, most people think stealth are crazy with minutia, and the detail goes way beyond that. It's most important to be yourself, instead, I think."

Ze sat back and played with hir salad, not eating any of it.

"Whatever you do, don't be like me," I said with a smile. "Don't let others set your limits. If you struggle to be what someone else wants, you may wake up years later and fret the years you've wasted living someone else's life."

Ze shared to me with hir eyes, without speaking.

"Gail, you told me you've been involved with dressing for most of your life. Are you transitioning? Slowly?"

Ze looked at the table. "I— Uh."

I could see it was hard for hir to bring classical ideas together, because they didn't fit hir.

"Are you transgender?" I asked hir.

Ze looked thoughtful. "I don't think so."

"Are you slowly *becoming* transgender? Over decades?"

"I—don't think so. I'm just—me. I don't think I want to transition, really. Not all the time. I—" Ze seemed to think some more. "I go out as who I feel myself to be, which depends, but I don't fit."

I knew some people would say ze is "confused" or "unstable," as if hir changing gender expression indicated mental or emotional lack of direction, or that ze did not know hirself. But, on the contrary, I believed ze was extremely well in touch with hirself, didn't feel the need to fit a mold, and that ze had the courage to self-express. I admired hir.

"Some people feel they're 'neutrois,'" I said. "Maybe neutral."

"I don't know. I'm not always there."

"How do you feel right now?" I asked.

Ze shrugged. "I think I'm 'fluid.'"

"Gender fluid." I smiled at hir, to comfort. "Do you feel part of the trans community at large?"

She nodded. "I guess."

"Sometimes, people feel community, but they don't know how to fit in. So sometimes I say 'trans*natal*'—"

"I don't know that one."

"—an antonym for 'cisnatal'—"

"I *do* know that one."

"Yeah, a lot of trans use that for 'same as birth.' Sometimes I use transnatal when just trying to say 'different from birth,' without specifying anything in particular."

"I will admit that I've been changing, overall, in the last ten years or so, being myself."

I smiled at hir.

"What do you think?" ze asked. "Which way do you think I should go?"

"It's not what I think; it's what you feel."

Ze looked uncertain.

"If you were born intersex, with aspects of both, would you change that?"

She shrugged again. "It depends."

"Yet," I mentioned, "you've modified from cisnatal male, had some FFS, had electrolysis, grown your hair."

"I seem to be different from everyone," ze said.

"Like Janet Mock says, 'Normal is so basic.' Everyone's different. I think we should value our differences."

Ze went quiet, looked at the table. Tears began to form in hir eyes.

Looking at hir sit across from me, I got the impression that even though ze had the courage to be hirself, it nonetheless hurt—that ze had suffered abuse from someone, or several someones, in hir life about hir gender expression.

Most of us had known it—derisions, diminishings, denunciations, degradations, derogations—demeaning us into the burden of living with the belief that we were wrong, bad, unworthy as human beings, or harmful to others by our presence.

The belief that other people cannot make you feel badly about yourself, only you can, was simply not true. We can overcome a lot of it, especially with help, and we can struggle to overcome even more. Hopefully we will, in each case. But everything is interconnected. We influence others, and others influence us. It's unavoidable. And when we are degraded over and over again for years, when we learn it from family, media, work, neighbors—in things said or done overtly, or things people *don't* say or do—without relief from a strong social support network, the weight can be crushing. When the harmful message is internalized, when the person comes to believe, in herself, that she truly is wrong, no good, the results can be devastating.

Many of us pay for such cruelty with our lives.

I took hir hands in mine, and said from my heart, "You're so beautiful, Gail."

PART 5

UNLEARN I'M NOT OKAY

"History, despite its wrenching pain, cannot be unlived, but if faced with courage, need not be lived again."

"It is time for parents to teach young people early on that in diversity, there is beauty and there is strength."

Maya Angelou

20

Ashamed

MY JOINTS had been a problem forever, and I never did much about it, but one doc thought I had Marfan—which could be serious.

A specialist ran me through several tests—looked at me, bent me, measured me, tested me. I told him my sexual history, age at transition, per skeletal structure, and he evaluated me with that in mind. Most of the joints in my body would come out of socket. My knees would bend backward so far I looked like an alien from outer space. I took a knee and hip out of socket for him, several fingers, laid my ankles on the floor while I was standing, touched the floor flat-handed with legs straight, held my own hands behind my shoulder blades...

"Your knees ever lock backward?"

"Hurts like hell, yes."

"Your feet ever cave?" he asked. "Buckle under?"

"My left one."

"Then you fall?"

I nodded.

"Your arms— If Michael Phelps, the Olympic Gold Medalist swimmer, has 80 inches of arm reach, and if he's only 76 inches tall, as reported in Scientific American, then he has a 1.05:1 reach:height ratio. Yours is 1.06:1. Do you swim?"

"Like a fish."

In the end we looked at his computer together.

Instead of Marfan, the doc determined I was Ehlers-Danlos Syndrome, Hypermobility—EDS or EDSH, a genetic connective tissue disorder. It was not the worst version of EDS by far, but it was the reason my joints subluxed, hurt.

Why didn't most people see it? I learned long ago that some clothes tended to hide it, where others seemed to show it, or even accent it. I choose to wear the ones that don't show it so much, but it is hard to find blouses.

Walking was important for my overall health, yet it became more difficult. Two foot surgeries fixed some problems but subtly changed the relative lengths of some of bones in my feet. Together with my EDS, normal walking, after a while, tended to inflame the soft tissues ahead of both 2nd metatarsals, the longest bone in the foot. If I let that happen, I'd feel a stab of pain at every step that could take weeks to resolve.

Another doc said I could fix it with another round of surgeries, but I was so sick of them, I changed the way I walked, instead. A budding experimentalist, under Joe's tutelage, I found if I wore pads in my shoes of a certain kind, and if I yawed the foot slightly inside or outside of my stride, I could lessen the pressure at the head of the 2nd metatarsals and reduce the likelihood of a problem.

It sometimes caused a limp on either foot, depending, and sometimes it helped to use a cane to lighten the load, but it had nothing to do with driving or flying. It was a walking thing.

I scooted on a creeper, on my back, squirting Simple Green up to the bottom of the airplane, wiping off aerated oil from months prior, tossing used paper towels to the side, repeat. My hands and shirt were both smudged. I learned later I had a smudge across my right cheek where I'd scratched—airport bum stuff.

I hadn't put on any makeup that morning, and my hair was a wreck, gathered together in a butterfly clip so the creeper wheels wouldn't run over it and pull.

I made my way aft from the nose, between the main gear, feet first, and was heading down the fuselage, a bit at a time, tearing off another paper towel—

"Hi," a man said, stepping into my open hangar door.

I craned my neck to look. I could see him squatting, looking at me beneath the left wing of the plane.

I didn't know him, but he had that happy/hopeful look, and my heart sank for him.

"Hello?" I answered.

If it had been my home he'd walked in to, I'd have been immediately terrified, but at the airport, it was common for people to step in and say hi. We were in a secure area, behind keyed gates with cameras...

"I'm Kevin," he said. "I've seen you here for about six months."

I'd been there for most of 25 years, so he was referring to his time here. I rolled my creeper to the side of the plane he was on, got off it, and stood up, careful not to tweak either knee.

He stood up with me.

"One of the guys said he thought I should maybe say hi."

"Shit," I said.

Kevin smiled at me with half a chuckle. "I heard you were a little blunt."

Oh no. What am I going to do?

Immediately my mind whirled through scenarios. My main focus was on how I could protect this guy from heartache. For the next two seconds, my stealth mind whirled:

Does he know about me? Yet?

What is he looking for?

A girlfriend, I think. Or sex?

Bobby would say to give him a try! He's nice enough.

No! It'll only lead to his heartache—and when he learns about me, he'll feel bad and then tell people, and then it'll be another rumor about me— That's what I need, more people talking about me. And this guy will have to live with the fact that he'd been interested in a transsexual—

Or is that why he's interested? Does he want *a transsexual?*

Jesus, I don't want to be loved for that!

Or does he not know?

Or does he not care, like Joe?

Why can't I be normal sometime? Anytime?

Because I'm not!

I don't want to be known as trans!

Half the people at the airport probably already know. I know there's been gossip.

But—

My mind couldn't resolve it. I looked at him more closely.

Don't lie to him.

A little disgusted, I took my towels and Simple Green to a shop table.

"I'm sorry for that," I told him. "I think there are two or three guys here who want to match me up, and I don't know what to do with it."

Am I supposed to date normally? As I would, regardless? And let him deal with his own emotions when I'm revealed? Or should I evade for his sake?

"But like I've told 'em," I said, "I'm not on the market. I'm married. I'm not a curiosity," I threw that in in case he knows, and if he doesn't, it'll just seem like I don't want attention, "and I don't do windows," meaning sex.

Kevin didn't seem deterred.

Neither had Joe.

I faced him. "I'm just a crusty old biddy, raised by wolves here at the airport. I'm not fit for civilized society, any more."

"I heard about you and Joe," he said. "I'm sorry he's gone."

He had to say, "he's gone."

"In '12," I said.

"And I don't want to press you," he said, "but honestly, I'm not interested in some frilly girl who—some gals are into their own thinking, and I can't connect with them."

So he wants me for non-feminine thinking?

Then he doesn't know me. At least partly.

"They want to have bake sales, not fly," he said, "and that's what I like to do."

"You're talking about dating, and I don't even know your last name."

He told me.

"You an axe murderer?" I asked.

He smiled at me again.

What is it with all the smiling?

He told me where he'd been flying, before, "but I'm moving out here."

If he dates me, he won't be able to hold his head up in Camarillo—

What kind of low person am I that I should think that about myself?

It's a practical reality he'd have to live with, whether I like myself or not, I told myself. *He doesn't know it, but I do, and I could protect him.*

Shit, Jenna! There you go again?

"Kevin." I forced a brief smile for him. "I'm sorry. 'Whoever' should have told you better. I'm not on the market."

I argued with Bobby on the ramp in front of his hangar—isolated, just the two of us.

"Jenna, you need to be with someone," he said. "It's not healthy to be alone!" Bobby was a great old guy at the airport, everybody's grandpa.

"I love you, but *stop trying to match me up!*"

"What?"

"You didn't send that guy over?"

"What guy? Someone came over?" Bobby seemed pleased.

"Bobby, I don't want anyone. Any more. I told you that."

"Joe?"

"Joe was great, and I want him back, but I can't do that with anyone else, regardless. He was special."

"Yes, you can—"

"Damnit, Bobby!" I said, losing my cool, melting down. "You have no fucking idea!"

"No idea about what? You're smart and funny—"

He doesn't know what I'm talking about because I haven't told him? Really?

I've been thinking about how I shame myself by covering. Maybe I shouldn't? Who better to test with than Bobby?

Goddamnit, Jenna! Don't piss in your own pond!

How could I be considered piss? Goddamn yourself right back!

But if you confirm rumors, some people will never let go of it.

But if I don't learn to be myself, I can't live!

"Bobby, It doesn't work that way!" I pressed back at him. "I can't be all happy and get into some relationship with some guy without all kinds of shit happening."

"Why?"

"Because some people don't like it!"

"People like who?"

"I don't know! It could be anyone!"

"What are you talking about?"

"Bobby, if I tell you, will you keep it a secret?"

"What?"

"Will you?"

"Okay," he said.

He was a great guy, but I didn't believe that meant trustworthiness at keeping secrets. Usually with people it went to the next person in line, "I'll tell you, but you need to keep it a secret…" However, if it got around, I *would* have something to complain about with him if he broke his word.

It's probably already fucking around!

Not that I confirmed it!

My stress level, respiration, blood pressure went up.

"Bobby, I'm an old stealth transsexual from way back."

His eyebrows went up.

"You—"

"Don't go into it, damnit, Bobby!" I became animated, walked around in a little circle, my arms drawing pictures in the air in front of us. Years of shit poured out of me. I rapid-fired to him, "It doesn't fucking work like that! I can't get into dating someone without other people minding! Then shit happens—"

"They don't matter! Be happy—"

"*It does matter*!" I started to cry and talked to him through an increasingly hoarse voice. "You think it's like, 'Oh, we're fuckin' lovey-dovey and it's just gossip? Who cares?' Everybody can be light-hearted because you are? I've had shit happen, Bobby! I've been hurt—my own *personal fucking body*," I screamed at him, "and I don't want that any more! No more of that shit, *goddamnit!*" I yelled.

Bobby held back and considered my venting.

"You were raped?"

"NO!" I screamed at him. *"Fuck!"* My mind was a shambles. I tried to fix mistakes I'd just made, and I also tried to bring it back a little. I wiped my face on my sleeve. "You know what happens if someone like me dates someone like Joe? He's happy, if he's into me. Joe was. You'd be happy, 'cause I finally got someone. A few others, maybe. But other people try to get rid of me!"

He started to complain to me—I know to say it doesn't matter, or that people aren't prejudiced around there—so I cut him off.

"Nobody says, 'I don't like Jenna because she's trans'—or if I were black! Use another minority and see how it sounds. Nobody says, 'I don't like her because she's black,' or 'I don't want to hear about that black shit.' It's always, 'I don't like her because of something *else* she said or did!' You know what they do? They dump shit on me! Behind the scenes! Where people don't know about it! They dump it all over me, sometimes him, and it not only hurts, it's scary! You don't know what or when or how or where—

"Only I'm not black. I'm transsexual—so even if they would never think of doing some shit to a black person, they feel right in dumping on me, because I'm a freak *by choice*!"

I was beginning to have trouble catching my breath.

Bobby was at a loss for words, having me rant to him as I did about something he had not suspected. Finally he regrouped. "Jenna, at some point, you've got to begin living life, again."

"I can't take it any more, Bobby! You hear me? I can't take any more of that shit."

I composed an email to the Board of my local chapter of the 99s: Please remove me from your role.

But why, they wanted to know. Did someone do something?

Is that concern or a request for gossip?

I don't know any more!

I don't want to go into it!

The chapter was good, but images flashed through my mind of a couple of the ladies, looking at me in years past. It alarmed me, but I didn't know why.

With my experience, an alarm means something! I should listen to myself.

But maybe I'm overly sensitive because of years of hell elsewhere!

It's a stealth identity crisis!

I couldn't figure it out. What I did know was my mind cringed at the thought of seeing them any more. I just wanted distance. I didn't want to go to the meetings—

Why?

I could imagine my worst nightmare, *"Jenna, are you trans*gender?*"*

"NO!" I could honestly say that much. *But if not, then what?*

It was fear, I knew. I was afraid to stand up for myself, for who I really was, in my own heart, afraid someone at some time would mention something, and I'd have to deal with it, affirm or deny, clarify, explain— It'd be a big argument, and I'd be humiliated. I'd have to give up my hangar, move away—

I have to get out before anyone brings it up.

And there was no way to deny who I was—if someone hit the nail on the head. Lying wasn't my style. Then I'd have my confirmation on top of those two—

They were reluctant to remove me from the roles, wanted to keep me.

I insisted.

I went back and forth with a couple of them a few times until finally, sadly, it worked.

Will I still be a 99, internationally? They wanted to know.

I assured them I would. And I am. I cherish my 20-year certificate on my wall, and my national membership is maintained.

I regretted my decision to leave the local chapter, ever since I did it. They're good folks. They don't understand, because I've withheld. I probably created some gossip, that I'd love to avoid. In short, I probably sabotaged myself yet again, knowing the whole time it was because I had been so hurt by my years of criticism—and by a feeling in some people that if I was one of "those," I was "less."

2016

I sat in the living room and watched the 88th Academy Awards on TV, "The Oscars." In "The Danish Girl," Lili Elbe, an early transsexual, played by Eddie Redmayne, had died from complications secondary to an early version of SRS. Yet the Oscars said, twice, she'd had "Gender Confirmation Surgery."

My heart sank. As far as I could see, "Sex Reassignment Surgery" was not used. The Academy, like most areas of media, had adopted transgender terms that were purposefully vague.

I stared at the TV, stunned. I had respected the Academy for so long.

I felt so low.

Watching the Oscars I felt stepped-on by both the transgender paradigm and the Academy, hurt, marginalized—made even smaller with their lack of recognition for our need as human beings.

Lili gave her life for something we can't even say, anymore. I am something I'm not supposed to be any more.

Acceptance had been a problem, so sometimes I would break out and go to San Francisco during Pride week, just to feel some humanity, finding the entire city welcoming human beings with open arms. The feeling there was so fresh! Talking with people—anywhere—sitting at table with others while we would eat, seeing how others were respectful and integrating with trans people of all kinds, noticing how people didn't try to get out of having to actually talk with us. It recharged my batteries.

I sat this year in Dolores Park before the annual Dyke March, considering the idea of riding my Harley in their parade. People of all kinds gathered, whether straight, locals, visitors, cisnatal, transnatal—anything—and I watched how they accepted each other. It was spring. The sky was blue. The grass was green. The air was cool. The people were warm. It felt to me what the 1960s had wanted, caring for each other, not having to mold yourself to any oppressive establishment. Music played on a stage, booming to the entire area—and after a set, an announcer spoke into a microphone, welcomed everyone to the lesbian event, or almost everyone: "Welcome to Dolores Park!" The crowd cheered. "And *welcome all lesbians*," more cheering, "whether you're transgender lesbian, or a-gender lesbian, or gender queer lesbian, or gender fluid lesbian…"

Ah!

I lowered my head. My heart felt impacted, again, with a weight that slammed into my chest. My vision of them as accepting was blown. I was left out, again. They clearly didn't mean to include everyone as they identified; they were pushing a transgender political agenda.

"What's the matter?" a transgender woman said near me.

Should I tell her? They don't like to hear it.

"Nothing."

"Something," she said back to me.

"They left me out, again."

"I thought she covered everybody." I could see the question on her face.

I shook my head. "I'm not lesbian. I don't mean that. She mentioned seemingly every trans variation except transsexualism."

She seemed to consider for a moment. "'Transsexual' is a slur. That puts people down."

I got up to leave. My glare to her was not meant to convey contentment. "How dare you! My phenomenon is not a slur. I am not a slur."

"Everybody's transgender!" she shouted at me.

Walking out of the park, I called Ellen on the phone. "What the fuck, Ellen!"

"I know," she said.

"We get it from everybody!" I said. "Muggles, transgenders—one way or another, we have to be what they want, or they put us down! 'Oh, political correctness'—*bullshit!* That's a device to leverage a certain point of view!"

She did what she could. "You know why they do it."

"Oh, hell yeah. I know why. They'll admit it to each other, but not to anybody else—"

"Not true," Ellen said. "Sometimes they won't even admit it to themselves."

I considered, stopped storming so much. "True. I know. But the shit's gotta stop."

I saw my Harley kitty-corner across the intersection, parked by the curb. I left the park and walked that way.

"Ask people to publicly admit they've been hiding something?" she asked.

"Worse: Ask them to admit *what* they're hiding, let alone a history of it."

I dug in my pocket and pulled out my keys, opened the boot of the Harley. It made little clicks. All my stuff was in there, helmet, gloves, riding jacket, ear plugs, an Aerosmith bandana from a concert…

"Where are you?" Ellen asked.

I looked around. "Uh, on Dolores, above 18th, I think. They've got it blocked off for the bikes, for the Dyke March, later."

People crossed the street at will, talking and laughing. It was meant to be a festive day.

"At a lesbian biker rally?"

I nodded, then realized she couldn't see that on the phone. "Yeah."

"Sounds fun."

I shook my head in disgust. "Not any more."

21

Admitting What We Are

"IT'S A MESS out there," I said to patrons inside. I ran fingers through my windblown hair for an approximate shape, tucked part of it behind my ears.

The door to the T bar started to close behind me when two other patrons opened it to enter, followed by a third. Incoming wind blew hair and dresses until the door closed behind them. It was 10:35 pm, and the place was starting to fill.

Lady Gaga's energizing "Love Game" beat solidly through dim, soft-colored, dancing lights and slinky evening gowns into the hearts of worthy people in self-expression. Patrons milled about engaging each other in easy conversation as if old family on the first day of reunion. Some played pool in the next room. Exotic dancers, wearing almost nothing, made love to six-foot poles and greeted people who enjoyed. The dance floor was one of the most colorful places on Earth.

A regular turned from the bar to stop my progress. Elise was a good five inches taller than I, half again as wide, and she knew it.

I went on alert, watched her closely for sign.

"Remember what I said last time," she told me with more than a little steel. "You're *transgender* in here."

Usually, in the past, when someone did that to me, I'd simply leave. It was a stealth reaction. If I was attacked, I couldn't report the reason why, and in the social media age, they might post about me on the Internet. But my fear was getting old.

"Lise, I've taken that off you all since about '04, and I'm getting tired of it. I'm *not* transgender. Don't try to intimidate me—"

She leaned down, close enough for me to smell her breath.

I recoiled, reflexively.

"Don't come in here and cause trouble!" she said.

I didn't know what to do. I scanned. The bouncer hadn't seen her—

"Jenna!" Someone called to me from the side. I recognized her from the AIDS walk and moved over to her, gladly.

I put on the best smile I could. "Tanya! Hola. How's the job?"

"Sucks."

"Did you switch?"

"No, I kept it."

"I mean *you*."

"Sort of!" She said with flair, left with someone for the poolroom.

Lise glared at me from behind.

Being in a T bar was supposedly about being yourself, whether your*self* was cross dressing in whole or in part, queer, genderqueer, non-conforming, neutrois, fluid, transgender, transsexual, atypical, something else, or just *being* without identity or label. Nevertheless, I knew a lot of people who entered were nervous, underneath, fearing any hint of negativity, any crack someone may make. All of us, or someone we knew, had suffered similar forms of oppression at some time in our life—gossip, ridicule, assault, rape, and murder—the pain of which could remain for a lifetime.

I saw someone by a table, talking. "Jan! Marhaba."

"Jenna!" she said, giving me a little hug.

"What the hell's she saying?" the other lady asked Jan.

"Arab greeting. I'm from Iraq—years ago. Before."

"They have a lot of transsexuals there," the lady said, "like, second in the world behind Thailand."

"That's *Iran*, dumbass," Jan said. "Not Iraq. God, I wish people would get it straight—*one lousy letter's different*, but they are so very *not the same*," Jan said. "And a lot are coerced. Don't want you to be gay—they may kill you—so they pressure you to do that against your will."

"Where so," I said, "that's not transsexualism; that's a gay man whose been forcibly mutilated on pain of death. Can't judge a book by its cover."

"If you ask me," Jan said, "it's punishment, a deterrent."

"Who is this?" the other lady asked Jan, then to me. "You alone? You're here with someone?"

"Huh?" I wondered what she meant. "No—"

"Then why are you here?" she asked.

I was puzzled for a second. "Oh." I remembered I look something like June Cleaver in there, some middle-aged housewife who took a wrong turn, thought it was Macy's. I wasn't June, but the lighting was dim— I glanced into the mirror over the bar. It was true. "No. Sorry. I'm—an old stealth transsexual from way back."

I hate saying that.

"You?" she asked.

I nodded.

"So, still what are you doing in here?" she asked.

Is she going to get mad at me, too?

"I— Sometimes I come in here for a little humanity."

Try to.

"Karen lost another girlfriend," Jan said.

"I'm sorry," I said. "Loneliness is a major problem for us."

"It's hatred," Jan said, "They even kill us."

We all knew what she meant. Another transgender woman, Mia, had been murdered—this time by a date who discovered her penis in a romantic encounter.

"We need to work it out together," I said. "One way or another, we're all family. We fight sometimes—"

"Bullshit," Jan said. "If we were family, we'd *reject* each other!"

I frowned. "Family aren't people who don't fight; family are people who don't *leave.*

"Right!" Karen said. She and Jan each took a swig from their beer.

"So where've you been, Jenna?" Jan asked. "Haven't seen you since we went to 'Star Wars.'"

I glanced at Lise. She had moved to a table with three others. I started to relax a little. "Helping Han recover."

"He'd dead!" Jan said. "I told you—"

I enjoyed our previous banter on this. "Dark Hamstring ran him through, he fell off the high walk, then the whole station blew up—but that doesn't mean he's dead."

"Oh, Christ!" Jan said.

Someone laughed.

"Hamster didn't slice around!" I said. "It was a small diameter hole—cauterized—and there was *no corpse*! In Hollywood, that's air conditioning at best. Ask Kirk and Spock—"

"Han could be a sleeper Jedi who could save himself," Karen said, "because he shot one trooper earlier without even looking at him! Remember? Off his right side."

"There you go," I said to Jan, as if the cosmos had confirmed. "Sage wisdom—talks like Buddha."

"You want to sit?" I asked both of them.

Karen winked at me. "Gotta go." She moved through the crowd toward the dance floor.

"It's just us," Jan said.

I led her to a couple of empty seats on the corner of the bar. Along the way I saw a lady I'd enjoyed talking with last time, and said hi. She gave me a rude look and turned away.

What happened?

I was beginning to see the pattern.

Jan sat on the long side of the bar.

I took the short side, facing everyone lengthways and noticed another lady on the other side of Jan, sitting with a beer—35-ish, calm, quiet, with dark brown, permed hair settling about her shoulders, black, sleeveless dress to the knee, matching pumps—over warm, almond skin tones. She wore a gold cross on a fine necklace around her neck, and a gold bracelet on her wrist. The effect was sophisticated.

I didn't recognize her, but I knew that didn't mean anything. I didn't go to the club all that often.

"Nice," I said to her.

Her smile to me was genuine but brief. She glanced at Jan, and returned to her beer.

The bartender came to get orders from Jan and me, seemed to remember me and mouthed something that looked like "The same?"

I nodded.

She left to go get them.

With a slightly wary look to Jan, I said, "You've lost weight."

"I had to get into this dress." It was a straight, blue-as-night minidress in sparkles, reflected the dancing lights. "Don't you like it?"

"I—" I looked at it some more. "I think I'm pissed at both of you."

"What did I do?" the other lady said.

"Nothing," Jan said. "She thinks she has no figure, and we do."

"Wear what you want," the other said. "You look fine."

I shook my head. That would set me up for embarrassment.

"You could wear this," Jan said to me.

I knew that—yes, I could, physically, wear it, but I couldn't carry it well. I tried to make a joke of it. "I'd be happy if I looked as good as Phyllis Diller."

"And you do!" Jan said.

I turned to the other lady. "I'm Jenna. You?"

"Holly."

"Holly?" I looked for a mnemonic. "Okay. Like the Christmas wreath. May I ask, what's your cultural heritage?"

"India, half—"

"Oh." I smiled, brought my palms together with a slight bow. "Namaste."

She smiled at me. "But I was born in Texas."

"Well, then, 'How do, Ma'am,'" I said with a fairly authentic country drawl.

"You from Texas?" Holly asked.

"I been there, so I'm from there. I'm mostly from south of Dodge City, Kansas." Nobody knew where Minneola was.

Holly tipped her beer to me.

"I'm Jan, the friendliest person here, except for me," Jan said to Holly. "You're new?"

"Here."

"You've obviously been around for a while, somewhere," Jan said to her.

Holly nodded.

"Here you go," the bartender said. She gave a beer to Jan, and a bottle of water to me, with the cap still on.

I paid her for both.

"You look hot," Jan said to Holly, maybe coming on to her a little. "You full time?"

"I just cross dress sometimes."

"More than sometimes," Jan said.

Holly's return smirk seemed as it were meant to be sarcastic, but I thought I read a touch of insecurity behind it.

"Your family doesn't know you're CD?" I asked.

"Better not," Holly said. "What are you down about?"

I thought I'd masked that.

"I—worry about trying to be who I am."

Holly nodded slightly.

Jan was aghast. "You transitioned 35 years ago! I'm only in 10, and I'm more comfortable than you."

"I don't want to fight about it again—"

"You on hormones?" Jan asked Holly, surveying her figure. I knew what she was wondering.

"Hell no!" Holly said. "It works fine, if that's what you want to know. Better than yours, I bet."

"It still works, sweetie—" Jan looked a little ruffled.

"Chill, Jan. She didn't mean any harm."

"You look a little down, too," I said to Holly.

"My wife left me. You know why." Holly flipped the neckline of her dress. "That's 0 for 2."

"I'm so sorry."

Jan put her hand on Holly's. "How long ago?"

Holly took her hand back. "Last month, but fuck it. Nothing I can do about it."

"So you're into women?" Jan asked her with a smile. "I'm a woman."

Holly took a sip of her beer, with a slight shake of her head.

Jan bristled. "That is just a little extra tissue!"

"So you're not bragging?" Holly asked.

Jan let that pass. I wasn't sure if Jan was trying to lay Holly or piss her off. Maybe both. "Don't you get hot when you dress?" Jan asked.

"Not for you," Holly said.

Jan looked hurt. "I can take you as well as any woman! You'll get off—"

Holly ignored Jan and turned to me. "You had it done?"

I knew she meant SRS. Her directness was refreshing, though a surprise. "Um, yes, back in nineteen—"

"Why would you do that? I never understood that." Holly wrinkled her nose like it smelled bad.

"My—*need*—was always to be female—" I said.

"Jesus," Holly said. "If you whack it off, it's gone."

"Whacking it off is different from whacking off," Jan said. "Those goddamn researchers—"

Jan seemed to love caustic banter.

"Don't dump on 'em," I said.

"You like them!" Jan said.

I saw Lise in the distance, move to the other side of the bar. She spoke lightly with a group sitting at a table and watched me.

I gave Jan a matter-of-fact smile that said we'd had that argument before. "I've never met them."

"They hit us with *autogynephilia!*" Jan said.

"Auto what?" Holly asked.

"Getting aroused at seeing yourself female." Jan leaned into Holly. "You fantasize you have a pussy?"

Holly looked miffed. "I don't want to actually *be* female!"

"Fuck Alice Dreger!" Jan said, loudly enough for others nearby to hear.

She got a few laughs.

"Jan, Alice doesn't deserve that." I explained to Holly: "Jan read *Galileo's Middle Finger*—at least part of it—and has been over-reacting—"

"What's that?" Holly asked.

"I think that's where Galileo is saying 'Fuck you if you dump on science.'"

Jan turned on me. *"Did you see what she said about us?"*

"Did you *understand* what she was *talking about*? Or are you just gonna blow your stack every time someone doesn't support what you *want* to be true—"

"She hit us—thinks we're *auto*—and she supported Bailey and his insulting *Queen* book! We have to protect ourselves!"

I was incredulous. "You mean, you're mean to them, and you'll also be mean to anyone else who isn't mean to them."

"She deserves it! She said Bailey was right!"

"Partly. She also wondered if he was 'tone-dumb'! But that was not the point—"

"You agree with them!" Jan was alarmed.

"Actually, there are several places where I don't. It's as if a body of 'knowledge' was built on distant premises, and several researchers over time—"

"Dreger lover!"

"You say that like a racial slur!"

"Is it true?" Jan asked.

"What I'm *not* doing is dumping shit all over them and calling them names. Is that what you want? You gonna make legendary haters out of 'em? Forever? Like that's what they live for? Create fiction about 'em? Make an example of 'em? Who cares they're people who *aren't trying to hurt you*?"

Jan drummed her fingers on the bar. "Just getting started."

"Alice was saying hostile intimidation disrupts science. She doesn't hate LGBT—"

"She made us look like fools!"

"We make *ourselves* look like fools," I said.

Holly jumped in. "What are you talking about?"

Jan held up her hands as if to stop a bull. *"Don't ask her shit like that!"*

"Are you autogynephil—" Holly stumbled.

Jan sat back in her seat, in a huff.

I finished the word for Holly. "Autogynephilic?"

"Yeah," Holly said.

"No." I shook my head. "I am not aroused at the thought of being female. I'm aroused by men; my *response* is female. But deep in myself, I just need to *be*, to my core—"

Jan screamed at me. *"Damnit, Jenna! Now they'll say you switched so you could get laid!"*

"They might. But I didn't—"

"So you changed gender—"

"Whoa, no," I stopped Holly. "My focus was on changing *sex*. That was my salient issue. Sex and gender are two different things." I rolled my finger to play my own tape along, because Jan had heard it before from me. "Physical sex goes to reproduction of the species, *male* or *female*. Gender is a social construct, attributes of a sex, masculinity or femininity, *man* or *woman*. I can show you what I mean—"

"All the same thing," Jan said.

"That's the transgender view," I said.

"So?" Holly asked.

"So," I said, "if you want to change gender, what do you do? Change your name, clothes, take hormones, feminize, get softer skin, grow breasts, let your hair grow, remove whiskers, manage your behavior to some extent— That's transgenderism. But if you want to change sex, you—"

"You're doing it again!" Jan said.

"I don't look at all this like you all do," I said to her. *"Why isn't that allowed?"*

"That crap from you hurts us," Jan said.

"Your own insecurity hurts you. How—" I thought. "How can a Jew and a Christian be friends? Very different views, even the opposite. What if a Christian thinks the Jew is going to hell because he won't accept Jesus Christ as his Lord and Savior? And what if the Jew thinks the Christian is gullible, worshipping a human being? Opposite views—but they can get along with common decency. Having a friend who's Christian doesn't mean you agree—"

"*You* tell *us* what to say!" Jan argued.

"I—" I saw what she meant.

"See?" Jan asked Holly.

"It's just—example—if Jews say Christianity is a form of Judaism, I have to stand up enough to say no I'm not, and when you insist, I point out why. I want you all to stop saying I'm Jewish, is all. That's not telling you what to say—"

"That's arguing!" Jan said.

"If I don't speak up at least that much, suddenly I'm billed as something I'm not—"

Holly piped in to ask me a question. "You a Christian?"

"No. I'm Jewish. I was hoping she could see herself, because she is Christian. Or was, or said she was—"

"Bad metaphor," Holly said.

"That shit puts us down," Jan said.

"That's what you've been saying, behind my back? Slanting what I'm saying?"

"Sex and gender are all rolled together!" she hissed at me.

"No way. Nuh-uh." I shook my head. "They're both present in all people, but so are a lot of other things."

"Gender is in the head, and sex is in the body," Jan said.

"Jan— We don't have to do this."

But is it so bad?

What would happen if I stood for myself?

"Okay," I said. "That, also, is a transgender view. The paradigm says that, but it's misleading," I said. "*Identity* is in the head, of whatever sort, and *expression* is in the body. There are different kinds of identity, and different kinds of expression—"

"You mean, like—" Holly pointed her finger back and forth, between Jan and me.

"Bitch!" Jan said.

I clarified. "In the head, a person can have a gender identity *but also a sex identity*—the transgender view keeps leaving that out—and she can express in her body as a masculine or feminine *gender*, to be a man or woman, but also as a male or female *sex*, at least anatomically. It's not the same in different people. A transgender example: a gender identity of 'woman,' a gender expression as 'woman'—yet *also* have a *sex identity* of male which can be expressed with male genitalia—"

Jan looked squeamish. "Do you have to *say* that?"

"Big news. It's the truth: A penis is a male sex organ."

"You're being offensive," Jan said.

"You were proud of it 10 minutes ago." I said.

"Not when you say it!"

"What's wrong with it?" I asked. "It's a perfectly valid life. And there's been so much pressure on me since '04-ish, to avoid saying what I am, I haven't had the chance—" I changed thoughts. "Shit. My blood pressure's been up since then, too, and my acid reflux, but there were other pressures—"

"You come in here saying this caustic shit!" Jan charged me. "We're trying to just live a little, and you— You don't accept us as women!"

"I didn't say that."

"You're *transgender*!" Jan said. "You've gotta accept that!"

I glared at Jan and said through my teeth. *"Please don't call me that."*

"We've all decided!" Jan said.

"If the larger voice is what matters," I pointed to both of us, "neither of us would exist."

"Don't discriminate!"

"You know, it's bad for me in here," I tapped my heart, "if I feel I can't be myself. Isn't that what you tell the world? For yourself? But it doesn't apply to me?"

Jan sat closer to me. "Don't fuck with me," she said. "I'll get your sorry ass! We know what we are! We don't need you to tell us! Who do you think you are, God?"

I asked Holly. "You see that?"

Holly nodded and leaned forward slightly, perhaps interested.

"Well," I said, "people with a view like mine can't share what we're about, because you put us down if we do. It's really wrong to tell people I'm not myself but a version of you. People have got to know that."

"It's that big a deal?" Holly asked.

"This is life or death, to many of us." I remembered my pain in life, pre SRS.

"So what umbrella term do you use?" Holly asked.

"If I mean to say 'everyone who is trans,' I tend to say *trans person*—"

Jan jumped. "That's short for 'trans*gender*'!"

"Not to me. To me it means 'trans *something*.' It doesn't specify, because there's no suffix on it, and that's good. Don't assume I assume what you assume. Trans people are disparate, varied. We're not all about gender as the primary—"

"We all change gender in some way!" Jan said.

"That's transgender emphasis," I said. "Gender is involved for all of us, in some way. But to say we're all about that is wrong—"

"There you go!" Jan shouted loud enough for everyone to hear. *"I win!"*

A few people near us clapped.

I held up an index finger. "But, it is valid to see it differently, as well. You think it's about gender, a part of all of us; I think it's about needing to change sex or not—also a reasonable distinction. The problem here, is you don't think any other view is a *valid* way to look at us. Instead of allowing mine to exist, you hit me until I stop."

Jan started to object—

"I'm not about 'gender,'" I said. "I'm actually pretty sick of hearing about it."

"We all agree!"

"Obviously not."

"We're all transgender!"

"That's a political grouping, and it's not my politic. *Why can't a Jew and a Christian just be friends?*" I asked. "What's so hard about that? I want to be friends! I advocate for your acceptance. I support you, as I do gays or minorities in general; I'm just hurt that you say my phenomenon is part of yours, because it isn't. Shouldn't I be able to say that I'm different from you? Just different, not better—"

"You can't *see* the difference between us!"

"From the outside? With our clothes on? Can you hear yourself?" I thought about it. "A gay man and a straight man look the same—they're both men, both male—so it doesn't matter what we call 'em? *Hey!*" I shouted to everyone nearby. *"All men are gay because they look the same from the outside!"*

A couple people noticed I yelled. I got a smile from one of them, but they turned back to their own discussions.

"All Asians are not Chinese, Jan. Saying we're all the same, because we look alike, is wrong on so many levels—"

"Okay," Holly said. "How are you so different you gotta have your own, special name?"

"Holly!" Jan scolded.

"Well," I held out my hands to slow them down. "I'm different from transgenderism in lots of ways, but maybe three major ways.

"To start with, there are two 'transgenders,' not just one—"

"Two?" Holly asked.

I nodded. "For the first: A view on how to group things—what we are, what we think is best for us—is like a *political party* on how to have a social movement, the 'paradigm'—where we get the 'umbrella' term—and the tenets of the transgender view are to (1) believe it's primarily about gender, (2) conflate sex and gender, and (3) downplay genitalia. Just what you been doing."

"So? What's wrong with that?" Jan asked.

"So," I said, "I believe that hurts all of us, to put it bluntly. My views are *opposite*. I think we're *not* all about gender, I think sex and gender are *different* things, and I do *not* want to downplay genitalia. So I'm not in the Transgender Party. Think a different party view—and I wish other people would respect that we exist and stop just reinforcing yours. Not everybody's a Democrat, for crying out loud."

"What party are you in?" Holly asked.

"I guess 'trans person' party. For me, I think trans people are pretty varied, and we should each be respected for our own, very different issues—not be pressed to fit the transgender mold."

"Petty bullshit," Jan said.

"Second," I said, eyeing Jan, "'trans*gender*' is also a *phenomenon*—something that exists, the being of yourself as a person—and is about changing *gender*, but—I don't want to hurt your feelings, Jan, but it's also not wanting to change physical *sex*. It's the most popular and preferred trans way of being. Very common. Most all trans—"

"I'm a woman!" Jan asserted.

I held up my hands in surrender. "I didn't say you aren't."

"Say it!" Jan shouted in my face. *"Say I'm a woman!"*

"I don't validate people—"

"Cop out!" Jan said.

"I don't validate a long-time stealth transsexual friend of mine. I don't even validate myself, most of the time. I'm Memorex, a Nexus 3 replicant—"

"Because you don't think I am!"

"Why does everyone always want me to validate they're a woman? You know why you don't validate yourself as a woman? Because you don't believe it."

Jan fumed. "I *am* a woman!"

"Then you prove 'woman' is not the same thing as 'female.'"

"Shut! The fuck! Up!" Jan demanded.

I said again to clarify. "Honey, you can't win by telling me not to say it. You want to be a woman, but if you want to have a penis, you don't want to be female. You just want to be *accepted* as female."

Her mouth fell open.

"That's what transgenderism *is*," I said. "That's transgender living. It's the life, the goal, your intention. Your preference. You enjoy it. It's what you want. And then you say I'm 'transgender,' too—"

"I'm legally female!"

"I'm not disputing that. I'm talking genital anatomy, biology, the being of you as a person, your phenomenon—"

"We lobby—successfully—to be accepted as the other *sex* based on our *gender identity*!"

"To be accepted as a physical sex because of something in your mind that's not about physical sex. That's what you sold society, but you have to hide *sex identity* to make that work. That's not transsexualism. That's transgenderism."

"My *sex identity* is female!" Jan said.

I shook my head. "I don't think that's true, and I don't think you do, either. You have clear choice. I think you arrange your body, outside, to reflect who you are, inside. It's just that you're leveraging gender identity to be accepted as female, in society, and you're trampling all over me to do it."

Jan steamed, put her hands on the bar, took her hands off the bar, looked around— "You!"

"I don't want you to get even more mad at me, but there's a third point we haven't even gotten to, yet—"

"What could be worse!"

Jenna, they say you're not supposed to say.

What is so horrible about being myself, and how we're different, that's taboo? Why do I have to keep quiet and tacitly support their view? That would be oppression.

"On the heels of 31 years stealth," I said, "I think hiding these major things is behind most of our problems—you and me, all of us—so—"

"Go ahead!" Jan ordered. She drummed her fingers on the bar. "*Out with it!* Let me hear this brains from you!"

I considered her for a second and then continued softly, to both of them. "Third—" I waited. Jan didn't erupt. "Third, you and I have an opposite sexuality."

"How in the hell is that?" Jan screamed at me. "We're both *women*!?"

Other people around us in the bar turned to look.

"See?" I asked. "You keep going back to gender." I leaned in closer to Holly and Jan, yet spoke as softly as I could. "And you're downplaying genitalia, again."

"It's private!" she seethed at me. "It's none of your fucking business! *God!* The demeaning— How the hell do you get off

telling me— You bring attention to my— *It's nobody's fucking business!"*

"If you say I'm transgender, I get to say how I'm not."

Jan seethed. *"Male and female sex organs are homologous!"*

"That's misdirection."

"We have sex same as you!"

I shook my head. "You have sex, but it's not the same—"

Jan opened her mouth to speak.

"I get to say how we're different: What happens when you get aroused?" I asked. "What's your sexual response? What's going to happen?"

I waited for Jan to think about it. "I—"

I waited some more.

Holly took a sip of her beer and toasted us with it. "I know."

"SHUT UP!" Jan snapped at Holly, lightning fast.

I confirmed. "Your penis is going to get erect, and you're gonna want to put it some place."

"What's wrong with that!" Jan demanded.

"Nothing. It's not a bad thing," I said. "It's what you *want* to happen, isn't it? Don't many of you regulate your hormones for the feminization and then back them off so erections will work better—"

"Fuck you!" Jan sneered.

"I'm supposed to pretend I'm transgender, because nobody wants to admit that. Gay and straight have the same physical apparatus, they each get their own term—but we're *opposite*, and we can't? Sexuality is a big part of it. Everybody wants to avoid *this*, a fight like this, about this. Jan, I'm neither transgender—the party nor the phenomenon—and we have a *very different sexuality*. For many reasons, I'm not transgender; I'm transsexual."

A red-faced Jan somehow asked a question without spitting much on the bar. "And this is how you want *friendship*?"

I nodded. "Like the metaphor, I am not your religion. I have to assert I have my own. And, yes, I want to be friends—"

"I'm not transgender, either," Holly said.

"But all three of us are trans *persons*, in some way," I said.

"No, I'm not," Holly said.

"I'm trans sex. Jan is trans gender. You're trans clothes."

"I'm a CD," Holly said.

"Spoken as a noun. Okay. I'll say that for you, if you like, but your attire does transit gender expectation." I indicated most of the club with a sweep of my hand. "80% of this was called trans*vestism* until a few years ago. There are many millions of you; nobody knows how many, because most won't admit it. A lot of CDs get aroused when they dress. Hell, it's the *reason* a lot do it. Researchers knew it, and they said so about 'transvestites,' saying it was a *paraphilia*. But that codified it as a *stigma*, so you changed your label years ago from transvestite to 'cross dresser,' to avoid—which means the same thing, by the way. You're hiding behind terms to hide your needs and avoid stigmata, same as Jan is—same as I have for decades."

"Getting hot is my own business," Holly said to me.

As the focus shifted to Holly, Jan cooled a little.

"Why should anybody keep autogynephilia a secret?" I smiled devilishly at both of them. "Like Woody Allen said about masturbation, back in the '70s before you were allowed to touch yourself: It's sex with someone you love!"

I got a smile out of Holly on that one, but Jan scoffed. "Don't embarrass me with that."

"What about LGBSAK?" I asked.

"What?" they both asked.

"LGBSAK. We've got women into women, men into men, people into both, people who are straight, some people who don't want any sex at all, and," I smiled to Jan, who could see I was being ornery, "kitchen appliances."

"God." Holly sat back on her chair and chuckled.

"I'm not kidding!" I actually was. "And I put vibrators in the kitchen appliances part—in the drawer by the fridge. Don't you have a vibrator?" I asked Jan.

"I don't need one."

I stood on the lower strut of my bar chair and shouted to the room: *"I have a vibrator!"*

Nearby people laughed.

I sat back down.

"Okay. I'm being silly," I said to Jan and Holly, "but making a point. Trans people hate 'autogynephilia' because researchers said it was a 'paraphilia': *sick, ill, perverted.* Who would want to be called *that*? So why don't they call having sex with a vibrator a paraphilia: 'Mechanophilia'? You can't have a baby with it; it's got to be sick? Well, maybe you could have little Commander Datas with it, but you'd need Borg ovaries—"

I interrupted myself. "I can't go on without some coffee. It's 11:30—past my bedtime!" I hadn't even touched my water.

Holly caught the eye of the bartender. "Coffee?" She pointed to all three of us.

The bartender gave them to us right away.

We each took a sip.

"Oh, thank God," I said, "It's been a long day."

I took a drink from the water bottle, too, and screwed the lid back on.

I tried to get Jan to smile. "My first science class was hitchhiking around the galaxy with Arthur Dent."

"I got an A in that class," Jan said.

"Mom always said you were smart," I said.

"Researchers don't like us because we're trans," Jan said. "Then their bullshit gets into it."

"They need to get their shit together," Holly said.

"That's researcher bias," I said. "It happens sometimes. But on the other hand, how can any muggle know what's really going on *if we don't own up to what we're really* doing—you, me, all of us who hide things. A lot of the time, *we create* their bias. We misrepresent, hide things, lie, change identity, scold—even assault—to avoid stigmata, so—and here's the rub—if researchers are outsiders, they may not know what's really going on, and if they're insiders, they may also be into researcher bias *to promote falsities*. How are we going to grow out of this nonsense without deeper honesty and free and open inquiry?"

"That sounds like Alice Dreger," Jan said.

"That's called integrity and academic freedom, and it's me talking."

"She blames us," Jan said to Holly.

"We're part of it. People need to realize 'binary' is a common theme, but under the surface it's *social fiction*. It's not 'Humans are males and females, and then some mistakes nature made.' *People are varied."* I went on a tear. "Researchers need to admit we're okay—and take us out of the goddamn

Diagnostic and Statistical Manual of Mental Disorders, however it's phrased. If we're in there at all, *we lose.* They want it in there for third party billing, so they can pathologize us, make money off us, support their views." The subject did tend to make me mad. "I'm surprised vibrators aren't in there. Gays aren't in there," I said. "They took 'em out. They aren't sick, and we aren't sick, either. Stop trying to make out like we are!"

"Fuckin' A!" Holly said.

"Holy shit!" Jan said. "That's better!"

Some people cheered. All three of us turned our head to look. Someone had taken the stage and danced to a pole, yet obviously kidding around about it.

We turned back to our talk. "An example of them misunderstanding us and why: Remember how some researchers said the terminology shift from the 20th century's 'transsexual' to the 21st century's 'transgender' was that we were trying to avoid being slammed with autogynephilia? To get away from 'sex' and move to 'gender'?"

Jan cringed. "Yeah."

"Okay. That spin distances you from autogynephilia, but I think there's a larger reason for the shift that gets overlooked, because the transgender paradigm has been hiding it—one that applies to more people."

I looked at Holly. "You probably don't remember. You're younger—but Jan should. And I do."

"Remember what?" Holly asked.

"In the 20th century," I said, "trans awareness was mostly 'transsexual.' We were beginning to be able to express ourselves, anatomically, as the other physical sex. It got the press. Several of us wrote books or were on TV. I was speaking in universities. Transgender people were out there, also, mostly in closets, sometimes lecturing, like Virginia Prince, Ph.D., as an avowed 'transgender*ist*'—"

Jan wrinkled up her nose. "That word is so offensive."

"It literally means 'one who is transgender,' so why do you say that? Isn't that what you are? Hell, it's accurate. And it's history. You going to re-write history here, too? Like you do amendable internet articles? And send out malware to mess with people's computers? Their search results?"

Jan didn't say anything.

"I'll tell you why you say 'transgender*ist*' is 'offensive,'" I said. "Because Virginia popularized it as being about changing gender *but not sex*—woman though male."

Jan squirmed a little in her seat. "'Woman though male' is offensive, too—"

"In the first place," I said, "no it's not. It's people. Don't cut yourself down; don't say women who are male are offensive. It's not nice. And in the second place, Virginia was a self-described 'femmiphile'—I would have only used one 'm' on that—then 'transgenderist'—"

"If Virginia was transgender, she wouldn't have said 'woman though male.'"

"It was in the title of her 1971 book," I said, "*How to Be a Woman Though Male*. In it, she talked about a number of variations of males who are into the feminine, including 'male women' and also into the female, such as 'transexuals'—she put one 's' on that one—asserting that sex and gender are two different things. I agree with her on that, but her opinion of transsexuals was that we were 'misguided,' and we'd be sorry when we realized that men, who want us to have a penis, would be disappointed when they learned we don't have one, on and on. But she was a transgenderist, so naturally she saw us from the outside, misunderstood us."

Jan wrinkled up her nose. "That's old school. We say it different, now."

"Yeah, things evolve. Like," I continued, "trans*sexuals* were making more progress in social acceptance—I think because we mostly needed the other norm. People understood that, somewhat. So what did transgender leaders do? They hid what society didn't want to see: genitalia. They said 'transgender-*ist*' was offensive—to stop its use—changed the term to 'transgender,' popularized the idea that transsexuals were under their same term, and came out *en masse*. So then you get a larger social movement, and since everything was made to be about 'gender,' who is changing sex *or not* became *unclear, vague*, which was the point."

My brow furled. I looked at the two of them with, perhaps, a little more anger than I'd wished. "The first time in human history when our phenomenon could emerge as what we're trying to do—then you all come out and take it away, absorb us whether we like it or not, act like yours is the only view, slam disagreement—put us down hard—so you can downplay what you actually want to have, as if it were even possible to hide it, and finagle your own social acceptance."

"You make it sound diabolical," Jan said.

"It's sophisticated social engineering—"

Jan interjected quickly. "*Some* transsexuals *agree*—"

"Some transsexuals take a transgender view, true. Why? Maybe gender is their focus, also. Maybe to sell books, or they're celebrities and need to please the largest platform." I waited for a barrage on that one, which didn't come. "But the transgender phenomenon is real, and 'transgender' is the only name you'll even accept for yourselves, even today. You're literally using your term for everyone, a conflict of interest that benefits you and hurts people like me. It hurts me a lot. You don't know how much.

"If an umbrella is for everyone," I asked, "why does it have to be *your specific term*? Why can't it be neutral, so one phenomenon isn't specified over another, so you don't create bias?"

"We say it's for you, too!"

"Yes, but that's like saying 'We say that pop music also means classical music. So we've decided. Now it's real. So now we're gonna try to understand why Beethoven was writing a different kind of pop, that he just needed to write to be himself—'

"And then you try to change our own, specific term to yours with stuff like 'post-op transgender.' I am not transgender with an extra surgery. I'm not 'post-op transgender.' I'm different in mind and body.

"I believe that if you could magically be exactly who you want to be, and if I could magically be who I wanted to be, you'd be exactly as you are, but I'd be actually female, right down to my chromosomes—"

"Then what are you doing in here!?"

"I'm being *friends*, damnit!" I looked at her like how could she miss it. "Different should make no difference! Hell: I'm a liberal Democrat Jewish transsexual. My husband was a conservative Republican Christian 40 years older— I'm not someone who thinks you have to be the same to be *friends*—"

"Jesus!" Jan said with scorn. "40 years?"

I sat back in my chair and looked at her with a scowl, my tone now hard. "Yes, it's true: If you touch an old person, you get wrinkles."

I waited for Jan to absorb her comment and my sarcasm, but she didn't seem to.

"I'm saying I can respect people who are different. We both can."

"You're just an *extreme version* of transgender," Jan said.

I shook my head. "No. *You're* an extreme version of transgender. I'm an extreme version of transsexual."

Jan scoffed. "Don't flatter yourself."

"I'm not saying I'm beautiful. I don't even think I am. A lot of transsexuals—or intersex, or transgender, whatever—are more beautiful by far. My body was horribly male in shape. I've fought it always, doing what I could with it. But I'm extreme in my need to be biologically female."

"Muggles believe us," Jan said.

"I shook my head. "Yours is the word people *hear*, and 'gender' is 'obvious,' from the outside. I think most of them don't like the subject, so they don't want to open the book and actually read it. They don't even hear our feelings most of the time, so the rare person, like me, who speaks up now and then is thought a rogue dissenter. Transsexualism is a *small minority*, compared to transgenderism, maybe 1 in 20, depending on where you set parameters—even 1 in 30, if the rest of you come out. No one knows. Even today, 90-95% of people who identify as 'transgender' don't want to be the other sex. Most by far."

"You can't pressure us to sterilize ourselves to be considered the other sex!"

"God! Retreat to implying *genocide*— No one's pressuring you to have SRS; it's just clear you don't want it. Most trans don't have kids after transition, and among those who do, most don't have SRS afterward. Almost all transgender people don't have SRS, regardless. In most cases, that sterilization statement is hyperbole, misdirection, manipulation—trying to avoid the truth. And me, as transsexual? I'd have been emotionally unable to father children. I needed to be able to *bear* them, instead. That's the only way I could envision having kids, but it wasn't possible."

"You can't expect everyone to have GRS!" Jan said. "People have families! Kids to put through school. Or maybe they can't afford the surgery, or maybe they're allergic to anesthesia!"

"I've heard that stuff. Most of the time, those are called excuses. It's not about *expecting* people to have SRS. I don't mind if you do or not. But on the money, it's, like," I quoted Yoda, "'Do or do not, there is no try.' I was down and out, too. I had no money. I worked multiple jobs— If someone wants it, they'll change jobs, get into insurances or apply other funding to it, not spend money on clothes, cars, houses, vacations… If you knew how some of us would die without it! The desperation we feel, needing it so—"

"Oh that death tripe again! That is so pathetic."

"I'm being truthful with you, and I'm not the only one who feels this way."

"Then where the hell are the rest of them? I don't hear other people talking like you."

"Living privately—stealth, a lot of them. Avoiding condemnation from people like you—" I waved my arms to encompass my whole being. "All this stuff I'm relating, though, my views, my experience, my feelings— Whether right or wrong, it's out here. It has to be part of the rhetoric. Someone needs to speak for us. We shouldn't pretend we don't exist. And you call us names, if we try to stand up. It gets pretty ugly."

Jan gave us both a warning look.

"So," I said, "that whole 'What do we call ourselves' term-change thing, from the 20th century to the 21st century? It wasn't *one group* that changed its reference from 'transsexual' to 'transgender.' It was *two groups*—a *larger group* that came out and took over, and then *said* it was one group that was avoiding the sex stigma. That's social engineering, skillfully played.

"That's also the secret behind the transgender party's adamance, pressing transsexuals to accept 'transgender.' Because if we say 'transsexual,' the next question is, 'What's the difference?'" I turned to Jan. "And you don't want focus on *what you're trying to hide*."

"You're *'trailblazers'* for us!" Jan said.

"You mean our social movement was decades *before* yours?" I looked at her hard. "No, that's not what you mean.

You mean you hope we'll spearhead your current social integration, help make it *unclear* if you want to change sex or not, validate you as 'real women' to the public—as if we somehow had that mythical, mystical power—so people can misunderstand us as you and you as us. And for this help, we get to forever *marginalize* our own existence."

"There's nothing wrong with being us!" Jan said.

"There's nothing wrong with being us, *either*!" I said. "Saying I'm 'transgender' is *offensive* to me because—"

Jan was pissed at that. *"Now you're saying we're offensive!"*

"You are right-and-left misunderstanding me! No! Being male is not offensive, *either,* but it's horribly offensive *on me*!"

"That is so demeaning!" Jan said.

I put my hand on my heart. "Jan! It's— The gender transition nearly *killed* me. Does that even matter to you? *You know it's true. You've got my tears in your hair!* I couldn't live that way! I couldn't *stand* it!" My eyes teared as I tried to share. "It was so horrible for me—"

Jan was getting heated. Her mouth flew open. *"How dare you say such a thing!"*

"I can't say how I felt?" I begged.

"Transgender is *beautiful*!" Jan said.

"So is transsexual!"

"You're disrespecting us!" Jan said.

"It's *you* disrespecting *me*! Please accept me for what I am, is all I ask. I'm about a *sex* transition—and *I should be able to say so without fear!"*

Jan boiled over, put both hands on the bar, sat back in her chair.

"News flash!" she said. "Gender can be changed. We're being realistic. Sex *cannot* be changed. You are *fucking delusional*!"

"You mean my chromosomes? Ovaries? *You think I don't know I can't reach my goal? That I'm biologically male? I know I am*—it's disgusting! *I live with the pain of that every day!* My *need* was, and always will be, to be *female*—biologically female! It's what I need! I've done all medical science can do! *Everything!* It's their limit, not mine! Can't you see—"

Jan went at me.

"You don't accept yourself!"

"No, *you* don't accept myself!"

"You're prejudiced!"

"You're trying to shout me down to shut me up!"

"You're ashamed to be one of us!"

"*Stealth* are ashamed of *themselves*!"

"You think you're better than we are!"

"No! We're doing *different things*!"

"You—" Jan was red in the face. "You say we're scheming and lying about you and us and everyone— We're trying to survive out here! You're making it harder for us! *You're being cruel—*"

"*I have to agree with you, or I'm 'cruel'?*"

"Fuck you! FUCK YOU!" Jan screamed, red faced. "*You're fucking TRANSPHOBIC!*"

I sat back in my bar chair. Holly seemed like she wanted to withdraw from Jan's venom. I looked at people around us in the club. Some stared at me in concern.

Finally, I sat up slightly and addressed everyone around us. "That right there—" I said, "*that right there*—is a major problem with the trans movement, the way it's been going."

Jan looked like she was going to speak, but now I was angry.

I held up my hand to stop her, turned to face everyone. "Look at what that says to people—that hyper angry, over-defensive response! Now I've got to be transphobic! Have any of you faced this before? *Anything like it?*"

It was clear some had.

"Some of us are so scared—" I said. "I've known otherwise dignified people to slam anybody who doesn't adhere to Transgender Party fucking *scripture*—slander them, defame them, make up outlandish claims, *threaten—like to Bailey and Dreger and a thousand others*—all over this *fake union bullshit*—like there's a spectrum we tout that we're all different, but we all have to have *the same ideas*, somehow? Be the same thing? Use the same words? I have to give up who I am and pretend I'm her, or she'll hit me with this?

"That kind of thing, right there," I told them, "says it's not okay to have any idea other than the loudest person in the room, the one willing to go too far—*oppression of difference*—exactly the *opposite* of what we expect from people out there in the world—*the opposite of what we need!* If we do that, we convince people we're unstable, emotional, *issue-laden hotheads!*

"We are not adolescents, and this is not high school!"

My hands started to shake. Tears began to move down my cheeks. *"Goddamnit to hell,* I am sick of this!*"*

Jan lowered her head a little, didn't speak.

I tried to settle down, but it didn't work.

I wiped my face with the back of my left hand.

"And that's only half of it, you hear me?" I said, looking to everyone. "Whether you think it matters or not—*and it does*—scientific inquiry is interrupted with this *bullshit*! The way it's supposed to work is that *one study builds on another until the truth emerges*—God forbid the *truth!* Getting it wrong's a pain when it happens, but it's a *step in the process* that inspires other research. And if we slam them, other research that *could* be done—important third party confirmation, or even a new direction—heads for the hills and says 'Hell no,' because *who wants to be attacked?* So wrong or incomplete research that's already out there—or stuff that doesn't piss off the Choir—*that's what's left to dominate*, which burdens the process because then we have to consider that *both* may be *biased!*

"Science is not supposed to be worried about pissing people off! It's supposed to be about searching for the truth. *That's* why we no longer blame witches every time someone in the village gets sick! Had to fight the Church on that one, too—

I turned back to Jan. "Am I transphobic, Jan? *Or is it that you don't want me to tell the truth?"*

I stared at those near me, moving back to Jan. I used a bar napkin to wipe my face.

"You're like one of them, Jan." I pointed to the outside world. "I take shit from them out there; I don't need shit from you in here. *I fucking exist!"*

22

What We Can Do to Live a Normal Life

"I'M SORRY!" Jan said. "I didn't mean it that way!"

I took a slow breath and thought about it, wiped my face again.

Lise walked up to us and glared at me. "There a problem here?"

"Don't worry about it." Jan gave her a stern look. "I got this."

"It's consensual," Holly said.

Lise gave me a dirty look and went to a nearby table, talked with friends, glanced my way.

People around us in the bar commented, returned to their own conversations.

I wiped my eyes again. I held my hands together, trying to get them to stop shaking. I don't like conflict.

"You going to leave, now?" I asked Jan. "I'd expect you to put me down and then leave. Then put me down some more to whomever you're around."

Jan glanced to Holly.

She wants Holly?

"I've got something I'm trying to get to," I told both of them.

Jan collected herself. "You're out of your fucking mind. I know you. You were abused. You hate yourself. You hated living like us before GRS. You know society hates us, so you want to get rid of us, so society won't hate you as much— It's just you, maneuvering for acceptance, same shit you lay on us."

I took a sip from my water and set it down, put the lid back on. "I don't hold the Keys to Cosmic Truth. You can think that if you want, but it's not my reason. It's true that I was abused and hated, miserably, even the thought of living without *SRS*. But the pain of being so horribly wrong," I indicated myself, "helped show me that our phenomena are different. The proof is you're happy. You'll do anything to keep what you have, where I couldn't stand it. And I don't want distance from you. I'll help you do your thing, if you'll let me. But I think these problems and more happen because we—all of us—hide what we're really doing. I think most of us are scared, and that's why we don't say."

"Well, then, I got a cure for that," Jan said. "Don't be stealth."

"Exactly," I said. "Hiding is the problem."

"You shouldn't mind," Holly said "You're female. Who cares?"

"God," I said, shaking my head, playing through a thousand past events. "No. I haven't been immune from anything. They tried to push me out. I'm—" I faltered. "In years past— It's been a lot of trouble." My eyes teared more. "Once I even had a knife pressed to my throat, to get me to leave." I showed them where. "I couldn't go to the police."

Holly looked angry at that. "Why not?"

"I would expose myself. One reason for hiding is to avoid embarrassment, but it can actually create other trouble, even when you never thought it would. Like my old doctors," I told them. "One example, true story: Decades ago—after SRS—for years I used to have doctors tell me I needed Pap smears. You know: Put me up in stirrups to do a gynecological exam.

"Then another doctor explained to me, later, most of that was unnecessary. Pap smears check for cervical cancer, and I never had a cervix. I think most of them just wanted to look."

"Sexual freaks?" Holly asked.

"Maybe malpractice, to use me like that just to see, under the guise of treatment."

Jan seemed both surprised and not surprised, at the same time.

"When I learned that," I said, "I was humiliated to my core. It went deep. How could the asshole doctors trick me like that? I felt so exposed, *so violated*—

"After that, and some other shit, I haven't trusted them. I quit putting SRS on forms—I didn't want treatment for it—so nothing's in writing. On talking to docs, I'd state SRS as a reason for hormones, but no more free shows. If there's no medical reason to show you, I don't show you—*and why should*

I have to? The truth would come out anyway, in time, on some relevant procedure.

"Then I noticed two doctors I had wouldn't acknowledge to me I was transsexual."

"Why?" Holly asked.

"They wouldn't say, and I tried for *four years* to get them to tell me, two each. Maybe one was adamant about party views? I don't know. But the other one? When I pressed harder to be acknowledged as transsexual, he said, and I quote: 'I understand you think you're transsexual.'"

Jan and Holly both reacted to that.

"You '*think*'?" Jan asked.

I looked at Jan and Holly, astonished. "I know! You'd think I'd have noticed. My guess is that he was aware most *transgenders* don't want SRS, sometimes they lie about having it—and if he thinks I'm 'transgender' and I don't let him actually see— I think he thought I probably had male genitals and was covering it up! The whole thing leaves me absolutely disgusted, hurt and angry.

"Do you know how it feels for your *doctor* to do that to you?" I asked. "You actually put yourself into an even partially trusting mode with him, and he's thinking like that? *My SRS was more than half a lifetime ago!* Do I have to go through my whole life dropping my pants for these dweebs? When do I get to get past this—"

"Your genitals shouldn't matter," Jan said.

"That's a transgender view," I said. "They shouldn't be a *problem*, but they damn sure do *matter*. I keep telling people our life depends on it, and they think I'm exaggerating.

"But what I'm trying to get to is: *How can I advocate for something I'm hiding*? I think the solution is I need to *uncover*, be more open with who and what I am—advocate for myself—and it's scary as hell to me. I haven't opened up, yet."

"People don't misunderstand you as much as they misunderstand us," Jan said.

"There's something that might help," I said. "Don't be stealth."

"I'm not stealth."

"Yes, you are," I told her.

"I openly identify as transgender!"

"You're hiding a key part that you don't want them to know. It's what we've been talking about—"

"People out there don't care about the spectrum!" Jan said. "They think it's supposed to be all one package, that woman = female = vagina!"

"Then tell them it's not," I said. "I'll tell 'em with you."

"It's not that easy!" Jan said.

"I know it's not easy," I said, "but it's necessary."

Jan wrinkled her nose again in disgust.

"You don't respect yourself?" I asked.

"No! *They* don't respect myself!"

"Well," I smiled back at her, paraphrasing "I think coming out—the rest of the way—needs to be the next evolution in the transgender social movement."

Jan looked at me in question.

"You're only *partly* out," I said.

"We're *way* out!"

I shook my head. "No. You're doing 'Don't ask, don't tell' to yourselves with a 10-inch dildo. Twenty times a day."

"I tell people what we're about! 'I'm a woman...gender identity...'" Jan said.

"Nope," I said. "You're *vague* about what that means. Like language, 'Sex Reassignment Surgery': You re-name SRS as GRS, first as Genital Reconstructive Surgery, then Gender Reassignment Surgery, then as GCS, Gender Confirmation Surgery—like they were saying on the Oscars about 'The Danish Girl.' Lili Elbe gave her *life* to become the other anatomic *sex*. That was an early version of *Sex Reassignment Surgery* she had, and they were saying on the Oscars it was '*Gender Confirmation Surgery*'—probably trying to adhere to radical transgender scripture, giving in to rigid, rabid demand, cocked and locked, with angry lash-back at the ready. Lili died *transsexual,* and she's not being recognized for it. That makes me feel so maligned— You don't give me credit for my life's need, either—"

"I call it 'G.A.S.,'" Jan said. "Gender Affirming Surgery, because I am already my gender."

"Okay. *But who the hell knows what you mean by that?* A nip-tuck? An orchiectomy—castration? Breast Augmentation? FFS? It could be body sculpting, fucking *liposuction* for all anybody knows—any surgery for *gender*—whatever you even mean by *that*! If you tell someone you've had 'gender surgery,' you can give the wrong impression while claiming you told the truth. Vague. *Misdirection*."

"So everyone can be included!"

"*It's not a fucking club, Jan!* It's a description. And the real reason is to hide what you want."

"It's just a little extra tissue!" Jan said.

"Transgender view misdirection. I don't think it's 'just a little extra tissue.' I don't think *you* think so, either. And I know most people *out there* don't think so. It's easy to enter into a game with people, if you make things vague or you don't allow people to ask—"

"No one should ask!" Jan said. "They *objectify* us!"

"I don't want it to *have* to be an issue," I said. "I want to just be a person. But, if we're talking about transitions, *it's okay to ask!* Question! It's a major thing—very *important* to some of us! If you make some taboo vague, games take over. Other people can pretend they're not prejudice, and you can pretend you're validated more than you are—a mutual game of denial and fantasy."

"You don't know shit about it," Jan said.

"I've been doing it to myself as stealth since 1985. Have either of you read *Covering* by Kenji Yoshino?" I asked. "*The Hidden Assault on our Civil Rights*."

"No," they both said.

"It's about the evolution of acceptance movements. Women, race, religion, gays—have all gone through the process he describes, and so are trans people, right now.

"The first phase of an evolution might be with society trying to *convert* the minority, to 'fix' the problem. We trans have gotten that in spades. *The preacher doeth hold the Bible high and proclaim God's condemnation!* People ban us from things. Transreparation, conversion therapy for children— They try to fix our broken trans thinking—make us base 'normal' against our will. Get us out of the DSM—"

"Yeah, we get that," Jan said.

"Oh, yeah," Holly said.

"Then there come problems with *passing,*" I said, "like a gay person trying to act straight or like me, trying to live more as the other cisnatal."

Holly's look to me was of a slight embarrassment. "There's less shit that way."

"Okay. And then comes *'covering'* for it—where society knows about it, but you downplay it, anyway. Using Kenji's terms, working to minimize the obtrusiveness of a stigma. Using my terms, covering + trying to pass = stealth. Which is *all of that misdirection*—which you've done, and which I have done, too, that most trans people still do—which I believe has direct bearing on our attempts at integration as who we are. All of us. Different details—same process—just as bad for you as it is for me."

"No way," Jan said.

"Yes way!" I asserted. "Low self-esteem, suicides, social ostracism, rejections, and hate crimes—all the things that hurt us—would be improved with greater *respect,* both for ourselves and from others. *But covering disrupts respect*, regardless of whether it's you or me, us or them."

"I'm—" Holly stopped herself from speaking.

"You're stealth on a lot, aren't you, Holly," I asked.

"That's you fuckheads," Holly said.

"Have you ever tried to *pass* as someone who doesn't cross dress? Like, every day? Or if they catch you in a dress, and you say it was for Halloween— That's *covering.*"

"You're reaching," Holly said.

"No, I'm not." I turned to Jan. "When someone mistakenly thinks you've had SRS, and you let them believe it? You're trying to *pass* as genitally female."

"It's none of their business—"

"And if someone suspects you *haven't* had SRS and you evade, you're *covering.*"

"My genitalia don't matter; I'm a *woman.*"

My eyebrow went up. "Transgender view again—straight from the pulpit! But you disrupt your own integration with that effort to misdirect."

"We are rejected if we don't!"

"Some prejudiced dude hearing that can think, *'She wants me to ignore something I believe is real*—your genitalia—*and accept something I believe is not real*—your statement you're a woman.' If he thinks you're hiding something on one end, he won't trust you on the other. You hand your invalidity to him—gift wrapped."

"More bullshit!" Jan threw at me.

"You're thinking like *you*, not *him*," I said, "Covering makes it *harder* for the T movement to connect with him, not easier. It's easier *emotionally* for you, in the short term. You can walk away without having faced something embarrassing—but he gets to come away from your covering believing it's *obfuscation or subterfuge*—and I've known a lot of people who actually have. To him, you confirm his ideas work and yours *don't*, because you cover.

I tapped my heart. "And just as important as how other people process your covering, is how *you* process it, yourself, through your life. What are you telling yourself, if you agree with people to downplay your own *genitals* to be accepted? Of all the things to do—downplay your genitals to please prejudiced people!"

I leaned in on the bar, a little closer to them both.

"Holly," I said. "Have you ever been in a group of guys who dumped on someone crossdressed, and you dumped on her also, to go along? Did you feel you were also dumping on yourself with that? And what about your wife? She divorces you over this—and maybe lords your dressing over you to clean you out—blackmail! You can't speak up because your family will find out. What about when you finally realize—later in life—that you're someone who has to let people dump on him *for decades* because he can't speak up?

"Look at this: It's 'stealth living,' same thing I've done to myself for years, and it hits you the same as it does me. When shit happens—and shit *will* happen because we're all an unwanted minority—you can't stand up for yourself for beans, because you don't want to confirm what they're accusing you of. So then you try to live with it, some way, which makes you look eccentric as hell. You can't explain why you're doing things. You avoid certain people, maybe groups. Maybe you try to control how people think or interact with you, even how they are allowed to refer to you. Maybe you wonder if people know, or not, but you can't ask to find out. All that maneuvering creates walls between you and other people, and loneliness results. You restrict yourself to places and people where you can live while hiding. Your social skills can become myopic, as it were, overly focused, narrow to your situations, degrade.

"You think, 'My hiding is none of your business' happens in a vacuum?" I asked, daring either of them to disagree. "It's also hard to over-ride all that negativity, because you can't let people in life tell you you're okay about it, *because you won't let the issue be discussed—*"

"You don't know shit," Jan said.

"Looking back, I'd say me, at 24 years in transition—that's when a lot of this came together for me.

"Is there anything wrong with you, Jan?"

"I'm proud of myself!"

"*Stealth are not proud of themselves.* Are you living your life the way you want?"

"I do!"

I shook my head. "You told me—at the movies—*you are not.* And is there anything wrong with you, Holly?"

"No!"

"I agree for all of us, but look at what we're doing!" I said to them. "When you think of 'coming out'—both of you—it feels like what you really mean is for Holly to stay in the *back* of the closet, for Jan to come out only *partially*, for me to, quote, 'come out entirely' while pretending to be someone I'm not—keep your secrets for you—and that somehow, magically, people will finally understand us, and we'll all be happy."

I looked at both of them. *"That's not even possible!"*

"People out there won't accept us if we're open with it," Jan said.

"Stealth retort if I ever heard one."

"We tried it in the 20th century!" she said. "With Virginia Prince! Didn't work."

"But this is the 21st century! The transgender movement helped a little for you because many of you came out, even if only partly. But it's creating a ceiling for you at the same time—capping your gains—because you're limiting what you can do, with non-disclosure."

Jan leaned in to me. "Transgender leaders say to play it down!"

I leaned back at her. "That's a lousy party platform!"

"We walk into a bathroom, they don't need to know," Jan said.

"Stealth lie to themselves—they need to believe it's working. *Wrong!* It's not. Usually, *people already know*—that's why they balk. It's not a secret that most transgenders don't want SRS. *The problem is there's lack of respect for it!"*

"Lack of respect all over," Holly said.

"Binary facilities are the problem," I said, "not non-binary people. The solution to the transgender bathroom problem? Easy: Communal hand washing, individual stalls. Treat everyone the same, no intrusion. Done. Go solve something else."

"Costs money to do that," Jan said.

"Not as much as law suits," I said. "And this schizophrenic thing you do to yourselves: 'Don't notice it. If we have sex, need it, but when you see it, don't say it.' And what are you gonna do in a locker room? It's out and obvious there. Most of you want that locker room scene, but you want someone else to do it—"

"And I'm a fucking cop," Holly said.

"No shit?" I asked.

"No shit," Holly said. "And it's nowhere around here. And if I own up, the guys will hound me for the rest of my natural, fucking life. You two can do it, but not me."

"You think it was easy for Caitlyn Jenner to come out?" I asked. "America's ideal, gold medal-winning athlete? The picture of male success? One of the most famous people on earth? She can't go to the *grocery store* without people staring. I bet she had to work through some of that stuff, same as you, but 100 times worse."

Holly looked like she considered what I was saying. "A cop who says to the guys, 'I like to wear women's clothes on Saturday night—but you better know I'm a hard-ass, male, cop, so don't give me any shit'?"

"How is you coming out and opening up different from a gay cop 20 years ago—or any of the rest of us, now?"

"Because I don't have to! I'm not into body mod! The guys don't need to know!"

"Stealth do love to believe their own shit. Real stealth doesn't exist; it's fantasy. I shake my head at this craziness. It's like I didn't even say anything. That closet you love doesn't protect you like you think. Has one of your ex-wives outed you to some of your 'friends' because she's pissed? Has she gossiped with her girlfriends? And they're keeping it from you? Do the guys talk behind your back? Are you giving in to blackmail, in your divorce, so your wife won't talk—after she's *already* talked, but you don't know, because nobody will tell you?

"That's not her doing that, Holly. *That's you doing that to yourself.*"

Holly looked sick. "I have to live with myself."

"You have to live with yourself—*believing you have to hide*."

Holly looked to Jan. "Transgenders could trailblaze for us, if we claim you are cross dressers, too. Neither of us wants SRS. We outnumber you 100 to one."

Jan strained the backrest on her chair, her face stretching its limits. "You mean *pretend we're in the same group* to help you get accepted?" Jan asked. "*Why would we want to do that? We're trying to be accepted as women!* You just want to *look* like one!"

I tapped Jan on the shoulder. "You want *us* to pretend we're in your group, trailblaze for you. We're trying to be female; you just want to look like one—"

"*Fuck you again!*" Jan said.

I told them as well as I could. "'Stealth living' is supposed to be the cream of the crop, the best, the idea that's oh-so-good: 'What? You're living as a woman, and they don't know?' But in reality, it's a web of lies and entanglements, hidden assaults and spy craft. It's not something great; it's poor judgment. It's non-self-acceptance. It's dumping on yourself so you can live a fantasy, and it creates problems we won't even know about until most of life is over."

"You just want us to open up," Jan said, "So people will know you're not us."

"I *do* need to stand up for my phenomenon—but don't use my issues as an excuse to hurt yourself. These are lessons I've spent my life learning. I'm seeing you do some of the same things to yourself that I did to myself, and believe it or not, I care."

"We need you to help us," Jan said.

"You hope I'll hide who I am to help you hide who you are."

"What?"

"I'm not going to play that game, Jan. Even if I did 'help' you with that, it would hurt you in the long run. These lies don't convey integrity, and don't teach respect for difference. They're the *opposite* of what we need."

Jan pointed her finger at both of us. "'We' transgender people!"

"We *trans people*," I said to both of them. "*Trans is cresting!* The movement needs *revelation* for revolution! You've got to be open with what you really need as a human being and advocate for that in society, get people used to it, let the next generation grow up with it—"

"I can't," Holly said.

"That's up to you on a personal level, Holly. Only you know your life. I'm talking social movements here, in a general sense, to the leaders. But if you ever want me to, I'll go with you to your work, support you while you talk to your captain."

"I don't know why you would," Holly said.

I shook my head. "Because I'm a friend. Like when Caitlyn came out— When people dis my brothers or sisters, they dis me, too, and it hurts. Forget whatever groups we are. Forget arguments we have. Forget pretending we don't argue. If people dump on *any trans person*—or gay, or queer, or intersex or intergender, no label, or people from Mars or Romulus— whatever—I am sick of it."

"You don't suck, Jenna," Jan said.

"You don't suck, too." I clapped her on the shoulder.

Jan glanced at Lise, who stood by a nearby table, caught her eye, smiled, then turned to Holly. "Jenna reached between my legs for something good to eat."

Attempting to take a drink, Holly spit beer across the bar.

"It's true," I said. "And there wasn't as much there as I wished." My smile said I was teasing.

Jan whooped.

"Popcorn," I clarified.

Holly smiled, wiped her mouth with a bar napkin.

"I'm trying to convey to you both— You don't realize, yet, the hell of hiding so long. Right now, to you, it's projection, guess work, a risky plan that would be embarrassing and may never pay off—"

"It's not just—" I tried to think. "I've been asking myself: *Why would I do that to myself?* It's not just the pain of being separated from yourself, your nature, who you are. It's also the way it builds over time.

"I know I'm okay *up here*," I tapped my noggin. "But it's damned hard to know it *down here*," I tapped my heart, "when I won't let the subject be discussed. So I live with the shit feeling inside, which gets worse over time, because I'm confirming it by my own sorry actions."

This stuff was close to home. I had leaned forward in earnest sharing, but at that point, I leaned back in my chair and stopped talking, looked at no one. I studied my half-full bottle of water, tried not to cry, which did little good.

The bartender caught my eye, but I shook my head to her. It's okay.

"Trans celebrities help," Jan said.

"Sometimes I see fear flash across their eyes when the truth gets raised—a totally stealth reaction. I'd recognize that light-years away. And if the celebrity even thinks about uncovering, radicals slam her, which she can't have because she depends on public acceptance. And when a journalist senses evasion and asks about it pointedly, the response from radical transgenders is an angry, 'It's none of your business! *How dare you ask!* You're transphobic!'

"So a lot of reporters shut down, the movement gets to cover—which I'm sure is the point—and," I said clearly, *"private individuals, who need that exact life to be supported for their own respect miss out with family, friends, co-workers*, because the public isn't learning to value real life variations."

Holly retreated. "The law should help."

My face was grave. "You think the law said it's okay to murder Mia?"

Jan reacted to that.

"*People die over this shit.* What do laws do for the way people *treat you* on a date," I said, "in bed, on the job, in the family, in the locker room or battle field, or elsewhere? Good law helps, but lack of respect *kills*—and not just murder. Our suicide rate is so high—" I looked straight at Holly. "That goes for *all* trans people."

Holly's face showed she knew it was true.

"Put your badge on that dress," I said to Holly, "and I'll go with you to the Pride parade. Ride on a float. Sip ice tea."

"And me?" Jan asked.

"You, too. We'll take over a float.

"We should *support our celebrities*," I said, "when they want to speak out about who they really are," I said, "how they really want to live. We should be thankful someone would. It takes courage! We need to literally hold their hand in friendship and support, not slam them like has happened."

Jan looked to take a sip of her beer, but didn't, looked around the bar instead, at people sitting together, talking, laughing.

"There is a lot of fear," she said.

"Which oppressors put in you and want you to feel. So you'll hide."

"Gays can live a life saying they're proud of themselves," Holly said. "But they're just gay." She said it as if it were nothing.

"They face hate crimes, too. But the gay movement is ahead of us in their social integration evolution," I said. "They've been learning to uncover for a long time. They were scared, too; many still are. Homophobia is an ongoing problem. Trans are just beginning."

I looked at Jan and Holly, at others around us. People in the club talked, laughed, hugged, danced, and tried to have a pleasant evening. The humanity in our little trans Cheers helped, but I knew it was not enough. The thing that scared me the most, was when someone thought it *was*.

I shared the Trans Golden Rule: "Do unto ourselves as we wish other people would do unto us." I could see them both hearing me. "We need to learn to respect ourselves, as we wish others would, and that doesn't mean pretending a major portion of ourselves isn't there because most others wish we weren't here. I wish people everywhere, including us, would learn to value difference as a source of creativity and synergism that is *good* for humanity. We should not fear our differences; we should embrace them.

"That's too big," Holly said.

"Alright," I said. "To make it simple: If you hide who you really are, you don't love yourself, you won't be happy in the long run, and you'll complicate your life."

People nearby stared at me.

Lise moved to stand near Jan, put her hands on Jan's shoulders.

"You know why we know you're full of shit?" Lise asked.

Jan reached up to hold her hands.

I could see it coming, lowered my head in sadness.

Holly seemed to withdraw into herself, consult her beer.

"Because," Lise said, "you're hiding, yourself."

23

The Gravity of Gossip

I PARKED MY CAR at the Athenaeum, Caltech, and walked slowly down memory lane, west on the brick walk, from the stately pillars of the Ath toward the Fleming House cannon, halfway to the book store. Campus standard off-white collegiate buildings had seen the best of us tease secrets from the cosmos. The entire campus was a setting for concentration, studiousness, and the occasional bit of humor.

People passed me, walking the other direction. I wondered what was going through their mind. I could see, with every step, equations flashing like moving strobes behind foreheads through brains crowded with active neurons—rapid waves of calculations from one lobe to another with insight about some of the world's biggest problems.

I wondered about myself in comparison. My thoughts didn't feel bright and quick, like active strobes—more like waves, absorbed by one lobe, flowing back to others, mixing slowly over time.

I used to feel intimidated by people with brilliant minds, fearing I was so much less—until I realized that Joe was one of them and that he had chosen me; until I realized that they, all of them, were just people working on problems that intrigued them, that they were struggling with life's issues, as we all were—until I realized they were just as human as I, that I was as human as they.

I joked to myself a little with the "Big Bang Theory" TV show in mind. I knew I could not even be accepted as a student at Caltech. I had teased Joe: The only math course I ever took was bowling. I had to forget statistics and deductive logic to make that joke work, but I had avoided algebra, geometry, calculus, trigonometry, and the rest, believing I couldn't do them.

Joe taught me, later, I could have.

That magnificent man.

I stopped to look at the cannon still chained to Fleming House against adventurous MIT students, the joke bringing a smile to my face. Big thing. Heavy cannon. How MIT moved it anywhere, I had no idea. I started thinking truck, ramp, electric wench, engine-driven alternator, a little button under a thumb. Maybe they brought some muscle from Harvard. Offered 'em an ice cream for the day?

I felt at home on campus because I had shared it with Joe so many times. I kept feeling my nerd personality fit with people I met—either that, or it fit with Joe, and he fit with them. I liked them, too, and they were kind enough to accept me. After 22 years with Joe, he floated in through the pillow, and I spoke their language-without-words. Having met so many of them, I knew where they were coming from. I could read their books, listen to lectures as in Feynman, sit with them for hours, soak them up, and while I realized bowling was not much of a math class, I'd learned to feel at home with them.

My life-long self-deprecation was starting to fade. A little.

As I started to walk again, two older men approached from the front, possibly professors, possibly on their way to the Ath for lunch. It wouldn't surprise me. Did one of them have a Nobel Prize?

The one on the right looked at me.

"Hi," I said to him, knowing he was human.

"Hi," he said in pleasant return.

I walked into Addilyn's office. She'd known Joe and me for years, and she'd agreed to let me take her to lunch at the Ath that day.

"Addy," I said with a smile.

"Jenna! Good to see you."

"You 'bout ready?"

The Athenaeum was a peaceful place with stately pillars, high ceilings, chandeliers, thick walls, paintings of academic nobility on ancient, real-wood paneling. Calculations may have flashed through genius minds around me, but the atmosphere in the Ath was calm while it happened. Smoke didn't leak out their ears. It was a quiet place to break for lunch.

Addilyn and I sat in the Main Dining Room by a window that looked out over the west courtyard where I'd seen Kip Thorne once, two tables north of where I'd seen Stephen Hawking, one day with his aids. She and I chatted, nibbled at our lunch, not in the least worried about which fork we used.

"Your salad is good?" I asked.

"Delicious."

"Great."

Addilyn's interpersonal skills were polished. She was too smooth to ask why I'd invited her to lunch.

"I, uh, thought I'd ask you about a little something," I said. "I only have 2 brain cells, and I need 3, so I can use all the help I can get. You're familiar with universities."

She gave me her attention but didn't say much. "Sure." She was clearly interested.

"I, uh—"

I was still fairly new to uncovering.

She waited patiently.

Take your own medicine, Jenna!

If I let it bother me, I can never show my face here again.

Old stealth thinking!

"I think—" I hesitated. "I've been wondering about the effects on the psyche of secrecy and misdirection in personal expression as influenced by changing cultural values."

What am I saying?

"Okay," she said, again, with a smile, not pressing.

Just do it—part of a successful technique is to not make it into a big deal. You're blowing it.

"I'm an old stealth transsexual from way back—"

Only a slight response in her eyes. Either she didn't know but is not startled—or maybe she did know, but is surprised I mentioned it.

How would I know?

"I've been going through some personal growth in recent years, and I'm thinking that stealth living hasn't been serving me for a long time. But if I open up about it, I wonder if it would have an adverse effect on Joe's Lab at Virginia Tech."

I studied her.

She was thinking about my concern.

Impressive. She didn't ask any tourist questions about surgery or how I was raised.

"Maybe it's a stupid stealth question, but specifically, my private worry is if I opened up, would it mess things up? I'm asking you because you seem to know university things."

I did pretty well. Only a little nervous, I thought to myself.

"You've been keeping a low profile to protect Joe?"

"Partly, I guess. Me, too. It's all rolled in together. How will the world fall apart if I'm known?"

She talked with me about it for a while, suggesting most insightfully, if I understood her, that the way things were, years ago, are not the way they are. In my younger years, I was surrounded by people who had known only binary stereotypes—or who had condemned the few who varied, such as me. But now, people have grown up aware of a number of minority inclusions, equal rights, and she didn't think my issue was perceived by the populace as negatively as it had once been. There was a lot more work for society to do, but things were improving.

My relief was palpable, just hearing the view from another person.

"So if you do," she asked, "what would be your overall message?"

"That stealth is a trap," I answered. "It can help for a few years on some things, but after that, it can cause more trouble than people expect—not just for me, but for trans in general. I'm also half scared," I finally shared, "that if I were open, the Ath would ask me to leave."

"I don't see a problem there," she said.

"Even I don't believe what I'm saying, but still, I've had the fear."

"You don't have much of a support system?" she asked.

I shook my head. "Basically none."

Is the world becoming more beautiful than I've known?

As simple as it was, that conversation took a lot of courage for me. I handled my statements to her from my forebrain, quashed my primal insecurities in order to do so, trusting that new neural patterns will feel comfortable in time.

Some weeks later, I was having lunch in the Ath, when I noticed a trans lady sitting at a table by a window on the east side of the main dining room. I was making my way from the buffet toward the table I usually preferred by the Executive Council portrait of Noyes, Millikan and Hale, on the south wall.

I stopped by on hallowed ground to introduce myself as her sister and chat with her for a while, thankful for the opportunity to be myself without worry.

"So you're transgender?" she asked.

"I'm transsexual."

She was cordial for a few minutes but didn't want me to join her for lunch.

Having a chicken salad at the Golden Horseshoe review, Disneyland, I noticed they had a new skit that didn't involve putting down the ugly Mayor's daughter, Sally Mae, a man in a dress. I was so relieved.

The Universal Studios Tour tram rolled toward a building where we'd get a 3-D show. Ellen and I sat on comfortable, plastic seats and chatted. I knew King Kong was soon to attack, but there was no need to worry her with that.

"I think I should tell my BFF, back home," Ellen said. "I can trust her."

"Good secrets are rarely kept—like almost never. Think, before you do: How would you handle it if it got around?"

"It won't."

I shook my head. "There's no such thing as a good secret."

"I'd be alright. I could handle it."

As the tram rolled, two men sat in the seats in front of us. I wasn't sure if they could hear us, but I continued talking in the same vein to press Ellen's boundaries a little.

"If it hit suddenly? I doubt you could handle it. If one day you realized the ladies in the beauty shop knew? And the grocery store? And on your job?"

"I'd—worry," she said.

She hadn't quieted me, yet.

The men didn't seem to be listening to us.

The show started. Jurassic Park's worst dinosaurs tried to kill the tram. Tyrannosaurus Rex tried to eat us. People screamed. We got dinosaur spit sprayed on us. I got some in my mouth. But King Kong was our champion. He ran into frame and started beating them up. *Fast!* Kong had speed and muscle that were quite convincing. He ruined them, bashing them back and forth.

We were saved. Oh, thank goodness. People clapped.

The tour continued through the Universal back lot.

"I could handle it," Ellen said again.

"I'm worried about how you'd take it inside," I said to her. "It's an adjustment. I've seen people in crisis over that, but you don't have to guess much. You remember me talking with you about the importance of 'test marketing'?"

"Not that again."

"After long-term stealth, uncover just a little at a time, in safer places—like going to some distant place, be anonymous, out yourself to a group like it's normal for you—and return to that same place a few times, so you know what it feels like, next time, to walk into a place where people have known. And if you panic, you can walk away, because it was anonymous."

"I am not going to do that. If it happens, I'll deal with it." She sipped some water from her cup and put it back in the holder on the back of the seat in front of her. "I'm not that shallow."

I shook my head. "It's not shallow; it's experience. I'm trying to help you. You're middle aged, and you have never done this."

"Hell no! People can't see it on me. I don't have to."

"Unless you want to be yourself."

"I *am* myself!" she said. "People won't think I'm—me—if I do that. They'll think I'm—*that!* Not the same thing!"

The tram tour guide talked, people looked.

The tram crawled through the remains of Spielberg's real Boeing 747 crash set from "War of the Worlds." I leaned over to Ellen, "The plane cost him some $60,000, but it cost another 2 million to ship, because—you know—it wouldn't fit in a box."

"You making light of this?"

"No. Sorry. On us: Our existence is something we need to come to grips with, ourselves. You have to find a way to be who you really are, without avoiding it."

She leaned over and whispered in my ear. "Accept being transsexual? I never wanted to be that. I just—" She stopped.

"I know," I said. "That wasn't the need. I feel it, too. It's just that we can't go all the way. It's the fact of it.

"I'm not going to accept that," she said.

"You're scared."

She cringed. "Gossip—" she started to say, then dropped it.

"I think it's a little like gravity. It's felt closer to us. Step a few paces out of your life, and people aren't as involved. You can take a break by just going somewhere else for a while. It's easier than it was when we were growing up."

A man ahead glanced back at us, briefly, but didn't seem alarmed.

Ellen acted normally, answered me with a relevant, common, yet unrevealing phrase. "I've read about it. That's enough."

I leaned into her ear and whispered. "Was reading about being *female* good enough?"

I sat in my hangar at Camarillo Airport—in a chair, as Joe would urge, and tried to understand how I'd complicated my own life.

Stealth living was making my life hard in so many ways—

Denial! I need more denial! Where do I go to get denial?

I could see Joe smile at me, in my mind, as I processed the issues.

I don't know if I can do this, I thought to him.

Yes, you can, I felt him think back.

Maybe I'm extrapolating your advice wrong? I hope?

No. I felt an immediate answer.

I'm getting him right.

He'd say I should have the courage to be myself, not worry about it. Take the pressure off, and find my true way. Stealth issues weren't his forte, but I felt he'd say beyond the first 10, healing years, I should have let stealth fade. Long ago.

I scrutinized the flier I held in my hand about a fly-in, bar-b-que and spot landing contest, coming up soon, with the Antelope Valley 99s, the chapter to the east of us. I'd given the wrong impression to my local chapter, the Ventura County 99s, by leaving a few years before. I'd retained my membership in the Southwest Section and at headquarters, but leaving local was another one of the mistakes I'd made in life.

I think it said, possibly, to them that I didn't like them, and I didn't want to imply that negative.

What a fool I've been.

I thumbed out an email on my phone to the local membership chair and asked to be readmitted. "Forgive me for leaving."

I was pleased they accepted me back, right away, without question.

Which only heightened my fear. Frankly, I knew I'd have to uncover. The question was how and when.

It felt like a crisis washing over me, of my own choosing.

I'm not ready!

A week or two later, after cleaning my airplane, I closed the hangar doors and coasted lazily around the airport in my car, as had been my habit for 27 years—when I saw a woman in the distance, putting an airplane back into a hangar.

Is she in the 99s?

I could ask her, and tell her about the Fly-in at Antelope Valley.

I drove up to her, slowed my car in front of her hangar— and it turned out to be *Caitlyn Jenner*—the most public, most well-known transgender woman on the planet—

Oh shit!

What am I going to do?

She left her airplane to walk over to my car, friendly.

Oh no!

Should I stay stealth with her and just recommend the 99s? I could!

Should I admit my own past? Normally, I would, to a trans person, but not on Camarillo Airport! You don't piss in your own pond!

God, I'm referring to myself as piss—

She's walking up to my window!
I had three seconds, no time at all to think.
"Caitlyn!" I said, as she got to my car.
"Hi." She was pleasant, easy going.
"Sorry," I said, as if she might not have wanted people to intrude on her privacy. "I didn't know it was you. I just saw someone putting her plane up, and I was going to talk to you about the 99s—"
Fuck, Jenna!
What should I say?
I hesitated. "I'm your sister."
"What?" She looked at me a little more closely.
"Um— I'm— " I stumbled over myself. "Well, I'm—"
She'll hate me, too, if I tell her the truth, goddamnit!
"Cait— I'm—" I honestly didn't know how to tell her, but I tried. My voice was weak, quiet, the words barely leaving my lips. "Cait, the thing is, I'm transsexual—"
"You?" she asked.
"—but the thing is, my view is, I also have to say—I'm also not transgender."
To my surprise, it didn't seem to matter to her— No. I think it may have mattered, but I could see, instead, that her manner with me was accepting, not condemning.
She started talking with me through the window of my car, so I got out and stood beside the car, chatted with her—for one of the better 30 minute talks of my life. In its own way, because of the timing, it was as important as my talk with Christine Jorgenesen, back in 1982, because she happened to be saying things I needed to hear.
Chance coincidence?
Currents that crossed in time-space? I had never met her before, but she changes, and there she is.
One of those near-psychic events?
"Stealth?" she asked. "Why? You need to come out."
"I know!" I told her my story. "I've been working on a book for that purpose. It's about how I made my own life a mess."
Caitlyn shared about her life, as well—fascinating. She'd apparently been a pilot for a long time. Nice plane, too, a Bonanza with the latest toys.

When we had a pause, I shared about the Antelope Valley 99s fly-in, two weeks hence, and my local chapter.

"And I'm scared as hell to go," I said. "Imagine that."

"Why? Be yourself."

"It's too simple to say that," I said. "I've been around a long time. I've earned my wings, nothing to be scared of, except—"

"They don't know?"

"I don't know what they know. Some probably do, or suspect, but it's not— They're nice people. I'm just—"

She tried to help draw it out of me.

"I'm not scared they'll do anything to me! I think I'm scared that if the topic is raised, I won't know how to answer."

"Jenna! This isn't the '80s. I was so secretive for so long— You know all those years? Coming out was the *best*! Don't do this to yourself!"

Too simple.

Sometimes trans people will encourage me to be more open because they want support for their life, but that wasn't it, this time, with her. Instead, I think it was that she was new. At that point, Cait had only been in transition about a year. When people first transition, they may be elated, enamored, enthused, for a period of several years. Cait looked down to earth, but she was in her honeymoon phase.

Opening after prolonged stealth living was different. I was not glowing, not in love with it. It wasn't new to me; it was practical, day-to-day living, and not always nice. Life had hit me over the head so often, I was hype-aware, sensitive to the way people treated me as an unwanted minority, how they looked at me. I'd learned to notice little cues—comments, looks, or their absence. I didn't think I could take much more of people hurting me—yet, I knew, I was hurting myself by not embracing myself. Opening up would not be the joyous release it was so often felt to be, on initial transition. Opening would be a test of pressure, a battered person standing up to a social bully in the hope it would help her respect herself, and in the belief it was the way to make him stop.

Yet, and nonetheless, I could see Cait's message was still apropos. I couldn't deny it.

Another angel, telling me what I need to hear.

We both shared a lot—more than I would have thought could be done in 30 minutes. And after a few minutes, we hugged. Twice.

"You should come on 'I am Cait.'"

"Me?" I shared I was worried that if I didn't use the right terminology, it might conflict—it had happened before, most of the time—but she said it should be no problem, gave me some examples.

I thanked her for the invitation, but it's a stretch for someone who is still "stealth." I had a hurdle or two, I thought. If she still wants me to later, perhaps I should.

I walked into my garage, turned and locked the door to the house, behind me. I remembered how it had been left open when the place was burglarized, how other things had happened.

A chill went down my spine.

They knew it would scare me.

Who can help?

I didn't know.

If I open, it must be to the core of my being, spread beyond my control, so that it's done and out of my hands—so no one will come to my door and try to force me back into silence.

I sat with Martha Phillips, President of the Ninety-Nines, Inc., the International Organization of Women Pilots, in Applebee's restaurant, and talked with her about whether or not I could or should disclose to the local chapter, the Ventura County 99s, and about the 99s' policy as a whole on accepting trans people.

The next evening, April 19, 2016 at Santa Paula Airport, at the monthly General Meeting of the VC99s, Martha told the group that the Ninety-Nines will accept people into the organization based on pilot certifying authorities' recognition of a pilot as female.

Way to go, Martha.

"And now," Martha said, "Jenna Ware will talk about this for a few minutes."

My information was well received, as far as I can tell. And it was the first time in 25 years as a member that I began to relax around them.

In the computer room of the Inn at Virginia Tech, I scrutinized my email one last time.

Joe was the most magnificent man I'd ever met. He was born two blocks southeast of campus.

One of the family's greatest, I was sure, had married—me. Without meaning to, Joe had pulled Ware family legend into 21st century respect for sex and gender variance.

I'm sorry, Joe, for being me.
But is this the right thing to do?

I knew I was self-deprecating in my thought process. I don't think anyone could live a life as I had, without being self-critical. But I also told myself, yet again, the secrecy had to stop. Joe loved me. My origin, my nature, was never an issue for him. He made it known to everyone, in the family, at Virginia Tech, among old Lockheed friends...

And— If leaning on him for this decision helped give me courage, I knew I would do it.

I just need your help, Joe.
If you have any ideas, please—

Somewhere in the back of my mind, I could feel him nod.

I sat on the grass in front of Joe's grave and talked with him, felt the hard stone with my fingers.

It may sound odd, talking to someone who has passed, but that's what you find yourself doing.

"It's been done, Joe."

Yes, I seemed to hear, then, *partly.*
There is more to do, I thought to him.
There is always more, I felt him say.

Interim Dean Taylor spoke comfortably with me in his office. For him, my being transsexual appeared to be a non-issue. Frankly—and I suppose to be honest about it—when we opened the Ware Lab back in the '90s, it was before my FFS, and I think I was even more obvious than recent years. I don't think it was ever a secret. The main difference, now, was I was willing to say it.

I sat with Dewey Spangler, Manager of the Ware Lab, in his office in the Lab, talking about things. Also—
After all the hell I've taken in my life for being who and what I am, I'd have thought that my heart would have been racing, but it wasn't. I was calm, and Dewey's manner helped.
He was friendly and informative as always. I don't think my revelation bothered him, either.
On leaving his office, I talked with a couple of students who were walking through. It's always a pleasure to connect and see what they're up to. On this occasion, though, I slipped myself in a bit more.
"You?" they asked.
I nodded. "Yes."
"Mrs. Ware?"
"Yes. I'm transsexual. I advocate for LGBTQI-LGBSAK, whatever—"
"You get around!"
"Sometimes."
We chatted for a while in the hallway.
They seemed to warm up to me. My impression was the students liked it—or was it my relaxed manner? I got the feeling they were pleased, perhaps as if it broke down some sense of stiff distance in my expected demeanor and made me look more immediate to them, more human.

I never went to my college graduations, because I never had anyone to attend who would care, but I was at Virginia Tech, and now out, so I went to the Lavender Graduation ceremony. LGBT were being honored for their degrees.
I found it quite uplifting—
I didn't expect it to be so meaningful to me. I expected people to be happy, some tears, a great speech or two, music playing, people walking across the stage to get their diploma, but I found it mattered to my core much more than expected.
Other than to Joe, it never seemed to matter when I achieved anything, but sitting there, watching LGBT people be honored, watching people in the audience who did care,

knowing I had opened to them—brought old feelings to the fore. These were LGBT who were being honored. Not shamed. Not debased. Not treated as outcasts.

After the ceremony, I stood with Dr. Sands, President of Virginia Tech, and literally cried on his shoulder for more than a few minutes. It was a release. I didn't mean to hog his attention; it just happened. Other people waited in line, respectfully. They wanted to greet him, shake his hand, and there he was, letting me continue.

24

Being

POST COLD FRONT, the day was CAVU—ceiling and visibility unlimited—beautifully VFR. There should have been a little leftover turbulence from the front, but I found the day remarkably calm. My little sports car of an airplane held her line as if she had an autopilot, steady as a rock. The stick between my knees was light. The slightest touch of a finger would turn the plane as if with a thought.

I scanned the gauges: altitude, air speed, fuel ... oil pressure, oil temperature, cylinder head temperature. I listened to the engine: smooth. From my indicated air speed, I did a rough calculation of true air speed and compared that to my outside air temperature. *Good plane*, I thought. She was born to fly.

From 5,200 feet over the practice area, north of Ventura, the Channel Islands were crisp and beautiful. Santa Cruz island, Smuggler's Cove— We'd enjoyed going there. Anacapa Island, just east of it, held our most common destination with Arch Rock, a large, picturesque arch you would only attempt to sail through if you wanted to swim 11 miles home, afterward.

I thought left. The plane made a gentle bank to the left. I looked for traffic. I thought right, and we made a standard rate turn to the right. I looked for more traffic. Seeing none, I applied more power, banked harder into a steep turn and applied a touch of backpressure on the stick. I could feel a slight pull of 1.4 g's in my cheeks. The horizon slanted across the top of the panel at 45 degrees and flew past the windshield at a rapid rate: the Channel Islands, Pacific Ocean, Ventura, Los Angeles, Pt. Mugu, more ocean—

I glanced at my altitude indicator periodically. I'd lost about 30 feet in the turn—not too bad—

Will I get it?

I felt a slight bump.

My own wake turbulence!

I powered back to normal cruise and banked left toward the Highway 118, north of Camarillo Airport. Saticoy Bridge approached, a reporting point in the local area.

There was no need for an instrument approach. There wasn't a cloud in the sky, but it was one of our old things, something I hoped to share with Joe the rest of my life. I checked Camarillo's recorded weather information. Winds were out of two five zero at eight, designated "November."

I preset Camarillo's tower frequency in my one radio, then dialed in Pt. Mugu's approach frequency. I didn't hear anyone.

I keyed the mike button on the leading edge of the stick and called Mugu Approach with my N number. "Saticoy Bridge, IFR request."

"Mugu Approach, say request."

I spoke clearly, succinctly, into the radio. "GPS Zulu Runway Two Six Approach, Camarillo, full stop. We have November …"

Mugu Approach gave me a squawk code for my transponder. I punched it in, and they continued, "Fly heading zero six zero, descend and maintain three thousand six hundred."

"Zero six zero, down to three thousand six hundred …"

I simultaneously reduced power for the descent and banked to 060. Camarillo Airport was on my right. I was on the IFR version of the pattern's "right downwind abeam."

The plane settled in for a typical instrument approach: slow, graceful turns, gentle power adjustments, with an airport that magically appeared, dead ahead.

I parked the car, in front of Hangar Two Two Eight, on the west ramp at Camarillo Airport, and sat there, alone. The sheet steel doors of the hangar stood solid, even cold—ours, but not ours any more.

I could see Joe, 27 years earlier, after a flight, opening the second large hangar door, turning to give me a smile of confidence, like he did.

And I could see the earlier me, happy to be there, yet scared in life, sitting on the tow motor control arms, so the tire would have more traction, in an effort to move the heavy T-28 into the hangar. I knew everything my younger self would experience, every mistake, every event she would survive— I wished there was a way to help her understand, before she needed it, the things she would do to complicate her life, simply by not knowing how to handle situations. There were a thousand things she could have done better. She had the ability, the power to act, so many times, but—she didn't know what to do. She'd scrambled to find people to ask, but whose advice was good? Who even understood the problems? Most didn't.

I wish she had known. Avoiding a major part of who she was still left her dealing with the consequences, only orders of magnitude more complex.

I tried to send her messages, into the past.
Don't believe the false word of prejudice.
Learn to respect yourself.
Stand up for yourself.
You can't run away from yourself.
Hiding creates distrust, in yourself as well as others.
It was true.

I sent strength to my earlier, younger self, who'd needed so much more.

But you're not open, yet, I felt as if I could hear Joe say.

I searched for the answer and found it, buried beneath my fear.

I don't want to! I flashed back to him. *They'll hate me, and I'm so sick of people hating me—I*

I felt him: *No.*

And I knew it was more than that. It was fear. But I was also sick of running from myself.

You need to be open with your views, as well as your life.

With a pause for my apprehension, I agreed. Oh, shit.

And where are you, now, Joe? I thought. The closed, steel doors had no answer.

My creative mind reached into multidimensional space around me, wondering, feeling for him. Could old Hollywood writers have the key? Could he be around, somewhere, able to hear me, even if I couldn't hear him? Could I, maybe, hear him, if I listened just right?

Sitting on the ramp in front of Hangar Two Two Eight, I made myself peaceful, inside, calming the noise of my mind, to hear what may be a faint signal from him.

Joe?

I didn't— I got the sense that—

I let that idea come in.

I—got the sense that I wasn't supposed to ask.

What?

Whether it was Joe, or my own mind, trained by him, it felt as if I did get a brief message:

Don't worry, Jenna. The cosmos isn't as you think. It isn't as anyone thinks.

And then there was a faint, *Things Are.*

I jumped. That sounded like Richard Bach.

Richard, I thought back. *I'm on the phone!*

I tried to recapture the feeling. What was that? Maybe it was Joe. It didn't feel like resignation to the status quo, because nothing could be done about it. It felt as if the feeling was happy, because the way things are—is good.

Separation isn't good! I blasted back at Joe.

Life is good! I got back, immediately, along with my reasoning that it isn't a question of life-after-death. Life-after-death is a question of the physical body, and most of the cosmos isn't so limited.

So how can we love beyond life—

No. I felt him. *It's—*

I felt him tell me, or I felt my own mind trained by him tell me, to trust the nature of the cosmos.

There had always been something about Joe, an awareness beyond science, that he had a sense of whatever that was. And whatever that was, it felt happy to me.

I felt a joy in his smile of my hearing him.

I'm sorry I wasn't more for you, I felt to him. *I'm so sorry!* My eyes teared at the truth of it—

No, I felt from him, immediately, as if that were the wrong thing for me to think.

I started to think, *I—*

That was wrong, also, I felt— It wasn't that I was inadequate for him. Instead, I felt his was an enjoyment at watching me grow.

I married Buddha, for Christ's sake.
I could almost sense him laugh.

Complications in our life related to me being trans, and not knowing how to handle it, either within myself or with others, felt like an "inadequacy" in our marriage, like I'd brought a storm of trouble into our life and mis-managed it into a nightmare.

Sharing all this with an elderly friend, once—even questioning reincarnation, life-after-death, other dimensions, or some kind of continuing beyond this life—I got a quite different thought. After knowing us for some 20 years, she told me that her impression of our marriage was not about me being inadequate for him.

"Love?" I asked her.

She nodded. "But other things, too."

"Our life was so hard," I complained. "He did so much for me, and all he got out of it— He gave me *life*, inside! He taught me everything. He taught me how to learn. I mean, before him, I was in a coma. I couldn't see two feet beyond my own existence. And after I got with him, I— It feels like now my vision of my life, other people, the cosmos, is open to the future! I've got the whole thing, laid out before me, and I'm part of it! He—" I tried to think. "He opened my mind, like it never had been before. For the first time—in *all* of my lives, if there's reincarnation—*I can see*. Our marriage felt so lopsided. I got so much from him. He was doing all the giving."

"You're hero-worshipping him, Jenna. He's not better than you."

"Than me."

She nodded. "I also think he grew, as a person, in the marriage. I think he didn't know how good he could be."

"We helped each other?"

She nodded.

"There was something he got from me?"

"Yes."

"Because I'm not so good as a person?"

"No," she said. "Because there's prejudice in the world, and he loved you, regardless."

Oh! I'm still learning I'm okay, that it's not necessarily me. I've been so low for so long.

I could swear there was a smile out there, at my thoughts, and just enough joy to give me the feeling I needed to have, one I could share with others: Life can be more beautiful than I think.

I felt, as if Joe and I formed the words together, in mind at the same time: *It takes courage to be yourself, but courage only exists when you fear. Once you are yourself, there is no more fear, no need for courage.*

I felt Joe withdraw, just a little, as needed.

I looked at the ramp in front of Hangar Two Two Eight, and noticed someone had painted three white stripes on it, as tire guides, the same as we had, 25 years before.

The stripes were as they should be. The sheet steel on the hangar doors were closed as they should be. The hangars were all in a row.

I was coming to grips with the most basic idea of being myself. After 59 years, my lifelong belief that it was wrong to be myself, and my lifelong devotion to survival by stealth, had been challenged by my own sense of peace in a conservative man who loved me.

Now it was time to uncover more layers.

I sat in my car by the east end of the runway at Camarillo, the seat back, my left foot on the dash by the window, and considered opening further. It wasn't just what I was that needed revelation, but what I believed. My phone, sitting on the passenger seat, was my window to the world. Thumbing emails was my primary means of communication. I picked it up.

J. Michael Bailey, Ph.D., Alice Dreger, Ph.D., and several others:

I felt it was wrong for some trans people to slam them, as they had, and I felt I should publicly decry the action. I asked to brainstorm about respect despite difference—as with my old metaphor, a Christian and a Jew can be friends. There was a time when that was radical, on the forefront of social change, and I felt we needed to put this radical trans paradigm/science conflict behind us, too. My earliest thought was to repair some of the damage of my sistren by demonstrating a little human decency with people of diverse thought. Though autogynephilia is obviously a real phenomenon, I do not agree with all the assertions out there about it or who has it, which is the point: to stand with people in mutual respect, saying we disagree on some things but that we'll be civil, regardless. That simple concept is foreign to so many. I hope to nurture an atmosphere of safe academic freedom by showing not all trans people condemn dissent.

Caitlyn Jenner:
   I walked over to Cait's, at Camarillo Airport. She had her Bonanza on the ramp, in front of her hangar, inspecting it.
   "Hi Jenna." She walked over to me.
   "Hi Cait. Um, sometime, when you get a few minutes, I'd like to chat about something, share some ideas."
   "Like what?"
   "Not now. You're gonna fly. Some time when—"
   She smiled. "I just got back."
   "Oh."
   She put her plane back in its hangar and stood with me a bit. "So what's up?"
   "Cait, you're a big shot in this area, a leader of the transgender movement because you're so well known, and there are some things I'd like to share with you."
   "There are several—"
   "I know. It's collective. It's you, Jenny Boylan, Janet Mock, others. I need some time to talk."
   "Like what?"
   I was uncomfortable bringing it up, but I felt I had to.
   "Transgenders have been coming out more quickly the last generation—maybe a million? One estimate was one point four. I expect another mil in time, who knows. And the movement's been so successful, it's outrunning its own success."
   I think she could see I didn't like having to confront her. She gave me a little hug, maybe to relax me—which it did.
   "Okay," I said. "I think the movement needs to take a new direction because political rhetoric from leaders needs to give way to practical integration for the transgender mainstream. Transgenders are winning access to places most don't even want to go."

She looked at me a second.

I continued with barely a pause. "What if a transgender woman wants to join the military, the police force, the fire department, or just go to the gym down the street—like any other human being. You see what I'm saying? It's the locker room nudity. Like the movement in general, she downplays how she can be a woman with a penis, but if she's scared to *say* it, how's she gonna *show* it? So she doesn't. She marginalizes herself due to embarrassment. The message—what is shared with the public—needs to be as clear in books and video as it'll be in the locker room to help people *on both sides of this* get used to what they're accepting. It may take a generation..."

We talked briefly about this before the conversation moved back to airplanes.

"By the way," she said, "I think I'm going to get an MU-2."

"Oh, you like hot rods with two big bazongas?" I put my hands together as if in prayer. "Please take it easy? Stay within the envelope?"

She gave me another hug.

Doctor's office:

I sat in a chair in this new-to-me examination room.

He looked at my intake paperwork, no doubt saw that I wrote down: "I don't have a primary physician. If you want to know, I'll tell you, but you'll have to listen to me for 10 minutes."

"Okay," he said. "So why no primary?"

"You give me 10 minutes? No leaving when I'm half way through?"

"Okay," he said again.

I gave him the story of the Pap smears, my refusal to drop my pants any more unless there actually seems to be a reason, and a former doctor thinking I probably had a penis I was concealing—my guess, and it's a shame I had to guess. "No telling what he put in my EMR—"

The doctor began to write on my forms.

Surprised, I spoke too quickly. "I don't want that stuff in my chart!"

"Oh, alright." He put his pen in his pocket. "But the Pap smears? That's—wrong."

"That's *malpractice*," I said, my old, Kansas, country, accent and nature asserting itself. "And there's more doctor stories than that. They violate trust and complicate the hell out of my ability to get even routine medical care. I don't even trust a doctor any more when he tells me I need to come in for some kind of maintenance. Maybe he just wants a billing—I'm sure I've seen that happen. I rely more on myself—which is a problem, too, because I know I'm not a doctor—"

"I won't lie to you," he said.

He seemed a man of few words, but also sincere.

Thank God!

"And now we get to the important part," I said.

"What's that?"

"I've resolved I will never again in my life allow someone to treat me if he doesn't get even the basics of what I am, or disrespects me by referring to me as something that would have killed me. I am transsexual; I am not transgender. Grouping disparate phenomena for a social movement is politics, and I don't want politics in my examination room or my medical records. It hurts me. Sex and gender are different things—"

"True."

"You mean you understand what the physical sexes are?"

His look was surprised.

"It's not a silly question," I said. "Even of a doctor. You'd be surprised—"

"I know," he said.

I continued. "If I tell you I had a tummy tuck 35 years ago, you gonna think I'm lying until I show you the scar? You need an X-ray before you believe my collarbone was broken once? A lot of people lie about their genitalia, which is foolish. The truth will come out eventually, on some medical procedure—"

"Right."

"What?"

"I'm not here to tell you what you are. I'm here to fix what's broken."

"You accept that I'm transsexual and not transgender?"

His answer was simple. "Yes."

Oh, thank God!

Again in my car by Runway Two Six, typing into my laptop, I heard a gentle Cessna over my head, descending to land.

It brought fond memories, and I know Joe would have loved it, too.

I sat my laptop on the passenger seat.

Did I put too much in that book, Joe?

No.

Is it worded okay? I thought back to him.

You can never say it perfectly for everyone. Don't try so hard.

I tried to understand, but it didn't sound right.

Don't worry, I felt him say. *Stop worrying for a change.*

It's odd, driving around a place where you've been 27 years, in a largely conservative area, where you've considered yourself private the whole time—to then bare your soul to others and face them, anew, with issues known that people have used to cause pain, your whole life. Fear lives in every anticipated interaction.

I've been hurt in an incident like that before. Will this person hurt me, now?

I've been put down from someone like that before. Will this person put me down, now?

Every hangar I saw was a concern, every person. It was easy to misjudge. You can't wipe away 59 years of denigration and start anew—not when you've learned the basis has been prejudice that you know lives with seeming justification in many a heart. That fear is something that may be with me forever.

Yet, I'd also learned that the truth is marginally disarming. Someone may still disagree. Some people may even react violently. But more people—even if they disagreed with how I thought about myself—would respect the honesty that came with disclosure, the character to face hardship in respect for truth. Some would even agree.

And with all of that, what I also gained with the truth was my ability to address incidents of prejudice, should they occur, the ability to let people know that I would not lay down for it any more, that I'd speak up as needed, correct a mis-impression, identify my public relationships with others just as they would, be part of the mix, part of who affects sentiment in my area, that I was no longer a passive receptacle for hate, and in the process, let people see other good qualities I have, that I was too distant, before, to share.

Stealth is not health. In a million ways, faking it, pretending, allowing people to believe things untrue and going along with it because it feels good short-term, causes so much more trouble in life that the bad far outweighs the good.

Yes! I could feel Joe say in my mind.

I love you! was my instant response. I will never stop learning from him.

I thought about my new life. I had only opened up seven months before, after decades. Was I happy like a Hollywood movie? Most books written on the subject show a transition and end on a happy note rooted in a new personage, but that felt like a honeymoon effect to me, sometimes prolonged by other social efforts.

But I am now about 36 years in transition. My husband died, and I'm alone in asserting myself against a social movement determined to make me into something I'm not. There is no honeymoon effect here; there is a long-term adjustment to life as an unwanted, misunderstood minority, dealing with people who will never admit prejudice but who find ways to make association unpleasant, learning to take my own interest in subjects and events, without that one person who meant everything—trying to find meaning in life without him.

Examples of self-liberation such as the well-done scene in "Frozen," with Queen Elsa on the mountain in the snow— flinging her arms wide in freedom—are inspiring. No one could sing it better than Idina Menzel. She let it go. She's free! Doesn't have to hide any more.

But it isn't that simple. As beautiful as that is, my 22 years with Joe also helped me grow past this moment's fleeting feeling. The joy that the weight of stealth is gone is not all there is to it. It does feel good to set the burden down, but life continues, a daily practice of encountering more things good and bad, dealing with them.

The difference is I'll no longer make life harder than it needs to be. If I hide, I'm hurting myself further, and I'm not gonna do that any more. I'll admit to myself and everyone else that I'm okay as I am. Mom, Navy, employers, landlords, anyone who wants to hurt me: I'm a valuable human being, just the way I am.

I hope, in time, Idina's message will ring louder in my heart.

I coasted in my car by someone's T-hangar. Three men inside were working. One came over to my car.

Take a chance!

I pressed the button, lowered the passenger side window.

"Hi!" he said.

"Hi. You put a window in your hangar?"

"Yes."

"How did you do that?" I looked at it a little more closely. "The steel is corrugated— Oh. You just cut a hole, and stuck it in there."

"Yes."

"Then caulked it?"

He nodded. "Yes."

"Won't that— Might someone break in, now?"

"Who's going to do that?" he asked. "We're behind security gates, it faces the flight line." I could hear yet another person telling me not to worry so much.

I'd met him some time before, but I didn't quite— "What's your name?"

"Michael."

"Oh, yeah. Sorry."

He stuck his hand into my car for a shake.

"I feel like this is the first time I've met you. Good to know you."

He's sharing he knows, but maybe that's okay. He seems very nice.

I looked at his hand and considered. I'd been so worried or so long, but I reached over and shook his hand. He brightened.

"So, now you can sit in your hangar and see airplanes land," I said.

He smiled. "Yes! Or whatever!"

"Think about those cold days when you want to be here. You can sit in there with some hot chocolate and see out."

"Oh, a lot of things. How are you doing these days?" He asked. "I haven't seen you in a while. Is life okay?"

I felt like I should run—but the impulse wasn't as strong as in years past.

"Uh—" I glanced in the car's rear view mirror to see how I looked. I'd remembered to put on some mascara that morning, thank God. "Same, same."

"You're doing well, then?"

"I think—all the same. No changes. I'm thankful my life is holding together. You gonna have me over for tea sometime?" I asked him.

"Any time! Come in now."

His smile was very inviting, but I thought I'd take it slow. "I'd like some of my own time, for a bit."

"Later, then. You come back."

"Okay," I promised.

I angled by another hangar that I hadn't been to in a while. The man Joe and I had known wasn't there, but on the other side of the row, I saw a group of other men I didn't know and a golden retriever.

I stopped my car in front of them and opened my door.

The men smiled at me.

The retriever walked over to me for some love and got plenty.

"She loves everybody?" I asked.

"Not everyone."

"She's adorable!" She seemed very comfortable with me.

"Come on in here and sit with us," they said.

It was my habit to be skittish. I didn't know them. "Another time. I—"

"It can wait! Come on." They were adamant. I was welcome.

Will they not like me if they know me?
Will I be welcome if they learn?

I quickly chastised myself for my old thinking.

The dog nuzzled into me closer and made it clear I should take a chance, so I got out of my car and went inside, took a seat in one of the old office chairs being used to lounge.

I noticed pictures of former days on the wall, airplanes someone used to own. One was a T-28.

"Hi," I said to them all.

"Hi," they said. "What's your name?"

"Uh—Jenna Ware?"

"God, she's not sure," one of them said to another, teasing me.

"Probably drinking to much," he said back.

"It's all that high altitude flight! You a pilot?" he asked.

"Yeah," I said.

He continued. "Lack of oxygen up there, dements the brain, can't think straight."

"Don't mind him. You're— Are you Joe Ware's wife?"

I thought of Joe, nodded. "Yeah."

"Good man," he said.

"You come in here any time," another said.

I nodded, but I wasn't sure, yet.

Someone else jumped in. "What's your real name? Your call sign?"

They were a jovial group. Though it wasn't my mood, I tried to play with them a little: "I can't tell you."

They complained.

With half a heart, I tried some more. The shtick was to adamantly deny it and then throw it out in sharp contrast, but I need to be in an up mood to do it right, and I wasn't. All I gave was, "I'm sorry, but I can't say. It's Bubbles."

"Bubbles!" They laughed. "How'd you get the name 'Bubbles'?"

Maybe they'd be good for a grin now and then. "A few years ago, I didn't know who this one general was—"

I got expected guesses as to what happened.

"No, it's just that I was talking along with him, showing him pictures on my phone about my plane—going on—and I didn't know he was the commanding general of this whole area, and the guys were ribbing me about it—"

"So 'Bubbles'?"

"Yeah. I wanted something dignified, but that's what I got." I pretended not to like it, when in reality it was good for morale. "The colonel who gave me the name said, 'You're an Airhead! But we can't call you Airhead! That doesn't sound right on the radio: *"Airhead! Break right!"* You're Bubbles.' Then I complained, and they rubbed it in—"

I smiled to them, relaxing into their way.

"*Are* you an airhead?" one of them asked.

"I claim only sometimes. So what are your names?"

Through the afternoon I connected with the guys a little— one step at a time.

The retriever nuzzled me again. I patted my shoulders, and she put her front legs on my chest, which got her one of the world's best back rubs a dog ever had.

GLOSSARY

99s: Ninety-Nines, Inc., International Organization of Women Pilots, because of 99 initial charter members in 1929. Amelia Earhart was the first President.

APA: American Psychiatric Association, who edit the *Diagnostic and Statistical Manual of Mental Disorders*

ATIS: Automatic Terminal Information Service, the "weather" or the "numbers," provides the weather and approach information pilots use to approach most airports.

BA: Breast Augmentation

C-120: Cessna 120, a 1947 aluminum "spam can" taildragger, no flaps.

C-177: Cessna 177, a "Cardinal," aluminum "spam can," tricycle gear.

CARB HEAT: Carburetor Heat, applied in many normally aspirated airplane engines to prevent ice formation in the carburetor.

CISNATAL: Same as birth or expectations resulting from birth, whether sex or gender; male now if male then; woman now if girl then...

CONFLATE: Combining two different things to make a new thing; two into one, grouped.

DSM: *Diagnostic and Statistical Manual of Mental Disorders*, edited by the American Psychiatric Association; used as a list of mental disorders by mental health professionals, primarily in the United States.

FBO: Fixed Base Operator, a business at an airport for pilots and aircraft; sells fuel, services, rents airplanes, etc.

FFS: Facial Feminizing Surgery, the process whereby a skilled surgeon can subtly trim underlying facial bone and also move relevant soft tissue to feminize a face.

GAS: Gender Affirming Surgery, related to GRS, GCS; another way to refer to some kind of surgery that affirms a person's sense of gender, such as breast augmentation or FFS, neither of which involves genitalia. In the real world, this term is sometimes used to give the impression of SRS when it has not actually been done.

GCS: Gender Confirming Surgery, or Gender Corrective Surgery, or Genital Constructive Surgery, may or may not refer to Sex Reassignment Surgery, SRS; could be any surgery that is felt to confirm gender, such as breast augmentation or FFS, neither of which involves genitalia. In the real world, this term is sometimes used to give the impression of SRS when it has not actually been done.

GEAR: The landing gear of an airplane, the wheels and support structure. Aircraft with retractable gear must lower the gear before landing. Fixed gear aircraft do not, as it's always down.

GENDER (personage): masculinity or femininity; man or woman, a social role.

GENDER (social): Society accepting someone in role of new "gender" or "sex," regardless of SRS.

GRS: Gender Reassignment Surgery, or Genital Reconstructive Surgery, related to GCS; general in scope, includes many different things; may or may not include SRS; could be any surgery that is felt to "reassign" gender, such as breast augmentation or FFS, neither of which involves genitalia. In the real world, this term is sometimes used to give the impression of SRS when it has not actually been done.

HITCHHIKER'S GUIDE TO THE GALAXY: An international best-selling comedy science fiction series, by Douglas Adams; four novels in a "trilogy."

IFR: Instrument Flying Rules, to fly through the sky on paths determined by instruments and with relevant procedures, whether in good weather or not. This is the way airliners usually fly, and other airplanes that want to be able to fly in clouds. Relates to VFR, below.

LETTERS TO JULIET: Romantic.

MIXTURE: The fuel-air mixture in most light, normally aspirated airplane engines can be manually adjusted to continually provide best power, changing with altitude and throttle settings.

NOTTING HILL: Perfect.
NSA: National Security Agency, headquartered in Ft. Meade, MD, is charged with signal intelligence (SIGINT) around the world.
NSGA: Naval Security Group Activity, NavSecGruAct, or NSGA, was part of Naval Intelligence and the NSA's Central Security Service, active between 1935 and 2005, for SIGINT, signal intelligence.
NSOC: National Security Operations Center, the NSA's operation and time-sensitive SIGINT, signal intelligence.
ORCHIECTOMY: Surgical removal of one or both testes; sometimes this procedure is felt to be a GRS, GCS, or GAS, implying SRS that hasn't been done.
PENIS: A male reproductive organ.
PPR: Prior Permission Required, a code given to an aircraft that allows it to approach a U.S. military airfield.
RTC: Recruit Training Center. A.K.A., in this case NTC San Diego, Naval Training Center, San Diego, "Boot Camp" to train U.S. Navy recruits, from 1923 to 1997.
RUNWAY TWO SIX: The name of a runway is designated, roughly, with the magnetic heading the pilot would fly to land on it.
SEX (physical): Primary sex characteristics of chromosomes, gonads, reproductive organs, genital anatomy, goes to reproduction of the species; being male or female (not to be conflated with gender).
SEX CHANGE: It is with great pain I share that biologic sex cannot yet be changed.
SIGINT: Signal Intelligence, one of the functions of the NSA.
SR-71: Developed in the latter 1950s, was an ultra-high altitude Mach 3+ reconnaissance "spy plane," the fastest plane to carry a human at the time, with a reduced radar cross section (semi-stealth); served in the U.S. Air Force from 1964 to 1998.
SR-9B: One of the variations of the Stinson Reliant, 1933-1941, covered in cloth, a "rag wing," in this case a 1937 with a Lycoming R-680 "round" engine on the front and large, 2-blade propeller.

SRS: Sex Reassignment Surgery, to replace the apparent/anatomical genitalia of one sex with the other, as in to convert male genitalia to female or vice versa. SRS is specific to this, where GCS, GRS, or GAS are general terms that could relate to anything one considers "gender."

STATIC DISPLAY AIRCRAFT: A common term for an airplane at an air show that is on display for public appreciation, not being flown in the air show. A pilot will usually stay with the airplane during the show to (1) protect it from harm, and (2) share its characteristics with the public.

STAR TREK: Yes.

STAR WARS: Of course.

T-28 FENNEC: North American Aviation T-28 Trojan, airplane, in this case with one, large Wright Cyclone radial "round" engine on the front. Used initially as a trainer, some were converted by the French Air Force into attack aircraft as a "Fennec," desert fox.

TRANS PEOPLE: Trans, in this case, as I use it, means "trans something" or "trans anything," not just "transgender"; any form of trans living, including trans sex, trans gender, and trans clothes.

TRANSGENDER (phenomenon): Demonstrated need to change gender; the vast majority of people who identify as transgender do not want to change physical sex.

TRANSGENDER (social view): adhering to the belief of (1) a focus on gender; (2) conflating sex and gender; (3) downplaying genitalia. It is where we get the use of "transgender" as an "umbrella" term for all trans people.

TRANSNATAL: As an antonym of cisnatal, used herein as different from birth or expectations resulting from birth, whether sex or gender; female now if male then; woman now if boy then...

TRANSSEXUAL: Demonstrated need to change physical sex. Gender is involved, but physical change of sex is salient. SRS is needed, and if medical science were able, transition would include chromosomes and reproductive system as well.

U-2: Developed in the 1950s, was an ultra-high altitude reconnaissance airplane; Served for the Central Intelligence Agency of the U.S. and is one of the few to have served in the U.S. Air Force for over 50 years.

VAGINA: A female reproductive organ.

VFR: Visual Flight Rules, to fly an airplane by visual reference to the ground, as not in the clouds. VFR airplanes do not necessarily follow electronic paths in the sky and have more freedom of movement, but are only supposed to fly in adequate seeing conditions.

VOGONS: Creatures introduced in the 1st book the *Hitchhiker's Guide to the Galaxy*. Their poetry is so horrible, literally gut-wrenching.

YAW: A twist or oscillation about the vertical axis, e.g., not nosing up or down, not raising or lowering a wing, but moving the nose left or right.

ACKNOWLEDGMENTS

THE ESSENCE of my thanks lies in the quality of gaining insight and inspiration from a variety of perspectives, hence my references here to people who have sometimes been in disagreement. Must it be a scandal that people of different views help the same person?

There are qualities of respect and patience in people who suffer through a rough draft and apply their time and consideration with the intent of helping. Thank you Al Germaine, Dot Minnich (a wonderful, sage friend from Joe's church who also makes a great cup of tea), Lindsey Bell, Randall K. Oaks, J. Michael Bailey, Ph.D., and Richard Goff, Ph.D. Their effort and inclusion here does not necessarily mean they agree with me on what I say, and where there are errors, it's probably because I was mentally out for pizza.

Others through my life, whether I've spoken with them, read their book, or seen them in media, have also given me cause for reflection or influenced my thinking, including but not limited to Christine Jorgensen, Jan Morris, Renée Richards, M.D., Nancy Hunt, Janet Mock, Jennifer Finney "Jenny" Boylan, Caitlyn Jenner (who also gives great hugs), Richard Kelty, MD, Richard Bach, Alice Dreger, Ph.D., Harry Benjamin, M.D., Stanley Biber, M.D., friends, family, neighbors, and my husband, Joseph F. Ware, Jr.

Finally, I'd like to offer a note of appreciation to Canary Conn. Canary: You came into my life at a crucial time, with your appearance on Tom Snyder and your book, *Canary*. It's hard to convey how empty I was inside with no framework to understand what was happening—and then you spoke my truth as if from my own mind. I don't know if you're still with us or if you've passed on. I don't know if you'll ever know how much you helped, but I want to share my deepest gratitude. If I were to ever meet you, I'd give you the biggest hug, probably cry in your hair. Thank you for being there.

www.ingramcontent.com/pod-product-compliance
Lightning Source LLC
Chambersburg PA
CBHW032147080426
42735CB00008B/610